Intimate Play (Viking 1987)

A Student to Student Guide to Medical School (Little, Brown 1985)

The Seven Basic Quarrels of Marriage

(with Robie Macauley; Villard 1990)

IN A TIME OF
FALLEN HEROES

IN A TIME OF FALLEN HEROES

▼

THE RE-CREATION OF MASCULINITY

R. WILLIAM BETCHER, Ph.D., M.D., AND
WILLIAM S. POLLACK, Ph.D.

THE GUILFORD PRESS
New York   London

Excerpts from *The Iliad* by Homer copyright © 1974 by Robert Fitzgerald.
Used by permission of Doubleday, a division of Bantam Doubleday Dell
Publishing Group, Inc. Excerpts from *The Iliad of Homer* copyright © 1951
by Richmond Lattimore. Used by permission of the University of Chicago
Press.

The Guilford Press
A Division of Guilford Publications, Inc.
72 Spring Street, New York, NY 10012

Printed in the United States of America

This book is printed on acid free paper

Last digit is print number: 9 8 7 6 5 4 3 2 1

Library of Congress Cataloging-in-Publication Data
Betcher, R. William
    In a time of fallen heroes: the re-creation of masculinity / R.
William Betcher and William S. Pollack
        p.   cm.
    Originally published: New York : Atheneum, 1993.
    Includes bibliographical references and index.
    ISBN 0-89862-844-X (pbk.)
    1. Men—Psychology.   2. Masculinity (Psychology)   I. Pollack,
William S.   II. Title
[HQ1090.B474   1994]
155.3'32—dc20   94-41733
                                                           CIP

This edition is reprinted by arrangement with Scribner, an imprint of Simon
& Schuster.

(Originally published by Atheneum Publishers)

To Martha and Ben,
to Marsha and Sarah Faye,
and
to our parents and grandparents

CONTENTS

▼

ACKNOWLEDGMENTS

We would like to express our gratitude to our many colleagues and friends who had a hand in the development of this book. In particular, we would like to thank Drs. Judith Jordan, Phillip Isenberg, Frank and Diana Paolitto, Rick Michael, Jeane Whitehouse, and Carol Gilligan, who read parts or all of the manuscript and made valuable suggestions. We would like to specially thank Jim Stone, Dr. Bennett Simon, and Dr. Leonard Muellner, for their generous aid in understanding the Greek classics, Dr. Steve Schwartzberg, and Dr. John Gunderson. Dr. Ron Levant, as always, has been a generous advisor.

Dr. Pollack would like to acknowledge the gracious support of his colleagues at McLean Hospital—its Chief, Dr. Steven Mirin, and especially the Department of Continuing Education: Drs. Robert Aranow and Shervert Frazier, Ms. Carol Brown, Ms. Cathy Toon, and Mr. Tom Picton. Thanks are also due for the excellent secretarial support with parts of the manuscript to Ms. Patti Brown, Ms. Laura Hegart, and Ms. Dale Swett.

We wish to thank our wives—Drs. Martha Markowitz and Marsha Padwa—and our children—Benjamin Betcher and Sarah Faye Pollack—for their loving support in the course of this project.

In addition, we would like to thank our agent, Gail Hochman, who has always been a much needed guide in practical and intangible ways, and our editor, Lee Goerner, whose thoughtful manner and creative talents made him a pleasure to work with. Thanks also go to Marianne Merola of Brandt and Brandt and to the staff at Atheneum.

Last, we would like to thank our patients, whose willingness to share their lives with us was the original inspiration for this book, and without whom it could not have been written.

The man who is incapable of working in common,
or who in his self-sufficiency has no need of others,
is no part of the community, like an animal, or a god.

ARISTOTLE, *POLITICS*

IN A TIME OF
FALLEN HEROES

1

▼

EVE'S RIB

We live in a time of fallen heroes. The monuments built of men, by men, and for men have tumbled. Men have not just been brought to earth, their strengths put in perspective by their flaws. Even their virtues are suspect vices: power has turned out to be oppression, strength rigidity, and self-sufficiency an inability to be emotionally close. Though it could still be argued that their economic and political clout makes this "a man's world," the empire seems to be crumbling. Women—the most oppressed majority—have made incursions into men's traditional prerogatives and even more inroads into their confidence. If men still appear in control, their smug certainty is gone. It is a difficult time to be proud of being a man.

Men's discomfort could be a necessary accompaniment to new insight and to change. Yet male antagonism toward feminism suggests that men, lacking their own vision for the future, may try to cast gender roles in the molds of the past. Because they feel powerless to shape a relationship of equality between the sexes, a backlash may emerge. Men may wield destructive power if it is all they have.

We believe that men can and must reclaim a sense of personal authority, and in so doing create a new form of masculinity and a new relationship with women. This is not a matter of power over women, but over and for themselves. Women do not have the answers for men, but men might start by taking seriously what women have been trying to tell them.

WHAT WOMEN WANT

What does a woman really want? This question provokes and intrigues us much as it did when the Wife of Bath asked it in the thirteenth century to entertain fellow pilgrims on a ride to Canterbury. Through the centuries men, including Freud, have asked this same question, sometimes driven by lust, sometimes by curiosity, often by exasperation.

In the second half of the twentieth century, women have become fed up with the answers men have proposed, and they have provided their own. The answer, of course, varies from one particular woman to another and is complex. But its implication for men is distressingly simple: women want men to change. Men are finding that their female colleagues, lovers, and wives are furious about men's subjugating, controlling, abusing, and defining women. Increasingly, women reject the traditional equation between one man and one woman in which there is a sign that means "greater than" rather than "equals."

The war of the sexes is eternal, or at least as ancient as the Bible, which provided two views of creation. As one has it,

In the beginning God created the heaven and earth . . .
    And God said, let us make man in our image, after our likeness . . .
    So God created man in his own *image, in the image of God created he him;*
    male *and* female *created he them.*

[GENESIS, CHAPTER 1]

In this story, it is clearly meant that men and women are created coequally at the same point in time. Woman is not an afterthought.

The garden of Eden story (probably an earlier tale, according to biblical historians) is quite different:

> *And the Lord God formed man of the dust of the ground,*
> *and breathed into his nostrils the breath of life;*
> *and man became a living soul . . .*
> *And the Lord God said, it is not good that the man*
> *should be alone . . .*
> *And the Lord God caused a deep sleep to fall upon*
> *Adam and he slept:*
> *and he took one of his ribs, and closed up the flesh*
> *instead thereof;*
> *and the rib which the Lord God had taken from man,*
> *made he a woman, and brought her unto the man.*
> *And Adam said, this is now bone of my bones, and flesh*
> *of my flesh:*
> *she shall be called woman, because she was taken out of*
> *man.*
>
> [GENESIS, CHAPTER 2]

In contrast to the first story, woman is a part man, a "second sex" created as a favor to man. The two stories differ not only in their view of women but also of the nature of men. In the first tale, man is made in the image of the godhead—invincible ruler over the universe. In the second, he is as lowly as the dust, a fragile and lonely being who requires another gender to make him whole. Here a woman derives her value not from being a coequal but from what she can provide for a man. It is this story and the role it prescribes that women are saying loudly they do *not* want.

TROUBLED MEN

The plethora of popular books about "bad" men is one manifestation of women's new militancy. Another, which we therapists are familiar with, is the increasing number of men, good and bad, who wind up in our offices. These men are frequently dragged into psychotherapy by women who want them to be "fixed." Those who come on their own are threatened, angry, and confused about their new role in the changing male/female constellation. They are unaccustomed to looking inside and avoid such scrutiny unless they see concrete rewards. They want their marriages to work, they want to be good husbands and fathers, but they don't know how to make things better.

"I have never felt fully alive or genuine," confessed Carl, a man who was having problems with his girlfriend. She had told him that after six years of living together she felt she hardly knew him. His reserve, which she had once admired as strength, now struck her as cold withdrawal. When, for brief periods while sitting alone, he was able to discover that he had feelings, he was unwilling to share them with others for fear of being humiliated. Over time it became clear that Carl had always felt that he had to perform in his profession and at home without feeling any deep connection to his experience. The deadness that his girlfriend felt in their relationship was an accurate reading of his lost joy in living.

Brett had been highly successful in his professional career and came into treatment in his fifties when his wife threatened to leave him. He related that for twenty years of their marriage his wife had been timid and acquiescent but that in the last two years had become critical and demanding. Brett admitted that when younger he had been abusive and difficult to live with but that he had mellowed. He was genuinely regretful about his past treatment of his wife. But he was bewildered and hurt that, despite his attempts to change, his wife was implacable. He alternately appealed for compassion from her, withdrew into cold silence, or felt despair.

"Bob rarely comes home in time to have dinner with us," another wife complained, "and then he wants to talk to the kids. Just after I've gotten them settled down for bed. But what really gets to me is that it's okay if he yells and criticizes, but if I do, I get the silent treatment." Bob admitted that he worked too much but claimed it was necessary to start up his business and that he only wanted to provide his family with a good living. He complained that his wife was always angry with him, that she had too many rules about how he should relate to the children, and that she didn't appreciate his efforts to be a good father. Increasingly he saw his wife as an angry person when what he needed was acceptance and a tranquil home. In the course of treatment, it emerged that Bob's compulsiveness at work was his way of not following in his alcoholic father's footsteps. He had little tolerance for anger because the home he had grown up in had been full of rancor. He wanted very much to be a good father but did not know how to modify his work demands so he could be with his family. Neither could he see how his own behavior contributed to his wife looking like "an angry person."

In each of these cases the man felt caught between his internal sense of what he had to be and the demands of a wife whom he had difficulty understanding or living up to. Like many others, these men are in a predicament. So too are their wives, for men's predicament inevitably is linked to women's predicament. Such men and women, who have come to us for help, have spurred us to write this book.

Each man, woman, or couple who comes to a therapist for help has a poignant story, a tale of failed dreams and pain. But we have come to appreciate how much men's struggles with women are shaped in the crucible of gender. One cannot understand the difficulties of one man and one woman without understanding the problem of Men and Women.

SEGREGATED DIALOGUES

Women still outnumber men as psychotherapy patients, but this is not a sign of illness. Rather, it reflects women's greater receptivity to self-analysis and disclosure. And women are increasingly choosing women to be their therapists, while men more often prefer male therapists. In part this reflects a more or less conscious belief that each person's most pressing unfinished business has to do with their same-sexed parent. But it also assumes that members of each sex feel they are more likely to get what they think they really need from one of their own kind. This is not just an affirmation of self; it is often a devaluation and fear of the other sex.

In clinical conferences and professional meetings that we attend, male and female therapists are increasingly polarized along gender lines. Differences between them are seen as gender-based bias. Women feel oppressed by men, and men by women. Such professional acrimony mirrors the tense condition of male-female relations in the whole culture.

Concern over sexual harassment; the morality of abortion and the right to choose; what constitutes consensual sex, and whether in rape charges a man or woman's past sexual proclivities should be on trial; what rights in the workplace should be equal for women and for men; should gay and lesbian marriages be legally recognized—such gender issues foment argument from the most intimate circles of our lives all the way to the Supreme Court. They expose the fault line of misunderstanding that separates a man's view from a woman's and which often defies compromise.

While our own peculiar vantage point as psychotherapists derives from a deep and empathic exploration of individual lives, we realize that it is impossible to understand the impasses that men and women have come to with each other without a cultural and developmental perspective. How did men and women come to be this way?

ATTACKING PATRIARCHY

Beginning in the early 1960s a revolution in the political, sociocultural, and psychological role of women in American society was being created. In 1963, in *The Feminine Mystique*, Betty Friedan dared to call attention to the problem that as yet "had no name," referring to women's domesticity as a "comfortable concentration camp" into which they had been herded by men, economics, and their own naïveté. Fifty years after the first wave of feminism that led to universal suffrage in 1920, Kate Millett criticized society's views of femininity and women's roles. She felt that women's second-class citizenship could not be remedied by electoral politics alone. Her 1970 book, *Sexual Politics*, redefined American society as a "patriarchy," a system of power in society in which all control was in male hands. She argued further that women were kept in a subjugated position by the creation of a false ideology of sex or gender roles. She saw Freud, in particular, as attempting to wed psychology and biology in order to create a second-class fate for the female gender. Millett now made a brilliant distinction between sex and gender, that is, between that aspect of being male or female that had certain biological components, and that aspect ascribed to the particular functional roles of each sex. Now gender was seen to be for the most part culturally and socially constructed and therefore open to redefinition. Other intellectual broadsides were forthcoming, including Shulamith Firestone's *Dialectic of Sex*, Germaine Greer's *Female Eunuch*, and the creation of *Ms* magazine by Gloria Steinem. Their intent was to tackle the gender biases of male theorists and to redefine gender roles and the sociopolitical status of women. And where best to start with redefining a psychology of women (and for that matter of men) than with the concept of *mothering*?

LITTLE BOYS AND LITTLE GIRLS

Nancy Chodorow, in *The Reproduction of Mothering*, asserted that women did not primarily nurture and care just for biological reasons, and therefore were not doomed to classical "feminine" roles; nor could they merely be forced into the role of mother by male domination alone. She felt the answer lay in the girl's early development, her role with her mother, and subtle, unconscious psychological processes. Put most simply, she felt that the nature of the tie of the little girl to her mother was different from the boy's—little girls remained bonded and attached to their mothers from earliest infancy, and had less need to separate and to become different than little boys, who had to distance from their mothers in order to achieve gender differentiation. As a result, girls created an intense identification with the role of their own mother, and later "reproduced" nurturant activity and mothering. Maternal "instincts" were not necessarily passed from mothers to daughters through their genes, but through the close-touch world they shared and from which little boys had been cast out. One implication of this view, best articulated by Jean Baker Miller in her ground-breaking book, *Toward a New Psychology of Women*, is that women are developmentally more bonded with each other than men are, and more comfortable with seeking out and creating a relational world. This capacity to maintain linkages, social networks, and structures of interpersonal meaning was now viewed as a particular strength, and women's disinclination to aggression, power, and competition was no longer seen as a deficiency. Instead, men's problem in relating was seen as the most important gender weakness.

Women psychologists began to take classical theories of human development to task, especially for the masculine bias that now appeared inherent within them. Carol Gilligan argued in *In a Different Voice* that because men's theories were based primarily upon the study of very successful men, they failed to take into account the more empathic, relationship-centered experiences of women.

While the concept of "empathy" may sound mysterious, it is actually an everyday occurrence having to do with human understanding. It is not the same as sympathy or caring. Rather, it is a capacity to be attuned to the thoughts and feelings of others, to be able to put oneself in another person's shoes yet still be in one's own shoes as well. It turns out that just how one tries on someone else's shoes is styled by gender: men seem to do better at identifying with others' predicaments, often from an intellectual distance, while women appear to be more emotionally involved with others' distress or needs. So women often wish that men could be "more empathic," men wish women could be more "objective," and both wind up feeling misunderstood.

Gilligan felt that the male-dominated theories tended to equate adult maturity with individuation and competitive achievement. In turn, personal relationships were given short shrift. This search for autonomous independence, and the almost magical idealized significance to which it is given in the typical man's development, left little room for *intimacy*. From Gilligan's perspective, *identity* and *intimacy* mature differentially for men and women. Women appear to develop early on a strong sense of interpersonal awareness and connectedness. They strive for and achieve intimate bonding. Only later, if at all, does any strong sense of "individuation" emerge. In addition, maturity, moral viewpoint, and personal achievement are based less upon the creation of "autonomous" success or "independent" identity. By contrast men are viewed as focusing first and foremost on creating a strong and separate sense of identity, often at great cost to their relationships. Only in later life, and then only with greater maturity, are they sometimes able to achieve a more comfortable capacity for intimacy. A new model was developed from Gilligan's view of independence versus intimacy and Chodorow's notion that little boys needed to stand apart from their mothers so as to create a healthier sense of gender identity. One consequence of this new model was that intimacy and identity took on the characteristics of diametrically opposed concepts, differentiated along gender lines. Men were interpreted as being threatened by intimacy.

Gender theory has evolved from a sense that women were deficient—either because they lacked or envied a penis, or were less interested in classical male struggles for autonomy and competition, or were too "dependent" rather than independent. In the past women were unfairly judged by male standards, and their different orientation to work, love, and moral decisions was chalked up to immaturity. The current dominant notion sees men as deficient women—lacking empathy, fleeing from emotional connection, unable to accept commitment, banished from the garden of psychological relatedness. Like Adam, men are seen as permanently missing a piece—more emotional than physical—that women possess exclusively. What has happened is nothing less than the feminization of gender.

MEN'S RESPONSE

Some men are on the defensive, angry in response to this new psychology of women, and feeling misinterpreted by them. They would like to turn back the clock to the time when men were men and women were sexual objects. They seek to hold onto male prerogatives, from date rape to electoral office, which they justify by tradition, biology, or because might can make rights. Others adopt a submissive stance in which they blindly try to live out ideas generated by the women's movement without any true integration. They bend over backwards to be fair and politically correct, will hold the door for a woman and pay the restaurant bill or not, depending upon what she wants, and attend lectures on gender issues where the men are outnumbered by women twenty to one.

Both types of men lack a deeper understanding of their own particular pathway of gender development. Neither approach leads to lasting change, to an integrated sense of masculinity, or, most important, to healthy relationships between men and women.

The predicaments that men and women get into with each other are well demonstrated in the cases of the Caldwells and the Greens.

Jack Caldwell was in his mid-thirties when he met his future wife, and as a result of several years of psychotherapy was able to overcome some of his fears about emotional commitment and to marry. Then, during a time of great stress in his life, he found, to both his and his new wife's dismay, that he was unable to talk to her. He told his therapist that his wife "required," at times even "demanded," that he "relate" to her. What he meant was that when he was moody, she would probe him for information that might help her to console him. Mr. Caldwell had learned to hide such feelings and to eschew support at such moments, in large part because of a disappointing, intrusive relationship with his mother. He now felt he was faced with the additional burden of having to "relate" to his wife at just those moments when he sought solitude. The therapist's attempts to help him understand his wife's needs only led to an emotional withdrawal from him as well. It was only when therapist and patient were able to see how hurtful it felt to be "forced to relate" that Mr. Caldwell was able to reach out, on his own, for his wife's support. He could now accept more intimacy since it felt more mutual and "masculine" and less "like it was imposed by my mother."

Rita Green says, "My husband thinks he is sympathetic to my wanting greater equality, but when the toilet needs to be cleaned or the meals prepared, he still acts as if it's 'women's work.' " She has realized that he not only resists taking on domestic drudgery, but his view of himself as a sensitive, enlightened male makes it difficult for him to see how much he expects her to take care of it. She has found that she can cajole her husband into doing the work by acting like a combination of a seductress and his mother. She says, "Oh, honey, could you please help me, please, please, please," or "I really need your help, cutie. I really *need* you to help me." Her husband then responds with a smile and is happy to do the work. Although the chores get done, she feels angry that she has to manipulate him, and in the process loses some respect for both of them.

The Greens and the Caldwells point up the gender-related dilemmas that in day-to-day life drive well-meaning men and women apart. In attempting to respond to each other's needs and remain true to themselves, each either disappoints their partner or sacrifices their authenticity.

VALUED DIFFERENCES

The very theories of human (now read as men's) development that women have begun to dismantle have created a stereotyped role for males that limits growth. It has discouraged men
from looking inward and from expressing strong feelings other
than anger. It has also eschewed conflict, whether in relationships with others or within the self. As a result, men may be at
significantly high risk, at the moment, of not recognizing the
profound impact that this redefinition of women and their psychology may be having upon both genders. Nor are most men
well-equipped to identify the tangled array of unconscious and
conscious feelings and behaviors that are being evoked in reaction to it.

In 1928 Virginia Woolf observed, in *A Room of One's Own*,
that:

> Women have served all these centuries as looking-glasses
> possessing the magic and delicious power of reflecting the
> figure of man *at twice its natural size.* . . .
>   . . . if she begins to tell the truth, the figure in the looking-
> glass shrinks; his fitness for life is diminished.
>
> [PP. 35–36, ITALICS OURS]

The new psychology of women had altered how women see
themselves and the relationship between men and women. It
had also altered how men view themselves. Formerly heroes,
or at least potential ones, they have been recast as oppressors
and frauds. In the long run, the effects will be positive for both
genders, but at present things feel a lot worse to many men. If
women are no longer the "second sex," men feel that this subservient role may fall to them. This is unacceptable to most men, who
associate this position with being made into a woman.

Women now refuse to accept being devalued or blamed by
men; modern men must find ways to place into personal perspective the depression that ensues as they take more responsibility for problems that they used to blame on women. Men

must be able to understand the very justified anger that women feel as a result of how they have been traditionally treated by men. In turn, women need to be aware that men often experience women's anger as "male bashing" that is neither fair nor properly directed. Gay men and lesbians may also be victimized by "straight" men or women whose anxieties about their gender adequacy remain unacknowledged.[1]

Perhaps due to the way public culture has been defined predominantly by white men, disenfranchised groups (including gay men, lesbians, people of color, and ethnic minorities) have struggled with the need to accommodate to those who hold greater power, as well as with the need to assert their differences. Women have had to maintain a dual awareness—of their own, private experience and of the public experience of men. We believe that men too need to develop such a dual consciousness, which would be furthered by men better defining and communicating their private experience.

We would hope that when women feel on more secure ground and men are able to convince them that they are lis-

---

[1] Perhaps one of the most important controversies about gender is over the expression of love *within* a gender, what historically has been called homosexuality. For example, to what extent is being a gay man an expression of biological difference or a socially mediated phenomenon, and why has it been so difficult to integrate such variant forms of masculinity within our culture? Further, as the psychiatrist Harry Stack Sullivan, pointed out, to act as if there are merely two adaptations—homosexual and heterosexual—is inherently misleading. Interestingly, Plato believed that philosophy began in an older male's attraction to a young man who is both physically beautiful and possesses "beauty of the soul."

Some gay men and lesbians have suggested that their own struggles to liberate themselves from rigid cultural prescriptions for masculinity and femininity might provide a useful model for "straight" men and women. In time, we hope it may be possible for straight men to develop a dual consciousness of their own and of gay men's experience, and to see the parallels more clearly. But for now, most men are too threatened by the prospect of identifying with the gay experience to make such learning possible. Sadly, the strongest parallel may be gay men's historical need to conceal their sexual adaptation in a homophobic culture and straight men's fear of revealing their more "feminine" sides.

Our lack of attention to such matters is not because we think them unimportant but because we feel our personal and professional experience best enables us to address issues between heterosexual men and women.

tening, the notion of one sex being deficient will be replaced by one of valued differences. Men's classical difficulty of getting in touch with and expressing their feelings, which is increasingly under attack by women, must be understood from the perspective of male development and male needs rather than through the pejorative lens of psychopathology. *For if we truly want men to become more empathic, we need to become more empathic to men.*

EVE'S RIB

Craig Jensen, a successful professional man who was always quite punctilious and correct, found himself becoming so hurt and angry one evening when his wife wouldn't give him the remote control to the television set that he lost his temper. He pulled out all the drawers in her dresser and spread the contents around the room. When he later reflected on the meaning of his behavior and his uncharacteristic loss of control, he recalled his father being a businessman who was always away from home and never showed much feeling. By contrast, his mother's emotionality had seemed to him "silly" and "uncontrollable." Craig had identified with both of them and been unable to resolve this contradiction. He shunned feelings because he could only feel "masculine" by remaining aloof. His wife, Jenny, learned to avoid pushing him because his rare outbursts of feeling were scary and did not invite her to share her feelings in return. Like many women, she concluded that all men are immature and incapable of change. He could never be as attuned to her or to his own feelings as she wished. For many years, the couple drifted into a quiet alienation, until finally Jenny insisted they see a therapist.

Increasingly, we therapists are seeing couples in which it is the wife who is demanding a change. Less dependent on men financially and supported by an ideology of women's rights, many women are leaving the kind of marriages that they used to put up with. While women are understandably frustrated

with men's apparent difficulties with intimacy, we feel that it is
not helpful to interpret men as solely resisting, being afraid of,
or being incapable of close relationships. It is disrespectful of
men and counterproductive to try to make them act more like
women.

Feminist writers have with some reason criticized traditional
psychology as being a psychology of men. But we are now in
an "Eve's Rib" era when women's ideas are defining men, in
large part because men have done such a poor job of explaining
themselves and in part because of the inevitable gender bias of
women. Women are right in saying they know more about the
psychology of women than men do, but they are on less solid
ground in their attempts to explain men. The result is that
both sexes fail to understand each other. Women have had the
courage to show men their own true nature but men have yet
to show women theirs. Much remains hidden under the swagger
and bluster of insecurity and is unknown even to men, who
have been loath to renounce their dominant role in society. Such
dominance not only victimizes the very women they care about,
but places an unfair burden on men themselves.

Men need to understand their inner reality—their thoughts,
feelings, and fantasies, and the matrix of personal development
from which they spring. Men need to be more aware, not just
because women want them to but for their own sake. The
stereotypic male defense of not knowing what he feels, or of
not giving it a sense of value because it "doesn't change anything," must be addressed in depth.

The discussion of gender is imbued with all the conflict,
uncertainty, and confusion that moral conflict and political
change engenders within our society. And yet there is an inherent conservatism to the concept and experience of gender identity. It tends to be solidified, according to the work of John
Money and others, by the age of two to three, and once set in
place it is often very difficult to change. Such psychological
entrenchment finds its counterpart in the slow pace of change
within the culture. Our ideas about what gender roles *should*
ideally be far outreach the reality of people's willingness to
change, or to engage in the level of depth exploration and per-

sonal pain that may be necessary to achieve change over time. This is as true for women as it is for men. At a recent annual international conference on the psychology of women, held in Boston, a therapist told a poignant story. Her patient, a feminist woman, having spent a great deal of time rethinking the nature of her development, and now her children's, found herself one day singing her daughter to sleep with a favorite lullaby. For the first time in many years she realized to her horror that she was singing "your daddy's rich and your mamma's good looking," reassuring the baby that men would continue to support them as long as she and her mother were beautiful. She came to her therapist confused about this deeply embedded, almost mysterious view of self and gender, quite distinct from her new political views. What became clear to therapist and patient alike was that the unconscious was the repository of both the old and the new, and of course allowed them to simultaneously co-exist. Even though we may rethink, and review, our minds represent our prehistories, and require depth involvement and personal struggle to make for meaningful change.

A NEW PARADIGM

Thomas Kuhn, in his historic study, *The Structure of Scientific Revolutions*, cogently describes the dialectical historical processes that underlie revolutions in thinking. Anomalies exist in prior *paradigms*, which cannot be completely explained within the classical models. Over time there is a recognition that the old model fails to explain the scientific, historical, cultural, or psychological phenomenon that it was meant to elucidate. This in turn leads to a crisis that requires the creation of a new worldview. This is a view free from earlier prejudices and biases and more able to describe, confront, and solve the problems generated by our current experiences. Prior to the breakdown of the old paradigms there might be hints of cracking around the edges, and pain, as people recognize that old theories do not adequately explain experience. But as the crisis broadens and the old structures crumble, we are caught between outmoded certainty and uncharted territory. The new feminism or women's movement, beginning in the late 1960s, has created just such a crisis as well as a need for a shift of paradigm in the redefinition of our sense of *gender*, masculinity and femininity, and in the roles and psychology of men and women.

While the new feminism has forced a rethinking of women's psychology, it has left in its wake the rubble of old theories of human development, and especially our concepts of men and masculinity. Heroes—the personification of manhood—are no-where to be found. This has left men without authority or an understanding sensitive to their own specific needs. This book takes its spark from the women's movement and its new psychology and attempts to look at central concepts in the psychological development of men. We will follow the thread of men's experience: the imperative to remain alone, the importance of special women and special men in their lives, their need to command respect and exert control, their having to live up to obligations to work and family in order to feel masculine, their urge to play and to transcend themselves, their difficulty wedding love with lust, their learning to be competent fathers, and their struggles to mature, to change, and to become men. We will try to provide men with bridges from their thoughts to their feelings and women with a greater understanding of the inner workings of men with whom they attempt to become intimate. Our hope is to help men to find and articulate their own values and to help women to understand men's "different voice."

MYTH

One bridge from theory to personal understanding is stories. We will use vignettes from our clinical practices of men whose struggles to become men will be recognizable.

Another type of story we will use is myth. Myths are narratives that endure from generation to generation because they offer what H. D. F. Kitto referred to as "an explanation of human life and of the human soul." But whatever truths the myths embody, like the Delphic oracle's utterings, they still require interpretation. Myths are, as Sigmund Freud said, a mixture of "conscious ignorance and unconscious wisdom," or as Arthur Miller put it, "the deepest paradoxes in the most adept shorthand." Just as each generation rewrites history in accord with its own image and gains from such reinterpretations even while it unwittingly distorts, so too must we reinterpret what ancient myths say about gender and the psychology of men.

In myths we can find an assortment of fallen heroes, whose virtues and vices may bring some balance to how we view our own. The beauty of myths, and perhaps the secret of their longevity, is that they contain an *elusive*, subjective truth, one that allows us to project ourselves into them, as if we were the actors in the script. Men such as Oedipus, Achilles, and Odysseus are familiar to us because they not only represent a search for truth or immortality; they seem to breathe the same air, feel the same passions and weaknesses, and aspire to the same heroics as we do now.

We have chosen myths largely from the Greco-Roman tradition for several reasons. The stories will be familiar to most readers and the gods and heroes easy to relate to because they so clearly manifest human foibles and virtues. Judeo-Christian myths, on the other hand, are laden with spiritual and moral dimensions that are perhaps too close to modern conceptions to provide new insights. After all, it is necessary to stand a certain distance from a mirror in order to see oneself clearly.

As Ralph Waldo Emerson put it:

> . . . the foundation of that interest all men feel in Greek history, letters, art, and poetry, in all its periods, from the heroic or Homeric age, down to the domestic life of the Athenians and Spartans . . . [is] that every man passes personally through a Grecian period . . .

The costly charm of the ancient tragedy, and indeed of

all the old literature, is that the persons speak simply—speak as persons who have great good sense without knowing it, before yet the reflective habit has become the predominant habit of the mind. Our admiration of the antique is not admiration of the old, but of the natural.

[RALPH WALDO EMERSON, "HISTORY,"
IN *SELF-RELIANCE*, PP. 106–7]

However, ancient Greek literature, created largely by men who were addressing other men, should be regarded as offering more insight into their own psyches and their own view of women than it provides an accurate picture of women's private experience. We do *not* look upon ancient Greece nostalgically as a time of greater senstivity to gender than our own. In that society, masculinity was even harder to achieve than in modern times, and therefore the danger of femininity to men was correspondingly greater.

The plays of Sophocles and Euripides, for example, are full of men's preoccupation with the perfidy of women. As Bennett Simon points out, in *Tragic Drama and the Family*, women's sexuality and reproductive powers are repeatedly cursed or wished away. It was hardly a golden age for women, who, whether queens or slaves, lived in a world made for men. As Euripides has Medea lament:

Of all things which are living and can form judgment
We women are the most unfortunate creatures.
Firstly, with an excess of wealth it is required
For us to buy a husband and take for our bodies
A master; for not to take one is even worse.
And now the question is serious whether we take
A good one or bad one; for there is no easy escape
For a woman, nor can she say no to her marriage.
She arrives among new modes of behavior and manners,
And needs prophetic power, unless she has learned at home,
How best to manage him who shares the bed with her.

[*MEDEA*, GRENE AND LATTIMORE,
TRANS., LL. 230–1]

Medea ends up revenging herself on her husband, Jason, by murdering their two sons. But Euripides' *Medea* is neither a polemic for women's rights nor a cautionary tale about the dangerousness of women. It is a tragedy about the inability of the two genders to live together in harmony. In less dramatic and less lyrical ways, the same tragedy continues to be enacted in the misunderstandings between men and women today.

In our search for men's roots and for masculinity in its best sense we find several classical notions inspiring: the Greeks' quest for wholeness, such as men's need for both physical and mental challenge; the heroic ideal of *arete*, meaning a combination of virtue and excellence; and the Greeks' tragic awareness of men's essential dignity and weakness.

MYTHIC HEROES AND TRAGEDY

The early psychoanalysts often turned to the classics of Greek literature—mythos and tragedy—to elucidate unconscious undercurrents in society and in the psyche. Freud came to view the fateful journey of Oedipus as the quintessential male struggle for identity. In recent years, commentators on the fate of men's psychology, most notably Robert Bly, have unearthed a new mythos of chthonic Iron Men to mentor forgotten males back into a network of healthy, vibrant masculinity.

We will take exception with Freud because we believe that we must go to even earlier layers of development, to the so-called pre-oedipal period in order to understand men's dilemmas with intimacy. We will reinterpret myths using both Freud's and Carl Jung's conceptions—myth as intrapsychic residue of individual conflicts and myth as repository of cultural symbols or archetypes. We do not feel they are mutually exclusive. Gender was far from being the subject of Freud's most enduring insights. Still, psychodynamic theory, like the ancient myths, is "underwater," just beneath much of our current notions about human behavior.

We admire Robert Bly's poetry and acknowledge his contribution to the new psychology of men. But although his mythopoetic approach does reach down to more primitive developmental levels, his solutions tend to obscure the complexity of the issues and can easily encourage macholike, antifeminist sentiment.

To Otto Rank, the hero represented the impulse for self-determination and personal mastery—what we would see as autonomous man. In many myths, Rank pointed out, the hero has two sets of parents—one lowly, the other noble. He is reared by the lowly parents but eventually returns to his biological ones, to whom he metes out punishment for abandoning him. From this perspective, the hero merely lives out what for most others is a fantasy—the "family romance" in which one imagines that one's real parents will someday appear and make up for the deficiencies of the ones we know.

Our likening men's experience today with that of ancient Greek heroes is not to inspire men to passionate bravery or bold adventures. Men such as Oedipus, Achilles, and Odysseus were not comic book superheroes. Nor were their families wishful creations of boyhood imagination. They were fallible men whose exceptional qualities enabled them to perform great feats, but who were chastened by awareness of their limitations. The *Iliad*, the *Odyssey*, the story of Oedipus are tragedies, for even heroes cannot escape their mortality, their character, and the consequences of ambivalent family relations—in fact, these limits are inextricably bound to their virtues. We refer to them as "fallen heroes," not because they ultimately failed in their quests, but because "falling" is an inevitable part of being a real man. In contrast, we believe that the predicament of many men today is due precisely to their inability to face their limitations—they seek to deny death and the inevitability of loss. To face the tragic does not mean embracing the ultimate gloom of classic psychoanalysis—that we are enslaved by destructive instincts. We are simply saying to men: you must have pain, you must face it, but that doesn't mean all of life has to be a tragedy.

A generation of American men were scarred by the war in Vietnam. That we are still yearning for the missing in action to come home is a sad commentary on just how much was lost and how little we have healed. Those who went to war still feel shame, and, paradoxically, those who did not go feel shame too. In a sense, all men are still trying to find an honorable way to come home.

In the aftermath of the new psychology of women, which has caused us to question just how admirable and strong the autonomous heroes of the past really were, men are looking for a different kind of hero—neither a man's man nor a lady's man. What is required is what Joseph Campbell referred to as "the call to adventure," a heroic *inward* journey. Wishful fantasies of our connection to exalted forebears will not suffice. We must search for our true origins.

MEN'S NEEDS

We began our story with women so as to provide a context for what both genders are struggling with now. But our real concern is, What do *men* really want? Perhaps, in the light of revision of gender theory, the question needs to be recast as "What is it that men really *need*?" We will argue throughout the chapters in this book that men need an opportunity to reevaluate their own *selves*, by which we mean their sense of masculinity, their identity both alone and in relation to others, and their feelings about work, love, play, and parenting. They need to find their roots, both historically and personally. Men need to rediscover their fathers and their mothers and other special men and women in their lives and to understand how they continue to be shaped by these relationships. This requires a redefinition of men's precious autonomy as perhaps necessary but limiting, and an acceptance of their need for other people as neither shameful nor weak. They need to discover the submerged peninsulas that once linked their islands of autonomy to the mainland.

In this Eve's Rib era when men feel beset by women's accusations and expectations, both fair and unfair, we believe they need to have heroes of a different sort than ever before. They need heroes of human dimensions, with courage, integrity, and humility, not to champion masculinity at women's expense, but to inspire men's self-respect. After all, neither an invulnerable nor a wounded man has much to offer a woman. Without the opportunity to reevaluate and understand their own development, their own roots, men will be posed with a painful and insoluble dilemma: how to respond to the "new woman," in a way that is both sensitive and fair, but maintains empathy for one's own self, one's own gender.

In "The Wife of Bath's Tale," in *The Canterbury Tales*, a knight who had raped a young woman is condemned to death unless he can answer the queen's question: "What is the thing that most of all women desire?" In our own time, men are again under duress to expiate past sins against women by being more responsive to their needs. But men will never be able to be the type of partners that women wish for—not only in intimate relationships, but in all the ongoing relational arenas of life, including friendship, business, and play—unless they gain a better sense of their *own selves*.

In Chaucer's story, the knight's answer to the queen in open court was:

> *Women desire to have the sovereignty*
> *And sit in rule and government above*
> *Their husbands, and to have their way in love.*
> [*THE CANTERBURY TALES*, P. 235]

The Wife of Bath remarked that "No widow, wife, or maid gave any token of contradicting what the knight had spoken," and so his life was spared. But though this solution may indeed save men from women's anger, it is not workable for either gender to have sovereignty over the other.

As we have seen, the Bible, too, chronicles the difficulties of men and women. Although the classical interpretation of the Adam and Eve story is one of original sin and downfall, modern revisionist biblical scholars have suggested this couple's transitional role from demigods to human beings. As such they represent a *necessary* loss—the relinquishing of a grandiose hope for eternal life (the Tree of Life), in return for a more realistic possibility of important *knowledge* (the Tree of Good and Evil). Like Adam and Eve, we cannot expect to live forever and must create a sense of legacy through giving to other generations. This includes procreation, parenting, and the husbanding of old and new knowledge. Adam and Eve's loss, if we choose to learn from it, is really our gain, especially if we come to see our progenitors as not so much having been "cast out" as having chosen to "know" a different life.

If it turns out that the Garden of Eden was not such a beautiful place for women, then perhaps it wasn't heaven for men either. Women can no longer be seen as the appendage of men's bodies, selves, or psychologies, but so, too, must men redefine themselves. It is not acceptable (or healthy) for either sex to be molded out of the rib or any part of anatomy taken from the other. The new psychology that women have begun to create, men must begin to work on themselves, and to re-create in their own image.

2

▼

ALONENESS

A woman's attraction to a man who cannot love was well-known in antiquity.

In the classic tale of Ovid, Narcissus was the son of the river god Cephisus and the nymph Liriope, and was most distinguished for his beauty. Upon his birth, his mother sought out the advice of the wise seer Teiresias, who prophesied that Narcissus would live a long life, but only if he never came to know himself.

As a young man, Narcissus's striking beauty caused all the girls who saw him to long to be his. But he was indifferent even to the loveliest of them, and their broken hearts meant nothing to him. Even the sad plight of the nymph Echo did not touch him.

Echo had been falsely accused by the goddess Hera of seducing her husband, Zeus. Her punishment was to be able to repeat only what was said to her. As Hera cattily put it, "My dear, you will always have the last word, but you shall have no power to speak first." Echo fell in love with Narcissus, but he fled at her approach, saying, "You must not touch—go, take your hands away, *may I be dead before you throw your fearful chains around me*." Echo, since she could only repeat his words, could not allay his fears about intimacy. She was left to hide her shame in a cave.

As the story goes, one day a woman[1] who had been scorned by him issued a vengeful prayer that sometime he would be able to feel what it was to love and receive no return of affection. The goddess Nemesis (meaning "righteous anger") heard this and granted her prayer. As Narcissus bent over a clear spring to drink, he saw his own reflection and immediately fell in love with it. He could not tear himself away, but of course neither could he bring this mirror lover to him. There he knelt, calling upon his reflected beauty, "Why, beautiful being, do you shun me?" but never able to achieve union.

Accompanying him to the end was his unrequited lover, Echo, who as Narcissus died could only repeat his last words, "Farewell . . . farewell," as a last good-bye.

AS THIS IS the myth of the pain of reflection, we may see mirrored in the myth itself the modern-day dilemma of many men and women and their often unrequited quest to find each other. Each is condemned to a painful isolation, in which they can be with each other but are unable to communicate. Ovid's tale suggests that the root of most of the trouble lies in a man's self-absorption and lack of empathy, which can only be remedied by painful experience. Women, too, are implicated by Ovid. While not to blame for their predicament, they are limited by the opposite incapacity possessed by men—they have *no* self, existing only as the echo of a man's hopes and dreams. Ovid clearly then foretells the modern dilemma: men are overly "autonomous," women overly reliant on "connection," and the casualty is intimacy. Lost, too, is the potential for new syntheses of masculinity and femininity.

There is a tale of a modern-day Narcissus that is also instructive. In the movie *Rain Man*, a young car salesman is the self-absorbed, materialistic male of our times. He has money, an exotic girlfriend, and he is in control. He does not know what he is missing. Early in the film, he and his fiancée are driving toward what she expects will be a romantic getaway. After a

[1] As with many of the classic myths, there are several versions. In some of them, the scorned party is a man.

lengthy silence, each staring ahead, she says, "Listen, I don't want to be demanding here, but do you think you possibly could say ten or twelve words before we get to the hotel? Consider it foreplay. Can you include me in some of your thoughts?"

"I'm just thinking," he says. "Nothing special, I'm just thinking."

"Maybe there's something you're thinking about that we can talk, maybe a little conversation."

"If there was something to talk about, we'd be talking about it. I'm just thinking. What's the big to-do about me thinking here?"

"I just feel like I'm going away for a few days with *someone*."

"Okay. You want to talk, let's talk. How was your day?"

"I don't want to talk. It's just like you're excluding me from what's going on."

He sighs. "One of these again. How did we get back to one of these?"

"I don't know why I put up with all of this."

"*You* said you wanted to go to Palm Springs. We're going to Palm Springs."

"But I didn't want to go *alone*."

The film highlights a man's need to feel self-sufficient as being a natural, even a necessary part of his gender identity. By the end of the film, a transformation occurs in this young businessman from cold self-absorption and a quest for money to a growing capacity for love. Indeed, he may be the prototype of our present-day culture of narcissism, and his transformation the longed-for change in men sought after by so many men and women.

Many men have difficulties with commitment and emotional openness. They have to be alone. But one man's privacy is a woman's isolation. The more she tries to get in, the more defensive he becomes. To what extent do men really *want* to be alone, and is it his problem or hers that he tends to be this way?

TWO VERSIONS OF ALONENESS

Fool me once, shame on you . . .
Fool me twice, shame on me . . .

Ted, an attractive, successful Boston architect in his mid-forties, found himself in one of our consulting rooms remembering this nursery rhyme as a clue to his adult paralysis about divorce and remarriage. Having constructed some of the most successful new buildings in the metropolitan area, he was unable to finalize his divorce and commit to a new love life. He had lived for years in an empty shell of a marriage and had only been able to separate from his wife when his children were in their teens. By that time he felt confident he could assure them of a more healthy upbringing. For the next ten years he had lived completely apart from his wife. In therapy Ted came to realize that despite the pain he had endured in the marriage and his relief to be separated, he could not bring himself to make a complete break. In the same measure, he was unable to become intimate with anyone else. His new lovers' complaints about his holding back were eerily reminiscent of what his wife used to say.

When the nursery rhyme came to his mind, Ted confessed that his first marriage was an "error" that he didn't feel was his fault, but that if he were to repeat it he would bring shame upon himself that he could not bear. He had been traumatized by the disappointment in his first meaningful love relationship and had created an island of aloneness where he could protect himself from being twice mistaken, twice abandoned, twice hurt by the women in his life. What was less conscious, but over time became more clear, was the fact that this man's first shaming and trauma had occurred much earlier in life when he had to leave his mother for boarding school.

A SUCCESSFUL INSURANCE executive came to see one of us at the insistence of his wife. Samuel and Kathleen Warner were extremely unhappy with their marriage and had tried couple

therapy without much improvement. He had long resisted going into therapy himself in part because he didn't like her ultima-
tums and also because he didn't want to change. But he had
come to see that his emotional reserve was a limitation and he
entered treatment wanting help in making up his mind about
the marriage.

One of the couple's recurring conflicts centered on his absorption with work, which, from Kathleen's perspective, left
her to manage the house and the kids by herself. Samuel also
reported that she resented having to take responsibility for dec-
orating the house and managing their finances. She accused him
of not caring enough and abandoning her. His view was that
his work responsibilities left little time for home chores and that
he could not manage both. Her vision of marriage was of a
partnership in which they did as much as possible together. He
believed in a division of labor, which he believed to be more
efficient and rational, and would result in more leisure time for
both of them. He did not feel he was fleeing from his wife and
children. But he truly loved his work, where his position as
partner allowed him a scope of responsibility and creativity that
was extremely seductive. He tried to limit the time he spent on
the job because he recognized the toll his absence was taking on
his family. But the question he continued to ask in therapy about
his work and his marriage was, "Is it impossible for me to have
both?"

ALTHOUGH MANY MEN, and more women, have come to accept
intellectually the necessity for emotional interdependence, in
practice men often experience loving bonds as a form of bondage. As Narcissus put it, "May I be dead before you throw your
fearful chains around me." They enter personal commitments
with the wariness of a wild animal being offered domesticity.
Once having made a commitment, they frequently feel caged
and believe that their mates want more of them than they feel
prepared to give.

In the first vignette, Ted's aloneness was largely a defense
against being hurt and shamed—he came to see how he was
trapped by the very walls that he had constructed against these

threats. In the second case, Samuel's wife felt shut out, but it is less clear that his version of aloneness was a form of scar tissue covering over boyhood pain. His aloneness was a problem in the *marriage*, but he did not feel it to be a problem for *him*. We have seen both kinds of men in psychotherapy and come to see how they represent two very different pathways to aloneness.

As early as the seventeenth century, the poet John Donne advised that "No man is an island, entire of itself; every man is a piece of a continent, a part of the main . . ." And yet most men continue to function emotionally much more like Robert Frost's neighbor in the poem "Mending Wall," who advises that "Good fences make good neighbors." Women who try to have intimate relationships with such men often find themselves being walled out in ways that cause them a great deal of pain and confusion. As therapists, we have been impressed by how many men are themselves in pain and bewildered—hurt by their mates whom they feel unfairly attack them, wishing they could be less closed off but not knowing how to be more expressive, uncertain about how much they really want to be alone. In his poem, Frost goes on to say, "Before I built a wall I'd ask to know, /What I was walling in or walling out." That is the poignant and vital question that we must consider in this chapter in order to understand why men so often find themselves alone or in search of a kind of sublime solitude. In the face of complaints from their most intimate "neighbors," it is not too late for men to reconsider whether what they have built are really "good fences."

TWO PATHWAYS TO ALONENESS

The first experiences of aloneness are largely *unchosen*—babies and young children of both genders seek out connection and are both physically and emotionally ill-equipped to tolerate being by themselves. Although children and adults may come eventually to value being alone, it is an acquired taste. For most,

the ability to be alone and to have self-mastery, although present
early on in rudimentary forms, is part of growing up.

The new psychology of women has pointed out that "autonomy" for women may be quite different from that of men since
for women the self always exists *in relation*. It is difficult for
men and women to understand each other when they talk about
the need to be connected or alone since these terms have such
different connotations for each sex. She is most comfortable if
her solitary voyages take place on a sea of potential joinings,
while he prefers the distance by which planets orbit around
each other—their relations protected by unseen forces. Gender
differences aside, the confusion that often surrounds talk about
aloneness is also due to our lacking an adequate lexicon to describe a variety of physical and psychological states whose subtle
differences tend to be obscured.

However defined, the growth toward autonomy depends on
the capacity of parents to hold onto the child sufficiently so that
he or she does not feel abandoned but not so tightly that there
is no opportunity to venture out on their own. It is an exquisite
balance and much can and does go wrong. As Sander puts it,
"Bonding can become bondage."

There are two early pathways that lead to aloneness as an
adult man or woman. Each person is likely to have traveled to
some extent on each of them. One pathway develops as a defense against parents and other caretakers who are misattuned
to the child's needs. The child experiences his parent's blindness
to his needs as a terrifying kind of abandonment. In such circumstances mature independence cannot develop—instead, the child
becomes an insecure, dependent adult, clutching literally or
figuratively to anyone who can provide protection from the
aloneness that cannot be tolerated. Alternatively, such a child
develops a false autonomy—a show of strength that may look
a lot like independence and is often hard to distinguish from it.
His aloneness is actually isolation. It differs from true autonomy
in that it tends to be driven by anxiety and lacks flexibility.
Rather than being *able* to be alone, such an individual *has* to be
alone.

The second pathway to aloneness is based on the more felicitous circumstance in which the environment is in tune with the infant. It fosters healthy autonomy. The British psychoanalyst D. W. Winnicott has best described it:

> Although many types of experience go to the establishment of the capacity to be alone, there is one that is basic, and without a sufficiency of it the capacity to be alone does not come about; this experience is that of being alone, as an infant and small child, in the presence of mother. Thus the capacity to be alone is a paradox; it is the experience of *being alone while someone else is present.*
>
> . . . When alone in the sense in which I am using the term, and only when alone, the infant is able to do the equivalent of what in an adult would be called relaxing. The infant is able to become unintegrated, to flounder, to be in a state in which there is no orientation, to be able to exist for a time without being either a reactor to an external impingement or an active person with a direction of interest or movement. . . . In the course of time there arrives a sensation or an impulse. In this setting the sensation or impulse will feel real and be truly a personal experience. . . . The individual who has developed the capacity to be alone is constantly able to rediscover the personal impulse.
>
> [WINNICOTT, *THE CAPACITY BE ALONE,*
> PP. 30–34]

In a slightly later stage of development of the first pathway, the child experiences his dependency or his attempts to become autonomous as "bad." He feels guilty about his steps toward mastery. As one man recalled about his homesickness at sleepaway camp at age eleven, "I had a hard time at first being away from my mother. But then, when I started to enjoy myself, I felt guilty that I didn't need her so much." Such an individual does not feel that he has what Arnold Modell has called "the right to a life." He is bound by an umbilical cord of separation guilt.

In the second pathway, autonomy is associated with a minimum of shame and guilt and the child senses his parents' ambivalence about his growing up as a healthy balance. He or she feels loved. The child's growing autonomy is also furthered by identifying with parental models who themselves are autonomous.

Thus far, we are describing pathways toward isolation and autonomy that can occur equally for boys and girls. Something happens on the way to becoming adults so that men seek aloneness and women shun it.

GENDER DIFFERENCES: IS IT NATURE?

Freud's often quoted and debunked dictum "Anatomy is destiny" contains within it the still deeply held assumption that there are fundamental, biologically mediated, immutable differences between men and women. Whenever a man says angrily "Just like a woman!" or a woman says in exasperation "Men!," they are blaming gender differences. But there is far less fact than fantasy in our prejudices about gender. The social sciences substantiate fewer clear differences than one might expect.

In 1974, Eleanor Maccoby and Carol Jacklin summarized the research findings on gender differences and concluded that males are more aggressive as early as age two; girls have greater verbal ability, on average, after age eleven; and boys tend to have greater mathematical and visual-spatial abilities after ages twelve or thirteen, and the disparity widens in high school. Their most notable finding was how few solid gender differences could be substantiated.

In 1983, the sociologist Alice Rossi surveyed the research since Maccoby and Jacklin. She concluded that support existed for the findings that men:

1. are more likely to act according to rules and less apt to perceive the undertones of any situation;
2. are more vulnerable to becoming dyslexic or stuttering;

3. have a superior visual and graphic sense;
4. can manipulate objects and visualize them in space better;
5. can read maps and know directions better.

Women:

1. are more interested in human facial expression and thus better able to read emotions;
2. speak earlier and more fluently;
3. are more sensitive to sound, smell, and touch;
4. pick up peripheral information more quickly and understand it faster.

The research seems to make clear that there are gender differences in how men and women attend to and perceive the world, and that they have different cognitive strengths—or, put another way, their brains are wired differently. Conventional wisdom holds that men are strong, objective, achievement-oriented, logical, independent, and less expressive of emotions other than anger. Women are believed to be overly emotional, intuitive, manipulative, irrational, sensitive, weak, and indirect in expressing anger. Interestingly, the Maccoby, Jacklin, and Rossi reviews found little hard evidence for most of these stereotypes.

In 1983, Leslie Brody, a developmental psychologist at Boston University, reviewed the research on gender differences in emotional development, specifically whether women handle feelings such as anger differently than men. Contrary to what stereotypes would predict, infant boys are more irritable, cry more intensely, and are more difficult to console than infant girls. However, the typical developmental path is for boys to increasingly inhibit the expression of most other emotions while girls inhibit the expression of anger. Brody concluded that much of what we consider to be innate gender differences in temperament are self-fulfilling prophecies that we impose on children as they grow up. Further, Brody suggested that many so-called feminine characteristics, such as expressing sadness and not anger, being sensitive to nonverbal meanings, and blaming themselves, represent accommodations to low status, little power, male aggressiveness, and to their role as primary child-rearers. Similarly, men's hiding all emotions except anger and their competitiveness may be necessary adaptations to the work-place.

In a 1990 review of gender development research, Eleanor Maccoby concluded that differences between the sexes may have been underestimated because researchers focused largely on in-dividual personality characteristics. She found that boys and girls develop distinctive social styles in their gender-segregated play groups, starting as early as age three. In brief, little girls are polite and cooperative, little boys are rough and competitive. These patterns foreshadow the ways that women engage in more intimate dialogue and defer through "silent applause" when with men, and the ways that men are aggressive.

Thus far, it would appear that much of what passes for innate gender differences is a reflection or echo of our own gender stereotypes. They are cultural, not instinctual. But there are some intriguing observations of infants, reviewed by the New York psychoanalyst Doris Silverman, that suggest otherwise. Silverman believes that girl babies are generally more calm, less irritable, and more alert than boy babies. As a result, girls can develop better social skills and feel more comfortable with their mothers than can little boys. Of particular note is research that shows that girl infants are better able to engage a gaze by their mothers and to feel enhanced attunement in such a gaze than little boys. Boys, whose neurophysiologic makeup renders them more fussy and irritable, may find extended eye contact with mother overstimulating and need to withdraw from social contact. Winnicott's poetic phrase—"The first mirror is the mother's face"—suggests the profound impact such face-to-face interaction has on the development of self.

If one adds to this the overwhelming research support for the fact that girl babies have better early verbal abilities, what emerges is a subtle but consistent biological basis for greater bonding between mother and daughter than between mother and son. Male infants' physiology may impel them away, not toward, their mothers, and presumably this pattern repeats itself in their relationships as adults. From this perspective, perhaps Freud needs to be rephrased as "Gazing is destiny."[2]

THE REPRODUCTION OF ALONENESS: THE ROLE OF NURTURE

It seems overly deterministic and simplistic to attribute men's proclivity for autonomy solely to subtle neurophysiologic differences, however. Men's need to cling to independence at the cost of intimacy is driven by emotional imperatives other than aversion of their mothers' gaze. From this perspective, it is not just what little boys *are* that is crucial, but whom they need to become.

Freud and his early followers linked core sexual and gender identity to the crucible of the Oedipus complex. But it has since become clear that the bedrock sense of masculinity and femininity is established in both boys and girls at a much earlier age. Nancy Chodorow argues that gender differences in autonomy are due to women being the primary caretakers in the early years of a child's life. For girls to experience themselves as "female," they must maintain a close relationship with their mothers and understand that they are alike. For boys to feel masculine, they must be *different* and therefore must make a clear-cut break from their mothers. To achieve this, boys may need to build higher and firmer walls than girls to ensure a sense of separateness and difference. We are beginning to see, then,

[2]The nature-versus-nurture debate remains unsettled. Clearly, gender differences cannot be attributed exclusively to either fixed biologic differences or cultural influences. Their intersection at certain critical periods in early development may be crucial. Cultural norms about femininity and masculinity are probably transmitted by social institutions, the family, and social interaction with peers. Further, the zeitgeist about gender, indeed whether sex differences exist at all, has shifted back and forth, a reflection of fluctuating trends in research. See Laqueur (1990) for a fascinating historical review and Kimura (1992) for a discussion of how hormones may lead to cognitive gender differences.

what men may be walling out when they seek out aloneness and autonomy. Men's gender identity may continue to need such barriers to defend itself against intimacy. Men are constantly trying to plug up the dikes in order not to be swamped by the ocean of femininity. In contrast, women, whose gender identity rests on a close connection with their mothers, will experience threats to the self through its loss. Autonomy and aloneness are felt to undermine the female self. Women's fear is to be cut off from the ocean. From early childhood, women are socialized toward maintaining a relationship and define themselves within a relational framework. Boys and men tend to see themselves from the removed vantage point of an independent self.

To test these ideas, Susan Pollak and Carol Gilligan asked over one hundred men and women to make up stories in response to a series of ambiguous pictures—a test known as the Thematic Apperception Test (TAT). The most dramatic finding was the frequency of violence in men's stories about intimacy. Further analysis revealed that in situations of close personal affiliation, men projected more danger than in situations involving personal achievment. For example, one picture showed male and female trapeze artists in midair. In many of the male stories one or both fell to their deaths. Men saw intimacy as the threat and were afraid of either being caught in smothering relationships or shamed by abandonment and betrayal. Women were just the opposite—they saw danger in the isolation that they associated with success and impersonal achievement. For example, they found a picture of a man alone at his office desk most threatening.

In short, women fear being alone if they are threatened with the loss of their connection to a man. It is not that they require his physical presence—what is crucial to them is intimate connection in a larger sense. A man fears being connected and seeks aloneness as a safeguard against these fears. His separateness can occur in a variety of ways—through physical distance, the avoidance of commitment, or a more subtle withdrawal in which he shares little of his inner self.

From Chodorow's perspective, little boys and grown men

unconsciously are always needing to fend off the original sense of oneness with their mother, which threatens their gender identity. This fending off may be reciprocal, Chodorow points out, for "though children of both sexes are originally part of her self, a mother unconsciously and often consciously experiences her son as more of an 'other' than her daughter."

Boys do not have the opportunity that little girls have of growing up with the bond with their mother that later readily translates into close relationships with others. Since fathers historically have not been very available, learning what it is to be masculine comes from learning to be *not* feminine. For boys and men, being masculine is integrally linked with going away from a relationship, and indeed from any aspect of life tinged with femininity, such as strong feelings, dependency, and openness. Like their tragic predecessor, Narcissus, men are left staring into a mirror trying to reassure themselves that they are *not* someone else!

Although it was the famous female actess Greta Garbo who is best known for saying "I *vant* to be alone," it is the credo of many men today.

THE TRAUMA OF EVERY BOY'S LIFE

Deep in a man's psyche lies the formative experience of a little boy struggling to maintain a masculine self. He is unable to grieve and therefore is forever yearning for the oneness with mother that can never be regained. Chodorow has focused on the bond between mothers and daughters, which she describes as close and significant. There is a poignant silence in the feminist literature, however, about what it must feel like for a little boy to no longer be able to hold onto his mother. Surely this societally enforced separation from the most cherished, admired, and loved person in his life must be felt as a terrible loss. All the more so because it occurs in a family context in which sisters are encouraged to remain connected to her. Fathers, if they are around at all, are usually not particularly attuned to boys' needs and fail to catch their sons when they fall out of the maternal Garden of Eden.

Men's traumatic experience of abandonment, though not consciously remembered, forever casts a shadow on their relationships. It is a sadness that cannot be named, a sense of yearning without a clear object. It cannot be remembered in part because it occurred so early in life and in part because wanting to be close to mother feels shameful. It is shameful because unrequited love often elicits humiliation and because the culture enforces a stoic code on male children to be "big boys" and not to cry. This normative male trauma[3] helps explain why men are so often written off as narcissistic. Pathologic narcissism refers to a damaged self that has lost the capacity to love; such an individual has been severely traumatized by empathic failures in his early development. But trauma is best regarded as a continuum, and in less severe forms, such as the boy's culturally prescribed loss of his mother, may lead to scarring of adult character that looks "narcissistic." It would be further traumatizing, however, to brand such wounded men with pathologic labels, just as in the past women have been done an injustice by calling their normative adaptations "hysterical," "dependent," and due to envy of a man's penis.

Martin revealed in therapy how when he became romantically involved for the first time in his early twenties he felt compelled to travel alone to India on a spiritual quest. He was miserable for the three months he was there, missing his girlfriend terribly, and wondering why he had subjected himself to such hardships. Only years later in therapy could he realize how he had unwittingly replayed the loss of his mother.

Throughout life men may continue to wall themselves off from women. It is the only way they know to reassure themselves of their identity ("not female") and to protect themselves against ever being left again. But the need for intimate connec-

---

[3]See William Pollack, "No man Is an Island" and "Boys Will Be Boys" for further discussion of this common and potentially traumatic disruption of the young boy's connection to a caring milieu—the so-called holding environment of childhood.

tion with a woman, though buried, continues to press for expression. This results in the stereotypic relationship in which men unconsciously yearn for closeness, seek out women who may meet this need, but then need to deny their dependency on them. This takes the form of leaving them, thereby recasting the play of traumatic abandonment, with the woman put into the victim role. Such role reversal from passive to active is a favorite device used by the psyche to help it master old trauma. Less dramatic, but even more common, is the man who remains physically present in a relationship but emotionally leaves. Women find themselves forever pursuing both kinds of men, who never have to acknowledge their own needs because they can count on women to always need *them*.

It is not really true then that men always seek out aloneness; rather *they need to believe they are alone*, or at least not dependent or needful while in the midst of a relationship.

One man, describing his difficulties in paying many of his bills and in maintaining commitments with women, was reminded by his therapist of his regularity in attending to his therapy bills. "Oh," he responded, "I view you like the phone or electric company—an essential support system that I wouldn't want to have abruptly turned off." Further associations revealed that this was his way of seeing his girlfriend, although consciously he had rejected this "dependency" upon her.

Women face a formidable challenge as they try to have an intimate relationship with men. They are in constant danger of setting off the tripwire of men's anxiety about losing their self-sufficiency. A man's independence may be only a face-saving illusion in his own mind. But it is an illusion he will go to great lengths to preserve.

The biblical character Samson appeared mighty until a woman cut his hair when he fell asleep in her bed. Many men act as if they were afraid of a similar fate. The parable further suggests that women may unwittingly threaten a man's masculinity because they do not realize his vulnerability and are therefore not able to respond empathically to it.

CULTURAL COVER-UP

Somewhere along the road to masculinity, the awful abandonment of childhood becomes the sought-for aloneness of
manhood. It is not just sought for; it is glorified. In a manner
that would make an advertising firm proud, the weak, mother-
needing, sad boy is transformed into the heroic "lone cowboy,"
"the Marlboro Man," the rugged individualist. They may not
leap tall buildings in a single bound, but in every other respect
they appear to be supermen—lone rangers who while they may
share their bed or domicile with women, prefer to work alone,
succeed alone, and suffer alone. On closer analysis this appears
to be a sad and lonely existence, but from the perspective of man
as hero it plays like an ideal stoicism. Aloneness, autonomy, and
self-sufficiency are equated with male strength. Indeed, men are
cast as the *only* possessors of strength.

In 1976, the psychologist Inge Broverman asked professional
mental health workers to describe a healthy woman, a healthy
man, and a healthy person. Their characterization of the man
and the person were much the same—a capacity for clear decision making, responsible action, and autonomous thinking. But
the healthy woman was pictured as dependent and passive.

Men are not the only ones who have bought into these cultural stereotypes. For generations women have idealized these
same mythic prototypes, from John Wayne to John Kennedy.
Perhaps that is why, with the birth of feminist psychology, such
stone idols have fallen so precipitously.

One young woman who had suffered the disappointment of
an early marriage and quick divorce entered therapy depressed
and concerned about "the type of men I seem to end up with."
Janet had grown up in a household in which her father was quite
removed and at times even abusive to the women in the family.
Her mother appeared to her as ineffectual and never provided
the nurturance that she yearned for. Her first husband had res-
cued her from the family but turned out to be unable to detach
himself from his own mother.

Now Janet was faced with how to choose new partners.

She began to find that almost every man she met eventually disappointed her. She would choose highly individualistic, headstrong men who at first seemed attractive and "strong." Before long she would feel hurt by their acting unresponsive and "uncaring." A breakthrough in the therapy occurred when she noticed that her expectations of men to be strong and autonomous drew her toward the type of man who was unable to be aware of her feelings and unable to share his own vulnerabilities. With this insight, she was able to become more interested in men who at first seemed "less exciting" but who turned out to be more open and nurturant.

Janet's struggle is all too common. We all—men *and* women—have been confused by our cultural overselling of the autonomous, strong man. Just as women have been oppressed by the cultural ideal of the slim, always nurturant female, which has straitjacketed their bodies as well as their minds, men have also been shortchanged by a stereotype. We have all come to expect men to be "strong" and been disappointed when men either cannot live up to this standard or, doing so, appear unable to meet the demands of intimacy. And so we have moved from idealization of the solitary superman to denigration of such cold, uncaring, unfeeling, *bad* men.

TOO WELL OR TOO SICK

Judging by women's magazines and many nonfiction best-sellers, the world is now menaced by immature, emotionally defective, disappointing men. Is it really possible that there are that many "bad" men out there, and is it necessary to educate women to steer away from so many "foolish choices"? Or is it more likely that we have been wedded for so long to a cultural myth of a totally self-sufficient man that, once the myth was debunked, the pendulum has swung too far in the opposite direction?

Autonomy has been overrated and its role misunderstood in the development of both men and women. Historically, men

have been considered "too healthy" to need relationships, therapy, or practically anything. Now it turns out that these men
may have been walled off in a world of defensive self-sufficiency, a kind of pseudo-autonomy in which they have been
dependent on women while denying their need for such support. They are being branded by some women as "too sick" to
form the mature, loving relationships that most women want.

Such hostility may be a necessary developmental stage as men
and women free themselves of old stereotypes. The strength
of women's attacks on men is fueled by anger at their past
mistreatment and their feeling more confident in insisting that
men pay attention to their needs. No doubt it is also driven by
women's fear about the parts of themselves that are still drawn
to such "bad" men. Some of the men we see are able to admit
to the ways they once mistreated their lovers or wives, regret
it, and sincerely try to change. But they frequently report that
their wives either can't see these changes, don't believe them
genuine, or perhaps need them to remain the powerful, unfeeling thugs they have always known. Emblematic of this pattern
was one couple in which the husband lamented that his wife
had always referred to him as "Charles," while his friends had
called him by the name with which he was most comfortable—
"Charlie."

There is a limit to how much anger alone can accomplish,
and declaring all men villains is probably just as limiting as
idealizing them. The obstacles on both sides to change are formidable. For those men and women who want to help men to
change, what can they do?

TWO SOLUTIONS: STONE
CENTER AND STONE AGE

One popular notion is that since women are expert in having relationships, men should learn how to relate from them.
Some would say that this view is at least implicit in many
women's theorists, such as those at Wellesley College's Stone

Center.[4] While each gender has much to teach the other about its unique perspective and talents, casting women as men's teachers is not an adequate solution. Rightly or wrongly, men have an inherent resistance to being "one down" and will not gracefully accept women as their teachers. Consider the difficulty that a typical man has in merely asking a stranger for traffic directions, and you have some idea of the problem. Men associate needing help with dependency, and being seen as dependent feels shameful. In many couples that we see, the pattern is that the woman feels that she knows what is wrong with the relationship and she tries to educate the man—through intimate talks, through therapy, through suggesting he read books. But he doesn't "get it." It is understandable that women get frustrated with men and there is much they could teach them. But as the feminists well know, one sex cannot define the other. Even if they could accept it, men cannot learn from women all that they need to know—about their own pain, their own place in the family, about being men. Men cannot find themselves through echoing the experience of women. They must look into the mirror and see who they really are.

One other proposed solution is that men must turn away from women and return to their own primitive roots, as prescribed, for example, by Robert Bly. They must learn from other men the mythos of the "wild man"—men with hair on their chest whose knowledge about the world and themselves is earned through blood and sweat. This might be termed the Stone *Age* approach. Such a return to archaic roots correctly appreciates the depth toward which men must grope to find themselves, but it is a naïve and simplistic solution to the complex problem of men's and women's difficulties with each other. Bly's solution turns too much away from relationships with women and ignores the role that women may have in helping men to understand themselves. Further, it unwittingly lends itself to bashing women, exchanging psychological clubs for wooden ones. Feel-good solutions are insufficient for the com-

[4]The Stone Center is a think tank for feminist theory and women's relational development, with many seminal ideas based on the work of Jean Baker Miller.

plex, empathic linkages necessary to achieve mature adult relations. How can a tomtom be the best means of communication in an age of faxes?

There must be an alternative to men becoming "second-class" women or clenched-jaw "he-men."

I AND WE

We have said much about the way the new psychology of women describes how men and women diverge in their development. Whether because of nature or nurture, men and women specialize in different spheres of adaptation—men in independent achievement and women in relationships. Such specialization is fundamental to each gender's identity and to their self-esteem. Men's center of gravity—the reference point around which their lives revolve—is located within themselves. For this reason, on good days they can appear to have a "strong character," to have substance and weight. On bad days, they can appear selfish, even narcissistic, oblivious of other people's needs. Psychologists refer to this reference point within the self as the ego ideal. Men are constantly seeking to live up to the standards of this ideal self, which typically require them to achieve higher positions, climb bigger mountains, earn more money, and make new sexual conquests. Ironically, what may turn into an impersonal quest for trophies is rooted in relationship, because the ego ideal itself develops out of early identifications with loved and feared parental figures.

In contrast, for women the center of gravity does not lie within the self. They, too, have an ego ideal but it is not appeased by impersonal achievement. The old psychology pictured women's center of gravity as lying too much in other people—women were seen as "dependent" and unable to stand on their own. It is more accurate to say that women's center of gravity lies *between* themselves and other people. It is not that they seek approval and a reflection of their worth in other people's eyes but that they measure their value in terms of the quality of their transactions with intimate others. This confusion of tongues, between men's needs to deny their affiliative bonds while shoring up their independent identity and women's wish for recognition of their relational capacities, may lead to much of the misunderstanding inherent in close heterosexual relationships.

These differences between men and women can no longer be interpreted as pathology but must be treated as basic gender differences. They become problematic, however, when either sex fails to appreciate the complexity of the other and instead makes the other into a caricature. Men can no longer afford to be seen as the lone wolves and women as the keepers of the flame. Both sexes must discover within themselves the capacity to get close and to be independent, although their styles of intimacy and achievement are different.

The Boston University Pregnancy and Parenthood Study[5] found that the *balance* between autonomy and affiliation is a better indicator of individual and family well-being than either capacity alone. Interestingly, it was also found that the particular measures of autonomy and affiliation in men and women had to be adjusted by gender. For example, healthy mothering of infants was characterized by acceptance and warmth while good fathering was more a matter of giving infants "attention." Mature men and women need to find ways to be a healthy "I" and a healthy "we," but they have to do it in distinct ways.

As they try to have relationships with each other, men and women get into trouble because intimacy and identity have become polarized along gender lines. In marriage, indeed in all intimate relationships, gender differences are exaggerated when men and women seek to reassure themselves about their masculinity and femininity. This smallest circle of our lives is hardly immune to the cultural puzzlement about gender, which is masked by stereotyped images of men and women. As the psychotherapist Wendy Rosen has described it, the culture car-

[5]Several researchers collaborated in this project led by Frances Grossman, Ph.D. The point made here is largely attributable to William Pollack, with indebtedness to George Klein and Gerry Stechler.

ries out a gender-based surgery in which vital parts of the self
are excised from each sex.

In a relationship between a man and a woman, both partners
seldom understand the roots of their differences, nor do they
have a depth of feeling for each other's predicament. A reconcili-
ation between the needs for relating and for autonomy becomes
possible only when men and women realize that they experience
relationships in entirely different ways due to their different
developmental paths. Each needs the other to move toward a
synthesis. *For men to move toward intimacy, they need to feel that
women can be empathic toward their need to deny their dependency.*
Men can be connected to women, but they often need to save
face. A woman's reaching out to a man must be respectful of
his fears about being hurt and humiliated. Women must come
to see that men are not "bad" but "sad" about their loss of
connection. In like measure, women need men to respect their
valuing relationships and their personal definition of success.
They also need men to appreciate the full extent to which societal structures and men as individuals undercut women's assertiveness and contribute to women's feeling afraid to be
themselves.

Earlier we talked about two versions of aloneness (autonomy
and isolation) and the two pathways toward them—one based
on a secure connection in early life, the other as a protection
against retraumatization. For many men, their seeking independence or solitude may not feel to them to be a problem. And
even such men who wind up in psychotherapy may not come
to believe that their wishing to spend time alone is due to a
problem with intimacy. After all, every man's aloneness is not
a sign of pathology. It may be a valuing of self or a gender-based
need to affirm his manhood that has such early foundations and
is so culturally reinforced as to be an essential part of him. But
whatever form of aloneness men may practice and whatever
pathways they may have traveled to get there, they need to
understand that aloneness is neither an absolute nor an isolated
freedom. Just as the origins of a healthy capacity to be alone
spring from a relationship, so is aloneness in adult life nurtured
by relatedness. The value of aloneness may be difficult to ap-

preciate because for so long men have asserted it as a right that needed no explanation. A man is much more likely to find a good balance between aloneness and togetherness in a relationship and to gain his partner's acceptance of his need to spend time alone if it makes sense to both of them and is openly negotiated. An aloneness that is understood and appreciated as an essential need or that is seen as ultimately serving the relationship is not threatening. Autonomy does not necessarily have to be divorced from relationships.

A MODERN MYTH

We return to the young car salesman in *Rain Man* since his story of personal transformation may be an allegory for the men of our time. His mother died when he was quite young, leaving him with a father who he felt rejected him. The story begins with his father's death and the final gesture of rejection—his exclusion from his inheritance in favor of an unknown brother, who is autistic. He had forgotten that he had a brother and he does not understand what autism means—a profound impairment in the capacity to feel and to have relationships. His brother is capable of remembering everything, but the telephone book has as much meaning to him as Shakespeare. His life is merely an echo of things he hears or watches on television.

The salesman thinks that his life can be redeemed if he can regain a share of his inheritance and to this end takes his brother as a hostage. His girlfriend tries to stop him from using his brother but he doesn't listen to her, and she gives up on him.

He and his brother go on a journey. The car salesman wants to go the quick way—by airplane—but his brother's irrational fears force him to drive the back roads. On this journey, which turns into a quest to know his brother, he learns that his brother became a mother to him as a young child, singing lullabies to him. But then after the brother accidentally scalded him by not realizing the temperature of the bathwater, the autistic brother was sent away to be locked up in a mental institution. In trying to connect with his brother—the last surviving member of his family—he realizes his yearning for connection and the ways in which he, too, had been cut off from his feelings and from intimacy.

Taking this as an allegory, it suggests that men have lost their mothers at an early age and been filled up with bitterness at their unavailable, cold fathers. They think that solace can be found in material things and in casual intimacy with a woman. They have cut off their feelings in order not to remember the pain of their early losses. This much is clear-cut. But what does it mean that an autistic brother frees our hero from his empty aloneness? It is not a woman from whom he learns how to love, although his girlfriend is no small help to him *after* he has spent some time alone with his brother. Nor is it a father figure, not a "wild man" of iron and animal passion. The autistic brother is a symbol for himself—the damaged self that has been locked up and that must be seen, acknowledged, and understood in order to become free. The autistic brother is Echo to the salesman's Narcissus—each is condemned to his own version of isolation. But the salesman, unlike Ovid's characters, is capable of tragic insight. Interestingly, one ancient interpreter of the myth of Narcissus—Pausanias—has suggested that Narcissus had a twin sister whom he lost tragically through death. In this version, his searching in the spring for a perfect reflection of his own image was a need to find this lost twin—the other half of his own self!

At the beginning of his journey, our protagonist, like many men, is all dressed up, skilled, full of himself, but with really no place to go. Through our enhanced understanding of men's and boys' development, it may now be possible to admire how our hero had to prop himself up and that he did the best he could with what he had. He had to depend on others to sustain himself while his pride kept him from acknowledging his needs. He is caught on an island that he did not originally choose to visit but which traumatic loss and disappointment by Special

Women and Special Men have caused him to be afraid to leave. The way back to connection, to a life with others that is worth living, is most of all an inner journey. It is a journey not of self-absorption but of self-reflection that requires remembering earlier pain.

3

▼

SPECIAL WOMEN

Men's relationships with women are characterized by a long history and a short memory. Men need to forget the needs they once had for a Special Woman as part of the price exacted to be called a man. They need to turn their back on their past and on any woman who reminds them too much of their earliest yearnings. But the doors to the past are always open. Not only do the ghosts of men's past relationships take shape in the living forms of present-day women whom they love, but so, too, do shadows of ancient men and women seem to direct the course of our intimate lives. James is one such man, who, like many others we have treated, seemed to have one foot in the present and the other in a time long, long ago.

The only gift from his first girlfriend that James didn't destroy was a small Egyptian statue of a prone cat. When she left him, he burned all of her letters and photographs, but the marble statue he buried at the base of an old, dying maple at his parents' house. He vowed that one day he would give it to the one woman to whom he could be true. He was twenty-two.

As a child, James had been very close to his mother and was fearful about venturing out on his own. His father was a remote and self-absorbed man whom he felt did not really know him. He had been terribly homesick whenever he was away at camp and had had difficulty going to college in another state. But by his second year away from home he had managed to stop feeling guilty about not calling her. He felt that he was finally a man.

Years passed. In his mid-twenties he dated many women, several times thinking he had met the Right Woman, only to find months later that she was not smart enough, or not responsive enough in bed, or not beautiful enough. He was always drawn away by thoughts of his first girlfriend, who became ever more desirable as his memories of her grew less distinct, and by his fantasy of the perfect woman that he would one day meet. He could be happy in the past or in his hopes for the future, but in his day-to-day relationships he was restless and unfulfilled.

In his late twenties, on a rare occasion when James took an hallucinogen, he went for a walk in the woods at his parents' house. He wrapped his arms around the dying maple and sobbed about how much he longed to be close to his father. He had never known about these feelings.

In his thirties he married. But after the first passion cooled, he was faithful but aloof. The statue remained under the tree, and its existence remained a secret even from his wife.

IN OUR PRACTICES we have met many such men who are drawn relentlessly to good-byes. They ascribe enormous importance to women, seek them out, and can love them, albeit all too often only temporarily. Like the man with the buried statue, their yearnings are often split off from their present lives, embodied in a fantasy if not lived out in affairs. From one perspective it may look as if men are constantly fleeing from and devaluing women; from another it appears as though men are in thrall to them.

THE SPECIAL WOMAN

The psychologist Daniel Levinson believes that young men are guided by a vision or "Dream" of the kind of life they want to lead as adults. The Dream is more than a potpourri of goals; it is an organizing passion that defines an identity and a life course. According to Levinson, as he matures, a man depends on male mentors to help in refining and realizing his Dream. But even more important than other men is a particular relationship with a woman in which a young man feels held, believed in, and nurtured. This person Levinson called The Special Woman.

The Special Woman is no ordinary romantic relationship. It is a union of lust, tenderness, and teaching. Her primary importance is as a guide toward the fulfillment of a man's Dream. We would argue with Levinson's notion that the Special Woman has importance only as a transitional figure helping a man to ascend toward self-defined goals. The connection with a Special Woman can become a value in and of itself. Further, a Special Woman need not be a lover or wife—a man's mother, grandmother, sister, or friend can also have a hand in his growth at key points in his life course. Whether seen as an aid towards self-fulfillment or as a soul mate with whom a man shares his life, the Special Woman is pregnant with meaning and possibilities. She is a "second chance" to make up for what the little boy never got or had to part with too soon.

Two literary examples may best describe how she appears in her romanticized form. The first is from Pablo Neruda's *Twenty Love Poems and a Song of Despair*:

> You gather things to you like an old road.
> You are peopled with echoes and nostalgic voices.
> I awoke and at times birds fled and migrated
> That had been sleeping in your soul.
> [FROM "YOUR BREAST IS ENOUGH"]

In Hermann Hesse's *Demian*, Sinclair describes his first meeting with an older woman, Frau Eva:

> I was unable to utter a word. With a face that resembled her son's, timeless, ageless, and full of inner strength, the beautiful woman smiled with dignity. Her gaze was fulfillment, her greeting a homecoming. Silently I stretched my

hands out to her. She took both of them in her firm, warm hands.

"You are Sinclair. I recognized you at once. Welcome!"

Her voice was deep and warm. I drank it up like sweet wine. And now I looked up and into her quiet face, the black unfathomable eyes, at her fresh, ripe lips, the clear, regal brow that bore the sign.

"How glad I am," I said and kissed her hands. "I believe I have been on my way my whole life—and now I have come home."

She smiled like a mother.

"One never reaches home," she said. "But where paths that have affinity for each other intersect the whole world looks like home, for a time."

Few of us can transform the fullness of our hearts into art, but at least once in their lives, most men feel that a woman can stir them to poetry. Call it starry-eyed romanticism or idealization, men dream of women, are passionate about them, and fall in love with them. Both Neruda and Hesse sense that there are larger forces at work than mere lust or infatuation. The inscrutable workings of fate forge the connection with a Special Woman, who seems to speak with the seductive echoes of a maternal voice.

DREAMS AND NIGHTMARES

If such connections to Special Women may make all the difference for men's vitality and development, when things go awry with such women the fall is profound. Levinson and others have noted that when a man's lover or wife becomes unable or unwilling to be his guide and helpmate, he can become depleted, depressed, or rageful. For many women, being the cherisher of a man's Dream is not as fulfilling to them as they once hoped. They, in turn, may become disillusioned and angry at men for not being the Special Man they need to nurture their own Dream.

When such misunderstanding and hurt occurs in a relationship, the role of Special Woman, with all its poetic and dreamlike beauty, can metamorphose into an equally powerful negative presence. A man's Dream of the Special Woman has the potential for turning into his and her worst nightmare.

We are accustomed to such shocking reversals in psychic life when what was once loved becomes most hated, and vice versa. It is less intuitively obvious, however, that both poles of feeling may coexist as a compromise in which the extremes are hidden, much as a muted color may give no clue that it is made up of much bolder hues. Thus, for example, a man's apparent nonchalance about women and especially his disdain or disgust may be a cover-up for deep yearnings and disappointments.

"YOU'RE JUST LIKE MY MOTHER"

The imprint of a man's mother follows him through all his adult relationships. Unknowingly, he may try to find a substitute or he may run away from her, but he cannot escape the psychological effects of her earliest influence. As he grows up, a boy is taught not to need his mother. His need to be different from her in order to be masculine leaves him with a strong ambivalence, conflict, and hurt in his intimate relationships with women. The flood walls developed to keep out the ocean of maternal engulfment remain as a rigid need to guard his psychological boundaries. The result is that he is often forced to pretend not to need anyone. Not uncommonly, a man's need to assert his differentness also takes the form of a negatively tinged sense about all that is feminine. As Nancy Chodorow has suggested, for a boy becoming a man often means *not* being a woman or a girl. Indeed, traditional Orthodox Jews say a daily prayer paying homage to the Creator for "not making me a woman." Many a woman has tried to tell a man about how she falls under the shadow of his mother. She does not realize how hard it is for a man to acknowledge his mother's power over him. Her very attempt to enlighten him may be rejected because he feels she is criticizing him "just like my mother."

Still, like Hesse's Sinclair, men are drawn to as well as repelled by Special Women, who, in Pablo Neruda's words, are "peopled with echoes and nostalgic voices." Like strong perfume, a whiff of mother tantalizes, while too much can disgust.

OEDIPUS

For Freud, the ancient tale of Oedipus, as told by Sophocles, was the first psychoanalytic study, predating by twenty-three centuries the tortured unconscious pathways followed by Little Hans and Dora.[1] The psychological complex that bears his name is such a familiar part of our culture that the rich dynamics of the original story are typically overlooked. To understand our assumptions about gender we need to revisit the central myths that underlie them, in particular the myth of Oedipus. As with any good story passed through many generations, there are several versions. We will tell the tale from Oedipus's perspective, and then add to it revelations about his background that he came to know later in life.

Oedipus grew up in Corinth, believing himself to be the only son of King Polybus and Queen Merope. There is no suggestion that his childhood was anything but happy. He has a strange name—Oedipus ("swollen foot")—which refers to his swollen feet. On becoming a man, he is accused by someone of having been adopted. Determined to find out who his real parents are, Oedipus goes to the Delphic Oracle. There he is told some bad news and some worse news—he is destined to kill his father and to marry his mother. Thinking still that Polybus and Merope are his parents, he resolves never to return to Corinth.

[1] Little Hans and Dora refer to two early psychoanalytic cases that highlighted to Freud the importance of castration anxiety and other aspects of the Oedipus complex.

On the road from Phocis to Boeotia, he comes to a narrow
crossing where three roads meet. He is ordered off the road by
a driver of a chariot and his several attendants. When Oedipus
refuses, the travelers argue. After the driver hits him with his
whip, the infuriated Oedipus kills all but one attendant who is
able to escape.

Oedipus then arrives at Thebes, where matters are in a bad
state. Laius, the king, is missing and believed killed by robbers
on a recent trip. To make matters worse, the city is being
held hostage by the Sphinx, who strangles anybody who can't
answer her riddle. The Sphinx is terrible to behold—with
breasts and the face of a woman, but shaped like a winged
lion. The queen's brother, Creon, offers the kingdom and the
widowed queen to anyone who will do away with the Sphinx.
Oedipus, who never shrinks from what most men fear, accepts
the challenge.

The Sphinx asks him the riddle: "What is the only creature
on land or air or sea that goes on four feet in the morning, on
two at noon, and on three in the evening?"

Oedipus answers, "Thou hast spoken of man, who when a
baby creeps on four feet, walks erect in manhood, and in old
age leaneth on a staff as a third foot."

The Sphinx is so distraught that Oedipus has solved her
riddle that she kills herself by throwing herself on the rocks
below. He claims his prize of the kingdom and Queen Jocasta.
They have two daughters and two sons and for many years they
live happily.

But Oedipus has not escaped his past. A terrible plague comes
to Thebes, which kills people and herds, and blights the harvest
and women's wombs. Those not killed by plague face famine.
At Creon's suggestion, Oedipus sends him to the Delphic Oracle to ask for Apollo's help. The news Creon brings back is that
the plague will be stayed only if the murderer of King Laius is
brought to justice.

Oedipus is determined to save the city once again. He pro-
claims a curse on whoever did this dirty deed. But many years
have passed since Laius's disappearance, and a murder investiga-

tion is now difficult to conduct in a conventional manner. Oedipus sends for the blind seer Teiresias, who is the most revered man in the city.

In Sophocles' version, Teiresias is uncooperative when brought before the king. He says, "O, send me home. Take up your load and I'll take mine. Believe me, it is better so. I'd rather keep you and me from pain. Don't press me uselessly, my lips are sealed." Oedipus's temper again gets the better of him and he accuses Teiresias of complicity in Laius's murder. Teiresias loses his philosophic detachment and angrily lets out the words he wished to withhold, telling Oedipus, "The rotting canker in the state is *you*."

Oedipus does not believe Teiresias and charges him and Creon, whose idea it was to send for Teiresias, with plotting to overthrow his rule. When he threatens Creon, Jocasta intervenes and tries to discredit Teiresias's words by revelations of her own:

> Once long ago there came to Laius from—let's not suppose Apollo personally but from his ministers: an oracle, which said that fate would make him meet his end through a son, a son of his and mine.
>
> Well, there was a murder, yes; but done by foreign highwaymen—they say—where three highways meet. And secondly, the son, he at three days old is left by Laius (by other hands, of course) upon a trackless hillside, his ankles linked together.
>
> So there! Apollo fails to make the son his father's murderer, or father (Laius sick with dread) murdered by his son.
>
> [ROCHE, TRANS., P. 51]

Oedipus is shaken at the description of Laius's murder scene since it so resembles the intersection where he killed several men, but he clings to discrepancies, such as the report that it was not one but several men who killed Laius. He is determined to pursue the investigation.

A messenger then arrives from Corinth with news of the death of King Polybus (Oedipus's supposed father). Jocasta again sees this as proof of the Oracle's error: "Aha! Forecasts of the gods, where are you now? This is the man that Oedipus was in a fright to kill; so fled, and now without the smallest push from him—he's dead."

Oedipus says he's still worried about the prediction that he will marry his mother. Jocasta tries to cajole him out of his suspicions: "Forget this silly thought of mother-marrying. Why, many men in dreams have married mothers, and he lives happiest who makes the least of it." The well-meaning Corinthian messenger reassures Oedipus that he needn't have fled Merope on this account, since he was adopted. In fact, it was this same man who had received the infant Oedipus, his feet riveted together with a spike, from a shepherd of Laius.

It is Jocasta's turn to go pale. She pleads with Oedipus not to send for this shepherd, to leave well enough alone. But Oedipus insists that he must know his origins.

The shepherd is brought before the king, and like Teiresias, tries to avoid telling Oedipus the ghastly truth until Oedipus threatens him. He then reveals that the baby given to the man from Corinth and then raised by Polybus and Merope was taken from Laius's own house. It was given to the shepherd by the child's own mother—Queen Jocasta—because of the Oracle's warning that he would be a parent-killer.

The story ends with Jocasta hanging herself, and upon his finding her, Oedipus takes the golden brooches she was wearing and blinds himself, saying, "Wicked, wicked eyes! You shall not see me nor my shame—not see my present crime. Go dark, for all time blind to what you never should have seen, and blind to those this heart has cried to see."

THE OEDIPUS COMPLEX

Freud claimed that the great power that this myth still holds for us lies in our fearful recognition that all men harbor the same wishes that Oedipus lived out—murderous rage and jealousy toward their fathers and erotic love for their mothers. In Freud's words:

> . . . it is easy to see that the little man wants to have his mother all to himself, that he feels the presence of his father as a nuisance, that he is resentful if his father indulges in any signs of affection towards his mother and that he shows satisfaction when his father has gone on a journey or is absent. He will often express his feelings directly in words and promise his mother to marry her. It will be thought that this amounts to little compared to the deeds of Oedipus; but in fact it is enough, it is the same thing at root. . . . The little boy may show the most undisguised sexual curiosity about his mother, he may insist upon sleeping beside her at night, he may force his presence on her while she is dressing or may even make actual attempts at seducing her.
>
> [FREUD, *INTRODUCTORY LECTURES ON PSYCHOANALYSIS*,
> PP. 332–33]

> . . . While the poet, as he unravels the past, brings to light the guilt of Oedipus, he is at the same time compelling us to recognize our own inner minds, in which those same impulses, though suppressed, are still to be found. . . . Like Oedipus, we live in ignorance of these wishes, repugnant to morality, which have been forced upon us by Nature, and after their revelation we may all of us well seek to close our eyes to the scenes of our childhood.
>
> [FREUD, *THE INTERPRETATION OF DREAMS*, PP. 296–97]

The classic Oedipal conflict consists of the attraction of the little boy to his mother, the realization that his father will literally or symbolically castrate him if he persists in this rivalry, and the resolving of this conflict around age five through identification with his father. Eventually, in a later period of development, he is able to love his mother in a more platonic manner and sublimates his incestuous desires in the form of the wish to find a wife "just like Mom." However, as Freud's case studies illustrate and the myth of Oedipus warns, sublimation is not foolproof. Over and over again during Freud's analyses with his female patients, they recalled being seduced by their fathers. Freud came to believe that such recollections actually represented unconscious *wishes*, not real *acts*, and that little boys harbor erotic impulses toward their mothers similar to those little girls feel toward their fathers. Just as Oedipus had to run away from his supposed parents to try to escape his destiny, only to find it waiting for him in disguised form, so modern-day neurotic men are driven to connect with mother surrogates and just as powerfully compelled to run from their beds. Oedipus's destiny, and our own, is not preordained by the gods but by our primeval, unconscious wishes.

A traditional psychoanalytic interpretation of the myth of Oedipus holds that his name, "swollen foot," is a phallic symbol. His parents attempt to damage his "feet," that is to castrate him. Some analysts also draw an equation between eyeballs and testicles. They point out, for example, that Teiresias is blinded by the gods after a series of erotic indiscretions, such as peeping at the goddess Athena while she bathed. Thus, when Oedipus blinds himself, it is a symbolic self-castration for committing the crime of having sexual intercourse with his mother. This may sound farfetched, but our clinical experience suggests that many men do cripple their potency out of fear of oedipal wishes. They cannot tolerate competing with father and winning. Such self-castration may take the form of inhibited career potential, of sabotaging themselves on the brink of success (shooting themselves in the *foot*), as well as sexual impotence or avoidance of women they find most desirable.

During the therapy of James, the man who buried the statue of a cat, it became clear that his reluctance to commit himself to any woman had much to do with oedipal style concerns. Like Oedipus, he felt worried about getting too close to his mother and lacked a strong connection with his father that could have provided compensatory love for leaving mother. On one level, his burying of the statue represented his psychological interment of his wishes to be close to his mother, whose true identity is disguised as a girlfriend who abandoned him. He does not destroy the statue and expects to give it one day to his true love. That is, the wish to reunite with mother, while cloaked in a panoply of psychological costumes, lives on. In a powerful way, he remains betrothed to her and cannot truly marry any other woman.

The psychoanalyst Otto Kernberg believes that sexual passion is closely allied with defiance of taboo, such as incest. This does not mean that the best sex that a man could ever hope to have is with his mother. It suggests rather that some flirting with the forbidden is exciting, with the crossing of a boundary being more symbolic or metaphorical—the Special Woman is reminiscent of aspects of a man's mother, but she is *not* his mother. In this way, oedipal impulses are gratified while guilt is allayed.

OEDIPUS AND GENDER

In Sophocles' *Oedipus*, it is striking how much more outraged people are about incest than about parricide. As a palace official remarks about Oedipus, ". . . his father's murderer, his mother's—no, a word too foul to say . . ." Jocasta kills herself after wailing "Unhappy bed! Twice wicked soil! The father's seedbed nurtured for the mother's son!" Oedipus himself laments, "I handed you my blood to drink—the chalice of my father's. O what memories have you of my manners then, or what I did when after that I came here? Yes, you batch of weddings! Birthdays breeding seedlings from their very seed. Fathers, sons and brothers flourishing in foulness with brides and wives and mothers in a monstrous coupling; unfit to tell what's too unfit to touch."

Such gnashing of teeth and drastic punishment visited upon the perpetrators at their own hands testifies to the revulsion against mother-son incest, or as Freud so brilliantly realized, the powerful guilt that accompanies such wishes. For such emphatic prohibitions are unnecessary to guard against impulses that no one feels inclined to indulge.

We doubt, however, that these impulses to connect with

mother, either as a boy or as a man, are largely about the desire to achieve erotic union. They are also wishes to keep her close, to be comforted, and considered special. In the light of our new understanding of how masculinity is precariously contingent upon suppressing any dependence on mother, we can better appreciate the Thebans' attitude toward Oedipus's transgressions. To kill one's father is terrible, yet at least one remains a man; but to share mother's bed is to lose one's masculinity. *So-called castration anxiety is about loss of gender identity*, and therefore not simply about feared damage to a man's genitals. One of Freud's great contributions was to undo Western culture's censorship so that the power of lust, aggression, and sexual curiosity could be fully appreciated. But his focus on impulse and our continuing cultural anxiety about men's sexual prowess have led to a mistaken emphasis on genitalia and sexual acts. As much as some men may seem to stake their claim to manhood by rampant sexual encounters, traditional masculinity is as much defined by strict limits on closeness as it is by racking up "scores." As the myth of Oedipus points out, a man's gender identity—his male authority—is very much a matter of whom he does *not* share a bed with.

THE MADONNA AND THE WHORE

A less felicitous solution to the oedipal dilemma than Kernberg's notion of flirting with taboo is for a man to split off his erotic desires from his romantic, tender feelings, with each directed at different women. As Freud put it in "The Tendency to Debasement in Love," "The erotic life of such people remains dissociated, divided between two channels, the same two that are personified in art as heavenly and earthly (or animal) love. Where such men love they have no desire and where they desire they cannot love."

Such men may love the "madonna"—the loving, caring, nurturing, maternal woman with great affection but cannot feel much sexual interest in her. Other women toward whom they feel no such tender or close connection will seem enormously erotic and will often be degraded. In the extreme case, a man has a motherly or sisterly relationship with his wife and is capable of functioning sexually only with a prostitute or some woman he considers to be far beneath him. More subtly, it appears as adolescent boys' and later adult men's sexual fantasies about "bad" women, whose gargantuan carnal appetites are applauded with titillation and contempt or who are forced to submit to sexual acts. Even for those men who are capable of sustaining a marriage, the largest measure of their passion is split off from it.

Men's sexual fantasies open one window into their deepest feelings toward women. In the Sexual Fantasy Project at the Columbia University Psychoanalytic Center, 11 percent of the men questioned had fantasies of torturing their sex partners, 20 percent fantasized about whipping or beating partners, and 44 percent imagined forcing their partners to submit to sexual acts.

Is all this naked aggression and need to degrade a way of ensuring that sex and maternal feeling are never mixed up, or are there other, even more potent causes for such darker impulses? To answer this question we will need to reconsider Freud's interpretation of Oedipus.

BOYS WHO LOVE TOO MUCH

Oedipus is not Narcissus, but he is not free of narcissism. The ancient Greek audience, for whom Sophocles intended his play, would undoubtedly argue with Freud that Oedipus is not primarily a story about how instincts cause more families to turn out like the Beans of Egypt, Maine, than Ozzie and Harriet; it is a cautionary tale about the dangers of hubris. As the play concludes: "Citizens of our ancestral Thebes, look on this Oedipus, the mighty and once masterful, elucidator of the riddle, envied on his pedestal of fame. You saw him fall; you saw him swept away. So, being mortal, look on that last day and count a man not blessed in his life until he's crossed life's bounds unstruck by ruin still."

Even mighty Oedipus, who was brave and clever enough to vanquish the hideous Sphinx, can fall from beloved king to an outcast. We can admire Oedipus's dogged insistence on learning the truth about himself, but the very trait that makes him heroic is also his fatal flaw. He thinks that there is no riddle that he cannot solve and he is blind to the evidence that *he* could be the guilty one. He rejects all advice and when opposed gets petulant and threatening. The first time anyone, such as Teiresias, dares suggest that he should look into the mirror, he becomes enraged and thinks that his brother-in-law is trying to betray him. This is what clinicians mean by "narcissistic character"—inflexibility, grandiosity, throwing tantrums when frustrated, exquisite vulnerability to criticism. And narcissistic character is not a legacy of the little boy's requited or unrequited erotic love for his mother during the oedipal stage of development. The psychological injury that gives birth to such an immature grown-up is due to a child's early experience of not being empathically responded to and loved for who he is.

Oedipus is abandoned to die by his own mother and father. It is not Oedipus's lust for his mother and jealousy of his father that sets the stage for his downfall but his parents' rejection of him. We will leave consideration of the role of father (Laius) and of male mentors (Teiresias) to the chapter on Special Men and focus here on Jocasta and Merope. Jocasta fails to provide the most basic care and protection for young Oedipus; she is unable to find a way to care in developmentally appropriate ways for both husband and son. The child needs to feel loved by both parents in order to relinquish his unrealistic wish for exclusive possession of his mother. Oedipus's fixation on mothers, which he was never able to give up, is not just due to lust, but to a need to clutch to a mother's apron strings after he has been abandoned.

Interestingly, Freud chose to ignore Oedipus's earliest trauma and blame the id. This omission is consistent with Freud's pivotal theoretical shift of replacing sexual trauma with unconscious fantasy as the nidus of neurosis. In recent years, as the true incidence of sexual abuse in families has become better recognized, women who were formerly viewed as having "character pathology" are increasingly seen as adapting to actual, severe trauma. While it is unlikely that boys are physically and sexually abused as frequently as little girls, boys, too, deserve an empathic understanding of their gender-specific trauma. The point is not to villainize Jocasta or any other mother, but to acknowledge that men *feel* they have been abandoned by their mothers. Like Oedipus, most men have no conscious memory of this early trauma, though their vulnerability in adult life is evidence of the unhealed wound.

The first Special Woman causes problems for men in yet another way. In Sophocles' *Oedipus*, Jocasta repeatedly tries to dissuade Oedipus from exploring his origins. "Forget it all," she advises. "It's not worth knowing now." It is less clear why Merope (or Polybus) never told Oedipus that he was adopted. Perhaps both his mothers wished to protect their son from pain. But in doing so they infantilize Oedipus and ultimately collude in causing him far greater suffering. Their silence protects *themselves*: Merope worries that if Oedipus knows he was adopted he will leave her for his true mother, and Jocasta fears that if Oedipus pursues his quest he will be lost to her. Oedipus, and other men, are deprived of the power of self-knowledge by mothers who cannot bear to have their sons leave them. This brings us to the meaning of the Sphinx.

THE RIDDLES OF THE SPHINX

The Sphinx is a terrifying representation of femininity. The name means "the strangler," and according to the myth, until Oedipus arrived, she strangled only *men* who dared to challenge her. She therefore stands for some kind of obstacle that men have to overcome in relationship to Special Women. The riddle that she requires men to solve is about development—the child becomes the man becomes the old man. Those who cannot solve her riddle cannot develop—they are smothered by the possessive mother who, like Jocasta and Merope, cannot let her sons leave her. Oedipus is the only one who can defeat her because he had to grow up without his real mother and does not know who she is. He is not in awe of her as other men are. Ultimately, the myth is about how Oedipus winds up being trapped by his mother, suggesting yet again how difficult it is for a man to escape his dependency upon her.

According to Theodore Lidz of Yale University, the Sphinx is representative of a powerful theme in Greek mythology:

> The Sphinx is a symbol of the chthonic deities, the under-world defenders of mother-right who antedated the Olympians in Greece—a carry-over from the time when the mother, having been impregnated by an ancestor spirit, was the child's only blood relative. She is a Ker, related to the Erinyes who pursued Orestes after he murdered his mother. . . . It is she, the Sphinx, who blocks the youth's way to independent manhood, and thus is related to the Great Mother goddesses such as Cybele who were worshipped in Asia Minor.
>
> [LIDZ, PP. 42–43]

According to Lidz, the Thebans traditionally believed that their earliest ancestors were born without mothers, and much of their mythology is characterized by the denial of the importance of motherhood and by mothers who, like Jocasta, abandon their infants. Oedipus, who solved the riddle of the Sphinx and married his mother, challenges the power of the Special Woman and for a time succeeds. But his downfall is a warning to men through the centuries of the price of denying their dependency upon her.

We are reminded of James, who buried the statue of a cat that his first girlfriend had given to him. Like Oedipus, he thought that he had left his mother, only to find that his delicately balanced need for and fear of a Special Woman dominated his life. Not until the third year of his therapy with one of us did he recall having buried the statue. When asked to make an association, he thought about the passionate lovemaking with his first girlfriend that she had referred to as two cats in heat. He said that he had never felt as passionate since. Then he said, "You know, it also reminds me of those ancient statues of an animal with the head of a woman."

EARTH MOTHER

The specialness and dreamlike quality that a certain woman has for a man is mysterious and powerful. Anthropologists and sociologists use the term "numinous" to refer to such qualities that inspire awe and border on the mythical or the divine.

Although much of Greco-Roman mythology highlighted masculine prowess and warrior gods, a significant prehistorical mythos is dedicated to the feminine. Riane Eisler points out that in early civilizations the central power was seen as residing in goddesses of nature. In these societies, such as in Minoan Crete, masculine and feminine were linked in a less hierarchical partnership. They were not so much matriarchal as matrifocal—organized around the feminine but not dominated by women. Such societies were symbolized by the chalice—the open cup of caring and giving. This was in contrast to the "dominator" model of society in which men dragged women off by their hair. The primary symbol in such societies was the blade—the chthonic exploits of muscle-bound heroes. As best we can understand, in these very early cultures God was not anthropomorphized as a male warrior who might at times be kindly, but as a woman with associated animal images—the Snake or Bird Goddess, or the Goddess of Vegetation. Such a Mother God, by effecting the cycles of nature, had mysterious power over life and death. Men worshiped her because they realized her power.

Yet such Great Mothers were not always *good* mothers. They

could be avenging and angry—as in the plague of Thebes, crops and people could be destroyed by drought or flood, over which men had no control. As Camille Paglia points out in *Sexual Personae*, "Daemonic archetypes of woman, filling world mythology, represent the uncontrollable nearness of nature." (p. 13)

Carl Jung linked such anthropological archetypes, reflective of women's numinous power over men, to the early mother-child relationship: "The mother-child relationship is certainly the deepest and most poignant one we know; in fact, for some time the child is, so to speak, part of the mother's body. Later it is part of the psychic atmosphere of the mother for several years, and in this way everything original in the child is indissolubly blended with the mother-image." [Jung, *Collected Works* 1969, Para. 723]

The Earth Mother mythos has since been overlaid by cultural layers of masculine and dominator warlike repression, but we suspect that it remains as a powerful undercurrent in our psyches. As Jung points out, the early experience of mother as an enveloping, all-important presence remains with us. He would have seen the man who buried the statue of a cat as proof of how the powerful mother continues to be represented in an ancient archetype. We are all closer to Oedipus in time and in psychological makeup than we realize.

One of Freud's contributions was to see the unconscious as a repository of our cultural and individual experience. Like the layerings of successive civilizations built on each other's ruins, psychic themes are preserved. Buried within men is the sense that women are magnetic, capricious, and controlling goddesses. As with the Great Mother goddesses of prehistory, men recognize the very strange and powerful roles of women and resent their influence. They long for connection with these Special Women of whose potency they are jealous. Small wonder, then, that at least in fantasy, as evidenced in the Columbia study, they wish they could force their will upon them. Men long to have power over women precisely because they still fear they are dependent, powerless little boys.

SISTERHOOD IS POWERFUL

For many men, sisters are another kind of Special Woman. Unlike the situation with mothers and fathers, many people underestimate siblings' importance, in particular their positive influence on development.

Oedipus had two daughters and two sons by Jocasta, who, since he was his wife's son, were also his siblings. At the end of *Oedipus*, his only request as he goes into banishment is to be cared for by his daughters. Sophocles' sequel, *Oedipus at Colonus*, describes how Oedipus is attended in his old age by his daughter/sister, Antigone, who herself is the subject of the last play of the Theban Trilogy. According to myth, Oedipus, in yet another fit of anger, put a curse on his sons that they would die at each other's hands. This eventually comes to pass, and King Creon decrees on pain of death that Polyneices, the brother who marched against Thebes, must be left to rot. His sister, Antigone, out of devotion to her brother, insists on giving him a proper burial in defiance of Creon's decree, and for this is sealed up in a tomb.

Until quite recently, most psychoanalytic thinking about sibling relationships focused on their darker side—rivalry, jealousy, and envy. Sigmund Freud viewed siblings as basically hostile to each other, fated to compete for their parents' favor. If in later life more affectionate feelings developed, they never could eradicate the deeper core of hatred. Subsequent analysts have largely seen brothers and sisters as condemned to play out roles in the larger oedipal drama of fantasized murder and incest. Anna Freud, for example, thought that siblings become the recipients of sexual feelings and hostility that are deflected from their original targets—mother and father.

The plight of Oedipus and his offspring may indeed be a homily about how children are themselves caught up in the unresolved murder/love triangles of their parents. Psychologists Stephen Bank and Michael Kahn, in a study of sibling relationships throughout the life cycle, found that they are shaped significantly by the parents' ability to offer support and love. Sibling relationships become especially intense when parents are unable to provide enough support and the kids turn to each other in special ways.

One man who lost his father as a child and whose mother died when he was a young teenager recalled his sense of pride and well-being at having kept the family together, as his mother had requested. He and his four siblings had remained in the same house instead of being divided among relatives, and became bound by lifelong loyalties. As an adult, this man continued to be very close to his sister, insisting on spending holidays with her and her family and often confiding in her. His wife became increasingly jealous, feeling that he was more open and loving with his sister than with her. He would get angry when she tried to limit his contact with his sister, as if she were trying to tamper with something sacred to him.

We believe that sibling relationships, while deeply affected by parents, develop a plot of their own outside the shadow of the oedipal drama. They provide opportunities to experiment, have special shared experiences, identify with each other and differentiate themselves, develop models of loyalty and fairness, and, perhaps most important, learn how to relate on a level playing field with a peer. As one sibling quoted by Bank and Kahn put it, "We're alike but different. This is challenging and creates opportunities for both of us to grow." Sibling relationships may be deeply hostile, as in the case of Oedipus's sons (to be discussed in Chapter 4), but, as with Antigone, they may also be devoted and loving.

Brothers and sisters often turn to each other in sexual ways. Mutual showing and touching of their genitals by children of the same age may solidify gender identity and later steer the choice of a mate as adults. For men, their sisters may become unconscious guideposts to Special Women that they seek throughout their lives.

JUST FRIENDS

Research suggests that those adults with good friends are healthier, live longer, and experience less depression than those without them. While many men are accustomed to thinking of connections to women in sexual terms, a surprising number have relationships in which they are "just friends."

The psychologist Lillian Rubin found that up to 42 percent of the heterosexual men responding to her survey said that they had close female friends. Although this percentage declined to 22 percent for those men who were married or living in a committed relationship, this is still a significant minority. Booth and Hess also found that in older adults (age forty-five and beyond) 35 percent of the men had close friendships with women.

Many of these friendships develop at work. Still, sexual attractions often have to be resolved first. Rubin reports that men and women feel that they "had to get sex out of the way" in order to then become friends. For some, that means having a romantic or sexual relationship that then turns platonic. In contrast to Freud's madonna-prostitute split, such men appear not to need to devalue a woman with whom they have been intimate. Other couples may be able to become friends without ever getting into bed.

One man described to one of us how he had been drawn to a fellow therapist, who had returned his affections. Both were somewhat unhappily married but were still trying to remain faithful. They shared their struggles, their ambivalence about their mates, their love of their children. Early on in their infatuation with each other they would giggle when they saw each other at lunch. But most important, he said, was that they continued to share their work. They each had a passion for the psychotherapy they practiced and a commitment to learn from and to teach each other. This passion was embodied in their shared love for a special teacher whom they admired and whose ideas were an important part of their work. Eventually, their romanticized attraction to each other eased into the background, but the powerful connection through their work remained.

Rubin suggests that friendship with a woman offers men a type of intimacy and caring that they do not often find in their friendships with men. As one man told her: "Even if you talk about the same things, the conversation has a whole different focus with a woman. Talking with a woman has a more feeling quality. It is more nurturing and less defensive, less of the male-male kind of competitive quality." [Rubin, pp. 158–59]

Rubin notes that opposite-sex friendships call upon aspects of our personality that are less accessible when relating to members of our own gender. Thus, for men, women friends allow them to be more vulnerable. As one man whom we interviewed put it, "I rely so much on my relationships with women to get in touch with my feelings that when alone I almost feel I've lost my voice."

For women, what a male friend receives from her may be paralleled by getting support for her independence and assertiveness at work. In this way, a man is able to develop his "feminine" side and a women her "masculine" side, aspects of themselves that without support from the other gender are typically disavowed or split off.

It is customary to refer to an opposite sex connection that is not sexual as being "*just* friends," as if it were something less than its erotic counterpart. But for many men female friends can be quite Special Women. Men may seek connections with Special Women not just out of biological attraction, not only in order to repeat their earliest ties with mother or sister, but out of a need to find some part of *themselves* that they have lost.

THE MISSING HALF

In Plato's *Symposium* the Socratic emphasis is on the idealization of abstract beauty and self-sufficiency, predating many of our Western cultural concerns about autonomy. Yet there is one notable exception—Aristophanes' speech about a mythos of love.

Each symposiast is required to give a talk on the definition of and in praise of love. Aristophanes' tale is usually presented as a humorous "after dinner" speech. However, on closer reflection it goes to the heart of men's dilemma over love and loss.

Aristophanes presents a prehistory of creation in which we were all large, round, roly-poly, double creatures. Each had two faces, four hands, and four feet. Each was outfitted with two sets of genitals (male and female) that fit together perfectly. Men and women were merged together, bouncing around and enjoying the greatest pleasure. We could engage in all types of athletic feats successfully and we considered ourselves perfect because we matched the Greek ideal of perfection—the shape of a sphere. Eventually, our tragic flaw of hubris brought down upon us the wrath of the gods. To humble us, Zeus split us in two. Our sense of oneness and wholeness was lost, leaving each of us as "but the indenture of a man . . . always looking for his other half." [Jowett trans., p. 355]

In this myth, each man yearns for his counterpart and has to search for his lost wholeness. The often-heard aging male lament—"I'm not the man I was"—evidently should be rephrased as "I'm not the woman I was."

It is not mere sexuality that drives us to connect with women:

> When one of them meets with his other half . . . the pair are lost in an amazement of love and friendship and intimacy. . . . The intense yearning which each of them has towards the other does not appear to be in the desire of lover's intercourse, but of something else which the soul of either evidently desires and cannot tell, and of which she has only a dark and doubtful presentiment.
>
> . . . there is not a man of them who when he heard the proposal would deny or would not acknowledge that this meeting and melting into one another, this becoming one instead of two, was the very expression of his ancient need.

And the reason is that human nature was originally one and we were a whole, and the desire and pursuit of the whole is called love.

[*SYMPOSIUM*, JOWETT, TRANS., PP. 356–57]

Our interpretation of Aristophanes is that little boys and, later, men are left yearning for the soft blanket and warm milk that the numinous early mother supplied. They must cast such wishes into humorous form—that is, belittle and trivialize them—to avoid remembering how much her loss hurt. Unknowingly, men wish to merge with women precisely because of their "feminine" caring qualities, while they deny having any such yearnings.

Men seek special women to love them with an exceptional blend of understanding, caring, and giving—qualities that men see as feminine, and therefore unacceptable within their own selves. This dynamic gives Special Women a great deal of power over men, which they idealize or resent, making women the stuff of both men's dreams and nightmares.

THE ANIMA

Carl Jung developed a sophisticated notion of man's feminine side which he called the *anima*. For Jung what was quintessentially feminine and unconscious within the man was the guiding "spirit" of what made men who they are. Jung felt that the feminine "half" of men, about which they have "only a dark and doubtful presentiment," had a meaning beyond the intensely personal experience of the early mother-child relationship. The archetypal power and numinosity of women was linked to the mythological images of the Great Mother. While for Freud the residue of early experience with mother was the dominant force driving men toward and away from women, for Jung cultural residues were every bit as important. Where Freud would see Sinclair's being smitten by Frau Eva as the siren call of Oedipus's mother, Jung would see the anima.

The anima is largely manifested as a shadow—we cannot see it directly in ourselves but rather as a projection onto others.

The psychoanalytic concept of projective identification describes an emotional process by which we take emotions and ideas that are unacceptable to us and project them onto other people, often onto intimate others. This part of the process is the projection. We then identify with the person we have projected these things on to, stay near them, and also unconsciously attempt to induce them to act in the very ways we find objectionable in ourselves. For example, in the classic marital conflict, a man who is frightened of seeming passive or emotional may split off those parts of himself, deny that they exist, and choose a Special Woman for a partner who can follow his lead and be expressive of her feelings. However, when she inevitably acts "too emotional" or "passive" he will denigrate these attributes, just as he has denigrated them within himself.

Projective identification, while at its extremes describes pathological relationships, is a common part of normal intimacy. Men typically split off the caring, loving parts of themselves in favor of autonomy and self-control and search for women who can express such warm and loving qualities toward them. Women become the container for the man's projected feminine side which he cannot consciously acknowledge. When he is without a woman he is driven to find her. He must keep her close by since he has placed within her a part of himself. His psychic equilibrium demands that she remain on the other end of this psychological seesaw. Here then is the psychoanalytic counterpart of Aristophanes' myth.

Jung viewed healthy male development as moving from an exclusive identification with prototypic "masculine" qualities to an integration with the feminine. For Jung, this is more apt to occur later in a man's life as he comes to terms with his mortality, with what he calls the death of the hero archetype, an important mythological theme that we will meet later in the book.

SPECIAL WO-MAN

A man in his mid-sixties was briefly hospitalized for what appeared to be an intractable depression, unresponsive to anti-depressant medication. In therapy he revealed that many years before he had become disenchanted with his wife of thirty years. He had met a woman in a self-help group toward whom he began to experience "confusing feelings." Gradually he became aware that this woman reminded him of a love affair that he had had over forty years ago with his very special "June." Like James with his marble statue, he had kept alive a buried, passionate connection to this early love, split off from his marriage and his conscious emotional life for all these years. To some extent, he felt that he had "married the wrong woman."

He really did have a loving relationship with his wife, but his erotic feelings toward the June of his earlier days could never quite merge with his tender feelings toward one woman. As therapy proceeded, it became clear that his interest in June had occurred shortly after the death of his father, who had been a very strong but distant figure. In beginning to remember this, the man told a story of a loss of a favorite family pet during a hunting trip with his father. In recounting this story, tears came to his eyes and he said, "I haven't cried like this for over forty years."

MANY MEN DO split off their affectionate feelings and their sexual desires into two separate women for fear of meeting Oedipus's fate, or, as we have described, out of fear of losing their tenuous hold on masculinity by rekindling their dependence on mother. But men may also use women to validate their masculinity and buffer them from their love of *men*. Relationships with Special Women often conceal feelings for Special Men from the past. In our patient's case, it was more acceptable for him to believe that he was still in love with a girlfriend from forty years ago than to admit the fact that he had longings to be close to his father that could never be met by his wife or any woman alone.

Many men also have to hide their connections with Special Women and to repudiate their own feminine side. As a result, these women may feel devalued by men, pushed away and misunderstood, with neither sex being fully aware of the deep unconscious forces that impel men to act in these ways.

There is a long tradition of a man having to be "his own man," which has required him to avoid being influenced by other people, especially by a woman. But in order to find his way to true strength of character, rather than a propped-up version, a man must understand how his nature is shaped by Special Women. Like Oedipus, he must have the courage to learn about his origins; but we would hope, unlike his unfortunate predecessor, he will be able to seek out and accept the help of a variety of Special Women, and, as we shall see, of Special Men.

4

▼

SPECIAL MEN

J eremy received one-thousand-dollar checks in the mail from his father. They arrived every few months, sometimes with a brief letter asking him to find out an obscure fact from his college professors, requests that filled Jeremy with pity or contempt at his father's ignorance. More often they arrived in their reused envelopes without a note. They were erratic and embarrassing, just like their relationship had always been. Money had truly been all that his wealthy father had ever been able to give Jeremy. These gifts made him angry—he told his therapist how he wanted to send them back ripped in half. He would not feed his father's illusion that he had been a "good father." But he was also tempted to cash them. He and his new wife could certainly use the money. Perhaps taking the money was the best revenge and compensation for the pain his father had caused him.

Accepting the offerings was dangerous, he said, because his father might manipulate him into feeling an obligation. He also feared some subtle damage to his manhood by allowing such Trojan horses past his well-defended walls. He could not cash the checks or send them back. They remained in the back of his desk drawer.

He enjoyed the edge of moral superiority that not cashing the checks gave to him and he talked about them as if they were "dirty." He did not want to be bribed into a relationship, especially by a man who trafficked in shady business enterprises. One day he announced that he had devised a solution to the impasse with his father: his therapist could "launder the money." He would endorse the checks to his therapist to put in escrow for payment of his therapy. By interposing the therapist as a middleman in this transaction he felt the taint adhering to the money could be expunged. While the therapist gently refused to do this, the request led to a useful discussion about what this man needed from a Special Man in order to face his father with his anger and his love.

Most of the men—young and old—that we see in treatment are at such impasses with their fathers. A man's depression, his overworking, his reluctance to make commitments or to become a father are often ill-conceived, unconscious solutions to old yearnings and hatred felt toward a Special Man. Most men remain unaware of the roots of their inability to be happy, to succeed, or to love. They feel that somehow they have not passed the test of being a man. Unknowingly they conduct all manner of crusades of redemption because they never make peace with this intimate enemy of their childhood.

We believe that most men intend to be good fathers and do not want to repeat the traumatizing actions of their own fathers. However, until recent times fathers have felt their role to be the provider and progenitor, rather than an intimate participant in the raising of their children. Men were either consumed by work, afraid of intimacy with their sons, or unable to find a way into the family. So many men whom we see in therapy today grew up with a father who was distant, either physically or emotionally, that they cannot or do not want to emulate him. Alternatively, these men feel impelled to repeat the actions of their fathers, to copy them, no matter what the cost to their happiness or to their individuality. Sometimes, more happily, the quest may lead them to seek mentors who can foster their professional growth in fatherly but less tortured ways. However, many men unconsciously, in turn, expect their mentors to be surrogate fathers and are inevitably disappointed. The search may also lead them to find male friends with whom they can feel safe to be loving in competitive ways that they could not be with their fathers. This course, for lack of a mature guiding hand, is often fraught with conflict as well.

MEN'S SEARCH

Recall that James buried the statue of the cat, symbolic of the Special Woman, beneath his parents' dying maple tree. He did not know why he placed it there until in a drug-induced state he embraced the tree and discovered his yearning for his father. For many men, the buried importance of mother and father remains similarly hidden.

We are all drawn at some point in our lives to questions about our origins. Perhaps we think that if we can answer our own riddles of the Sphinx we will be able to break the stranglehold of the past and stand on our own adult feet. This search is what makes Oedipus's story so compelling and instructive; it is what makes us feel he is our brother.

Freud remarked that the story of Oedipus is like a psychoanalysis in the way that slow and painful revelations about the self successively emerge despite enormous resistances to knowing the truth. But we see his story as comparable to a much less rarefied pursuit of self-knowledge that is an inseparable part of growing up. As the psychoanalyst Robert Michels put it, "Insight is a food, not a drug."

As an adopted child, Oedipus had especially good reason to seek and to fear knowledge about his origins. Loyalty to adoptive parents can compete fiercely with inchoate bonds to biological relations. The integration of these relationships can be easily disrupted, as with Oedipus, by the opposition of both sets of parents to answer questions about the past. More universally, in their unhappy moments, most children imagine that they were adopted. They dream that their true parents will someday reveal themselves and take them away from their frustrating, cruel, and insufficiently loving surrogates. All children sense the

▼

minefields of parental secrets that make them tiptoe around their past.

Another interpretation of Oedipus is that his search is driven by unconscious guilt. Like the proverbial criminal who must return to the scene of his crime, Oedipus cannot stay away from learning what he already knows. The Furies of his own conscience goad him to ignore the advice of Teiresias and his mother not to ask too many questions. Here we have Freud's formulation, and it is fundamental to his view of the role of the father, *the* Special Man in a boy's life: relinquishing the impulses that Oedipus indulged—murdering his father and marrying his mother—is made possible by becoming like father. In terms of psychic structure, the atavistic enemy of civilized society—the id—which forever lusts to emulate Oedipus, is henceforth opposed by the superego, which commands a boy's trembling respect by the threatened loss of his penis, or of its symbolic equivalent. The father principle is essential to morality and to the boy becoming a man. But he remains like the God of Abraham—stern, fearsome, and unyielding. This spartan notion of the father's role in a boy's development is bleak and incomplete. We must exhume Oedipus's past to find out secrets that he never knew and that his chroniclers—Sophocles and Freud—chose to cover up. For it was Laius, the father, not the son, and it was actual trauma, not incestual wishes, that doomed Oedipus to tragedy.

THE LAIUS COMPLEX

It turns out that Laius's own father died when he was one year old, leaving the kingdom of Thebes in charge of a regent. After the regent is killed, Laius is banished when still a youth and is taken in by Pelops, the only kindly father figure in the whole Oedipus myth. While with Pelops, Laius falls in love with Pelops's favorite son, whom he abducts when he returns to Thebes. According to some myths, Laius is thus credited with introducing sodomy into Attica. However, it is not Laius's love for a young boy that the Greeks would have considered aberrant. Rather, it was his abduction of him—his rape and his repaying the father's hospitality by such a crime—that was abhorrent. According to one version of the myth, Hera, the Queen of the Gods, was so enraged by these acts that she sent the Sphinx to punish Thebes for allowing this miscreant to remain their king.

Pelops is furious at Laius and places a curse on Laius: if he ever has a son of his own, he will be killed by this offspring. Thus, when Laius marries Jocasta he refuses to consummate the marriage out of fear of Pelops's curse. Jocasta seduces him by getting him drunk one night, and Oedipus is the result of this single encounter. One rendering of the myth holds that Oedipus's parents expose him on Mount Citheron as a sacrifice to appease Hera. The more familiar version has it that Laius and Jocasta try to do away with the infant Oedipus out of fear of the curse. Either way, they botch the job.

We recall that Oedipus's name—"swollen foot"—derived from an injury inflicted by Laius in infancy. It is an important clue to his origins that Oedipus ignores and to which Freud gives little attention. Its importance is suggested by the fact that the riddle of the Sphinx which Oedipus alone is able to solve, refers to numbers of *feet*. A symbol of castration consequent upon tabooed wishes? Perhaps. But in view of Laius's abuse of two young boys (Pelops's son and Oedipus), this interpretation blames the true victim. The swollen foot is emblematic of the psychological wounds dealt by fathers to their sons.

It is not that Freud was wrong about sons feeling competitive with father, wanting to supplant him, fearing that father would retaliate, and therefore feeling guilty about such impulses. But the unexpurgated version of the myth reveals that *both* generations participate in this murderous rivalry. The son not only fears and hates the father but the father fears and hates the son. Regrettably, fathers are capable of physical and emotional cruelty toward their sons. They also fail to protect their sons (as Pelops did with his son). Again, as with Jocasta, we are not suggesting we villainize a parent. It is well to remember that

Laius, too, was abandoned at a tender age. After all, in any man there is a part that is the father and a part that is the son. In their relationships with each other, they must reckon with their aggression, and in particular with the developmental struggle by which the gathering strength of the young heralds the waning of the old. Many ancient myths in fact depict the necessary killing of the old king by the son whose youthful vitality renews the kingdom.

Some commentators have attributed Freud's whitewashing of Laius and of fathers generally to his need not to tarnish his idealization of his own father. Like Oedipus, he, too, exonerated the father by focusing on his own guilty impulses. We are all then vulnerable to such one-sided interpretations, whether out of love for or fear of our fathers.

While young Oedipus appears to grow up powerful even without the emotional support of his father, self-reliance carries within it a tragic flaw. *His fall from power is not caused by blindness to Freudian wishes, but rather from denial of his traumatic wounding by an aggressive, absent father.* Without the mentorship or guidance of the nurturant father and without a comfortable connection to a woman, he became the classically aggressive, unaware man.

In this way, a vicious circle is created. The son cannot trust the father to guide him to a comfortable sense of what it means to be a man. In turn, when he himself becomes a father he must fear the aggression of his son as a projection of his own unresolved rage toward his own father. Oedipus's two sons battle to the death as a result of the curse he places upon them for not supporting him. That is, bad fathering is a curse that is passed from generation to generation, not so much because boys cannot control their aggressive fantasies toward their fathers, but because fathers are either abusive or fail to provide the male nurturance that their sons need. As one poet put it, "Fathers who cannot love their sons have sons who cannot love." (R. Shelton, "Letter to a Dead Father".)

THE AGGRESSIVE FATHER

In our therapy practices we have heard many men complain about fathers who abused them—fathers who could only criticize, who intimidated by straps, threats, or loud voices. In most cases, as boys these sons felt inadequate, unlovable, and afraid. They felt they themselves were bad. Often it is only as adults that they allow themselves to feel angry at their fathers and to know the depth of their pain.

Many fathers fear that they will be unable to contain their anger. They overcompensate by withdrawing from their sons, their remoteness an insurance policy whose premiums are sins of omission. Sons are left wondering why their fathers do not want to be with them. They are also left alone with their own aggression with no models of how to deal with it and without help in differentiating a range of angry feelings. An aggressive boy may be angry, frustrated, hurting, or letting off steam. A father's lack of understanding of his son's struggle to channel his aggression will lead to a failure to integrate this crucial aspect of masculinity with profound consequences as an adult.

James Herzog, of Harvard Medical School, has written in more positive terms about the beneficial role of fathers in managing aggression. In contrast to mothers, who typically provide comfort and soothing, fathers stir up feelings—they roughhouse with their sons, tickle, and tease. Carried too far, this is out of tune with the child's needs.

One of our male patients recalled how when he was a young boy, his father would wrestle and tickle him and his older brother. These sessions would start out playfully but they almost always ended with one of the boys in tears. His father didn't know when to stop—he would tickle to the point of overstimulation or he would not let his son get up when he pleaded with his father to "let me go." He wasn't sure in retrospect whether his father took sadistic pleasure in their helplessness or whether he was completely oblivious to what he was doing wrong.

MORE FELICITOUSLY, the son can learn to tolerate intense affects, to experience the limits of his own and his father's strength, and to modulate his aggression. Herzog refers to good fathering as "state-transforming caretaking," and suggests that sons can learn from fathers how to "shift gears" from one level of emotional arousal to another. Our sense is that fathers and sons mutually elicit and play off each other's aggressiveness. One of us in play with a three-year-old son, for example, has found that the boy frequently dives into his father, attempts to push him down, and seeks a kind of deep pressure contact that he seldom attempts with his mother. He calls this "playing dinosaur," "pirates," or "squishles" (as in "I'm going to squish you!"). While he clearly enjoys this play, a fine line separates optimal stimulation from aversive contact. Sensing such a boundary and learning how to negotiate it is manly knowledge that fathers can offer to their sons.

THE ABSENT FATHER

From time to time I have felt for my father a longing that was almost physical, something passionate, but prior to sex—something infantile, profound. It has bewildered me, even thrown me into depression. It is mysterious to me exactly what it is I wanted from my father. I have seen this longing in other men—and see it now in my own sons, their longing for me. I think that I have glimpsed it once or twice in my father's feelings about his father. Perhaps it is some urge of Telemachus, the residual infant in the man still wistful for the father's heroic protection. One seeks to return not to the womb, which is enclosing, a warm, passive oblivion, but to a different thing, a father's sponsorship in the world. A boy wants the aura and armament of his father. It is a deep yearning, but sometimes a little sad—a common enough masculine trait that is also vaguely unmanly. What surprises me is how angry a man

becomes sometimes in the grip of what is, in essence, an
unrequited passion.

[LANCE MORROW, *THE CHIEF*, PP. 6–7]

In her report on male sexuality, Shere Hite found in a survey
of over 7,000 men that most men claimed they had not been
close to their fathers. In addition, Jack Sternbach, a psychologist
who examined informally the father-son relationship in seventy-
one clients, found that close to a quarter of the sample had
fathers who were physically absent, another 40 percent had
psychologically absent fathers, and 15 percent had fathers who
were dangerous or frightening. More reassuring, in the Boston
University Pregnancy and Parenthood Study, we discovered
that fathers who remembered being nurtured by their own fathers growing up were likely to have children who had good
relationships with them. A father's presence, or absence, has a
profound effect on a young boy's adaptation to the societal
expectation of masculinity, and by extension to his inner sense
of being a valued, competent man.

Alexander Mitscherlich, the German psychoanalyst and social philosopher, has argued that postindustrial modern countries have created a cultural structure in which men are
isolated from one another—a "society without the father."
He suggests that rural and farming societies may have had a
strong patriarchal structure that tended to suppress women
and children, but served to integrate the role of the man and
the father into a meaningful social fabric. Sons worked with
their fathers, learned from them, and shared a brotherhood
of toil, yearning, success, and disappointment. They learned
what it was to be a man. Our own society has gained freedom
for both men and women at the cost of finding no way for
men to relate to their sons. Mitscherlich points out that most
men are hard at work at jobs that take them away from the
family during the day and often for periods of weeks. Consequently, boys cannot identify with the instrumental aspects
of what it means to be an adult male in their society. They are
never initiated by their fathers into a sense of the workplace,

which, ironically, is where their fathers spend the greater part of their lives.

A young man who came to one of our consulting rooms because he was unable to finish college revealed the following story. Although he was highly intelligent, and fared well in elementary and high school, he was having difficulty completing assignments in classes that he needed to pursue a professional career. It turned out that he was vastly ashamed of and confused about his roots. His father, who was a plasterer, would tell him over and over again that he would not teach his son how to do his trade for fear that he, too, would "put on the overalls" and never go to law or medical school. Since his father's whole life was his work, he had little else to offer his son, who felt that he was without a father. He felt barred from following in his father's footsteps, ambivalent about taking a path that was being imposed and that led him far from what his father could understand, and unsure about what his own talents and inclinations might be.

MEN WITHOUT FATHERS are left with their fantasies and with adult females' view of men. These they tend to put together, as best they can, into a pastiche of the father. He may be imagined as a "bogeyman"—a frightening, heavy-footed creature who imposes discipline with a kind of aggressive strength that little boys fear and wish to emulate. Alternatively, he may be idealized as Telemachus did with his absent father, Odysseus, such that the father's shoes appear impossible to fill and his own and other men's failings become unacceptable.

Since these images are somewhat ameliorated by a more nurturant, fathering presence, boys, as they become men, are confused about what their personal ideal should be. On the one hand they may grow up feeling like Kasper Hauser, the abandoned wolf child of German literature, or they may be seduced by the dark side of masculinity—they become the angry, controlling, patriarchal force that they imagined their fathers to be. Either the aggressor or victim role leaves men emotionally unfulfilled, vulnerable to psychosomatic and erotic disturbance, and to all forms of pathologic solutions. Such men feel deficient and father-hungry, much as Lance Morrow so eloquently describes. More commonly, they remain unaware of their intense need for a benign, fathering presence or suppress it with a macho, false-self façade.

It is easy to see how inadequate fathering becomes a family legacy, much as with Laius and Oedipus, and Oedipus and his sons. As with Oedipus, the abandonment by our fathers often occurs so early in life that we may not clearly grasp or have the words to describe why we feel something is missing. *We can only feel the consequences of our father's absence*—unrequited yearning, depression, and anger.

TELEMACHUS

The *Odyssey* of Homer is a tale of such yearning. It opens with the gods and goddesses discussing the sad plight of Odysseus, a wily and mighty Achaean warrior, who has now been gone from home for twenty years. Ten years he passed fighting at the gates of Troy, and, after the fall of the city, he struggled for ten more to return to his beloved Ithaca. At home his wife, Penelope, is hounded by dark-hearted suitors who think Odysseus dead and despoil the great man's house. His son, Telemachus, and his wife have no knowledge of what has happened to Odysseus but they hold to the faint hope that he may yet return. Telemachus was a very young child when his father sailed off to war, and now he is just at the point of leaving his boyhood, although not quite yet a man. The gray-eyed goddess Athene, who is resolved to help Odysseus return home, tells the other deities:

> But I shall make my way to Ithaka, so that I may
> stir up his son a little, and put some confidence in him
> to summon into assembly the flowing-haired Achaians
> and make a statement to all the suitors, who now forever
> slaughter his crowding sheep and lumbering horn-curved cattle;

and I will convey him into Sparta and to sandy Pylos
to ask after his dear father's homecoming, if he can hear something,
and so that among people he may win a good reputation.

[LATTIMORE, TRANS., BOOK 1, LL. 88–95]

The first four books of Homer's epic poem describe Telemachus's growing resolve to take charge of his life. At the outset, he feels helpless to deal with the suitors, he is embarrassed to question his elders, and he is more apt to shed tears than to take effective action. His mother refers to him as "an innocent all unversed in fighting and speaking." [Lattimore, trans., Book 4, line 818] When he addresses the men of Ithaca at a council about the actions of the suitors he ends up throwing a tantrum: "So he spoke in anger, and dashed to the ground the scepter in a stormburst of tears." [Lattimore, trans., Book 2, ll. 80–81] When later, with Athene's help, he sails to visit Nestor, one of the Achaeans who fought with his father at Troy, he shrinks from the advice that the suitors might yet be punished:

"Old sir, I think that what you have said will not be accomplished.
What you mean is too big. It bewilders me. That which I hope for
could never happen to me, not even if the gods so willed it."

[LATTIMORE, TRANS., BOOK 3, LL. 226–28]

Homer paints a poignant picture of a shy and insecure young man. But there are also many references to the "godlike" Telemachus, who reminds all who see him of his great father. Homer makes clear why Telemachus seems to cling to his boyhood—at the house of Menelaus, whom Telemachus and Nestor's son visit for news of Odysseus, Telemachus is overcome with grief when he hears Menelaus speak his father's name, leaving Nestor's son to explain:

"Great Menelaus, son of Atreus, leader of the people,
this is in truth the son of that man, just as you are saying;
. . . He longed to see you
so that you could advise him somewhat, for word or action.
For a child endures many griefs in his house when his father

is gone away, and no others are there to help him, *as now*
Telemachus's father is gone away, and there are no others
who can defend him against the evil that is in his country."
[LATTIMORE, TRANS., BOOK 4, LL. 156–67]

So here we have the prototypic abandoned son, yearning for
his father, struggling to be a man. He is grieving for a father
who he still hopes may return someday. Unlike Telemachus,
however, most abandoned sons of our own time are not in
touch with their grief—they are mad instead of sad, and may
not even know with whom they are angry.[1]

Classics scholars have long argued over why Homer would
begin his story with Telemachus, delaying the entrance of
Odysseus, the protagonist, until well into his story, and forcing
him to tell about much of Odysseus's adventures in retrospect.
Some have suggested that the Telemachy (the first four books
of the *Odyssey*) was originally a separate work that was later
somewhat crudely joined to the *Odyssey*, while others have seen
Homer as a master who was not afraid to be unorthodox in his
crafting a story. Our sense is that Homer chose to tell a story
about a son yearning for his father, and, as we shall discuss in
the chapter on fathering, about a father yearning for his son.
Homer's story sings in our hearts today because it is, truly and
deeply, a story of our own time. It is worthy of men now,
stirred up and perhaps lacking confidence, to ask after our own
dear fathers' homecoming, whatever forms they may assume.

THE SECOND CHANCE

The mysterious yearning for an absent father, so endemic
and yet considered unmanly in our culture, can perhaps be
better understood. Indeed, our understanding it may be our best
chance at interrupting the archetypal transgenerational pattern

[1] Samuel Osherson, in *Finding Our Fathers*, has written with great insight
about how wounded men search for their fathers.

by which sons forever yearn for absent fathers and grow up to be fathers who absent themselves from yearning sons.

Perhaps what makes the relationship of a boy with his father so special is that the father may offer his son an opportunity for what Morton and Estelle Shane at UCLA Medical School have called *otherness*—an alternative to mother's way of nurturing that has its distinctive masculine tinge—its own forms of love and ambivalence, its own voice, its own smell.

The modern psychoanalytic philosopher Heinz Kohut has written that each child has at least two chances during his or her development to consolidate a solid sense of autonomy and connection to others. The first opportunity usually takes place with the mother, whose ability to empathically mirror what the child offers of himself allows him to know who he is and to know that self is cherished. The second chance is most often with the father, who, at best, provides a protecting, nurturant, steady presence that the child can idealize and grab onto in times of stress. Ultimately, the result of both parental contributions is that the child feels himself to have a coherent, loved self. To Kohut, a deficiency in mirroring or in the opportunity to idealize a good parent can be remedied by a relative strength in the other. It is only when both opportunities are denied to the child that the safety of the self is threatened.

If, then, when the little boy is forced to separate from his mother, thereby having to relinquish the primary anchor to his sense of self, his father is not available to provide a second chance for being held, a double trauma occurs. It is not that mother or father should be blamed; after all, both of them are obeying the cultural prescriptions about how boys achieve masculinity. When he lets go of his mother, in his journey to become a man, the boy sets off on a perilous journey. When his mother has provided well, father need only walk beside him; when the opportunity with mother has been lacking, father must be able to hold his hand.

If the second chance is lost, it may feel even more painful than the separation from mother, since it is visited upon an already bruised and vulnerable self. As an adult, a man will likely be most conscious of his missing pieces as masculine deficiencies, but his earliest failures by Special Men and Women are inseparably connected, just as with James, who buried the Special Woman at the foot of the Special Man. Either father or mother may wind up being blamed for the deficiencies of the other, just as in adult relations, "becoming a man" and loving a woman are each handicapped by limitations in the other capacity.

As with Special Women, relationships with Special Men are not always what they seem. Those men toward whom a man develops powerful feelings may be stand-ins for Special Women from early life whose true identity is masked by the need to repress early trauma.

We all tend to see our mothers and fathers as distinct individuals and remain less clear about the effect on us of a less tangible entity—our parents' relationship. Yet how our mothers and fathers treated each other in our early lives—their love and disappointments, the way they valued their differences or showed contempt for masculinity or femininity—affect men deeply throughout their lives, especially in their love relationships with women.

MY BROTHER'S KEEPER

Yet another Special Man can leave indelible imprints on a man's heart: his brother.

Jason, a thirty-eight-year old divorced man, came to psychotherapy after his marriage and business had both dissolved. The theme that ran throughout his life was that "nothing is ever enough." He had created a successful furniture business, and although it meant taking significant risk with little capital, he felt he had to buy a second store. He would also overstock many items in the hope of bettering his sales each month. When he began to see that he would not meet his expectations he would push up his expenditures instead of retrenching. He could not tolerate a loss. In his marriage he was dissatisfied with what he felt was inadequate caretaking by his wife—there was never enough sex, she wasn't sympathetic enough about his business problems, and she didn't understand him. He had two daughters but he wanted a son. His solution was to withdraw his affection and have a series of affairs.

He attributed his insatiable hunger for love and admiration to a cold, judgmental mother and a critical father who had always worked at his own store for many hours each week and every weekend. But, over time, the importance of his younger brother, Ricky, became more apparent. Jason had been an only child till the age of five and had felt up until then that he was the center of his parents' existence. The advent of any sibling in this context of limited parental resources would have been problematic. What made it especially devastating was that his brother had cerebral palsy.

All the attention that had formerly gone to Jason shifted to Ricky, who required daily occupational therapy, speech therapy, and almost yearly operations with hospital stays. Jason did a lot of his brother's caretaking himself, but he felt cheated. He had looked forward to having a brother to play with and who would look up to him, and Ricky was capable of neither. Jason also could not admit to himself and certainly could not express his anger at this damaged sibling, who, in taking Jason's place at the center of the family, had effectively stolen his birthright. And so the feelings that could not be permitted in his own home became enacted in his relationships outside of it. He conducted his whole life as if he were owed something. In a sense, he lived out the blighted attitude evinced by Shakespeare's Richard III, who felt entitled to recompense because of his palsied arm. Ironically, in Jason's case, it was *not* being the palsied child that embittered him.

THE BIBLE OFFERS two central myths of brothers' rivalry. In one of the earliest stories, before the Jewish patriarchs, Cain and Abel are the warring children of Adam and Eve. As with many myths, characters can symbolize a cultural problem in integrating two social forces, in this case the Hebrew–Canaanite shepherd and farmer. But beyond this, they represent a personal

struggle for sibling supremacy. Cain kills Abel because he believes him to be more favored by God, and when questioned
about the disappearance of Abel, responds with the rhetorical
question, "Am I my brother's keeper?" Clearly, the hurt of not
being as loved by the most special man in a boy's life can lead
to murderous rage. Such pain poisons brotherly ties.

In the story of Jacob and Esau, a pair of brothers are sworn
to fight against each other to win the birthright of their father
through cunning. Jacob, the younger son, is much beloved by
his mother, and with her support competes with the older,
Esau, to wrest his birthright from him. Here again, we see the
sad legacy of a father's hostility toward or abandonment of his
son transmitted to his son's sons. Remember, it was the father
of Jacob and Esau—Isaac—who was bound to a stake by Abraham, the father of the Hebrews, in order to sacrifice him to the
new Hebrew God. God, the "father" of Abraham, commanded
this as a demonstration of Abraham's devotion to him, just as
modern day fathers may "sacrifice" their sons in less murderous
ways to remain loyal to the memory of their own vengeful
fathers. In the biblical tale, Isaac is saved at the last instant by
an angel, and it is believed that the resolution of this potential
son sacrifice led to the rites of circumcision of Canaanite, and
later Hebrew and Jewish, custom. No doubt, traditional Freudi-
ans would see in this symbolic castration the primeval threat
implied in all father-son and perhaps all brotherly enmities.
But the original threat is not castration but murder, or more
symbolically, the soul murder by which a father forsakes the
nurturing love he holds for his son.

Much like the battle between Oedipus's sons—Eteocles and
Polyneices—the curse of the father falls upon the males of the
next generation, with resultant internecine conflict and death.
Regrettably, brothers compete with each other rather than being
able to find solace in their shared yearning for and anger at their
father.

More muted rivalry, and even jealousy and envy of a sibling,
can also serve to make a man. Through such comparisons, a
boy can learn how he is different, an important developmental
step toward becoming an independent self. Also, as with their

▼

fathers, sons need relationships with other intimate males that are charged with aggression such that they can learn how to regulate the expression of anger and how to contain competition within ongoing bonds of love and friendship.

"HE'S NOT HEAVY; HE'S MY BROTHER."

Another model of sibling relationships is exemplified by a story told by Father Flanagan of Boys' Town about a boy who saves his heavier, older brother in a fire. When asked, after he has dragged him away from danger, how he was able to carry him, he responds by saying, "He's not heavy; he's my brother."

Notwithstanding the Bible, a profound sense of loyalty commonly is found between same-sex siblings, according to Stephen Bank and Michael Kahn's definitive study on sibling bonds. Loyalty can be enhanced if brothers have considerable contact with each other at significant developmental points, such as is likely to occur when they are close in age. Intense, healthy loyalty can also be evoked in response to a lack of parental support. The absence of a Special Man may lead to a mutual kind of foster fathering in which each becomes a replacement for the missing paternal, idealized presence.

Such brotherly loyalty can go awry if their independence or capacity to separate is affected. It can also be limiting if one truly becomes the other's "keeper," with one son becoming the proto-father and sacrificing himself at great personal cost to protect his brother. Jason may have been a version of this.

Brothers can teach each other about what it means to become a man, such as in adolescence at the beginning of sexual experimentation. The sense of not being alone with feelings of awkwardness, shyness, lust, and loneliness can be a powerful support. One brother may be a "trail blazer" who models the integration of sexual feelings into the boy's identity. However, when sexual confusion due to early difficulties with a formative

Special Man ensues, an older brother may not be sufficient to make up for these deficits. Worse, the shadow of the father may fall upon the siblings for the rest of their lives.

For example, in one family, the father had been emotionally remote and rejecting of the younger of two brothers, who, during college, became aware that he was gay. In his mid-twenties, the younger brother went to live in a foreign country and eventually notified his parents that he would have nothing further to do with them. His older brother made several attempts to reconnect with him, but found that no matter how he tried to make an approach, he was accused of behaving "just like Dad."

THIRD CHANCES

Fathers and brothers are not the only Special Men who can have a hand in a man's growth. Psychoanalytic and other developmental theories have gone beyond the study of the earliest years and the primal influences of the nuclear family. The interpersonal theorist Harry Stack Sullivan believed that throughout a person's life opportunities present themselves for new integrations and adaptations. Similarly, Erik Erikson saw development as continuing throughout a man's life. We need not be like Oedipus—prisoners of fate or of character forged irrevocably in the family crucible. Not all of the dye can come out of a fabric; but much of it can.

The British psychoanalyst D. W. Winnicott may have expressed this best:

". . . it is normal and healthy for the individual to be able to defend the self against specific environmental failure by a *freezing of the failure situation*. Along with this goes an unconscious assumption (which can become a conscious hope) that opportunity will occur at a later date for a renewed experience in which the failure situation will be able to be unfrozen and re-experienced, with the individual in a regressed state, in an environment that is making adequate adaptation."

[WINNICOTT, *COLLECTED PAPERS*, P. 281]

Winnicott was not referring exclusively to psychotherapy, but to the healing of early trauma through a variety of loving connections. We think of these opportunities to heal and to grow as "third chances."

But the chilling effects on character of a father's withdrawal of love are not easily counteracted. Boys develop a formidable array of defenses to ensure that the hurts suffered at the hands of mother and father will never be repeated. They learn, for example, not to need anyone, or, at least, not to appear to need anyone. For if you never need anyone, no one can let you down. And if you never show that you need anyone, no one can manipulate you through your needs or shame you for having them. It is important, the young boy or man thinks, never to be conned. Trust, therefore, is replaced by cynicism, since it causes less pain and seems to be more often justified by experience. The cost of this pose is that opportunities with other Special Men to unfreeze the past, to move beyond it, are often passed up. Like the poignant, near embrace of the lovers on Keats' Grecian urn, fathers and sons remain forever yearning, forever out of touch.

If a man is lucky, third chances may come along at many points in his life—a special teacher, an employer, a coach, a friend. Often, they are other yearning, incomplete men who may offer solace if they can recognize the son, the brother, or the father in each other. They may lend a temporary home of sorts, a comfort sometimes expressed in words, or in the warmth of brandy and cigars or a special handshake.

MENTORS

Daniel Levinson felt the mentor to be one of the most powerfully charged relationships for men in their formative adult
years. He is often an older man, usually a half generation the
senior of his protégé. An avuncular, supportive counsel or
guide, he facilitates work and emotional development. Through
the manifestation of his own essential qualities, he becomes an
ideal that the protégé can admire and seek to emulate. But most
significantly, for Levinson, the mentor assists the young adult
male to fulfill his basic dream or goal for personal development:

> The true mentor, in the meaning intended here, serves as
> an analog in adulthood of the "good enough" parent for the
> child. He fosters the young adult's development by believing
> in him, sharing the youthful dream and giving it his blessing,
> helping to define the newly emerging self in its newly discov-
> ered world, and creating a space in which the young man
> can work on a reasonably satisfactory life structure. . . . The
> mentor is *not* a parent. His primary function is to be a transi-
> tional figure. . . . The mentor represents a mixture of parent
> and peer; he must be both and not purely either one.
> [DANIEL LEVINSON, P. 99]

The most striking aspect of Levinson's insight into the role
of the mentor is his unabashed acknowledgment that it is a form
of love relationship. The connection between a mentor and a
young man is deep, ambivalently tinged, and charged with
emotional currents. It is equivalent to and rightfully called love.
As it is the youthful love for an older male, it is likely to lead
to eventual disillusionment, sometimes through a difficult and
extremely painful pathway. Most significantly, if it has served
its purpose, such an idealized connection with a special man will
lead to the internalization or taking in of the central qualities of
such a man, in a way that the earlier relationship with the
father or, indeed, the mother may have been blocked by more
significant childhood conflicts:

> Much of its value may be realized—as with love relation-
> ships generally—after the termination period. . . . Follow-
> ing the separation, the younger man may take the admired
> qualities of the mentor more fully into himself. He may
> become better able to learn from himself, to listen to the
> voices from within. His personality is enriched as he makes
> the mentor a more intrinsic part of himself. The internaliza-
> tion of significant figures is a major source of development
> in adulthood.
>
> [D. LEVINSON, P. 101]

Carl Jung, in his discussion of the mythical "death of the
hero," and Joseph Campbell, in his exploration of "the hero
with a thousand faces," speak about the need of the youthful
man to receive a mentoring support from a special older male
who helps his younger protégé integrate masculine and feminine
attributes into a more stable sense of self. Jung saw a man's
capacity to integrate his anima, or feminine self, as being most
apt to develop during the midlife transition in particular. Still,
he believed that the capacity for the younger male to accept his
aggressive needs (the "hero") as only a portion of himself, and
therefore needing to be linked with other nurturant and passive
longings, is part of the capacity of the hero to "die," and be
reborn as a more mature masculine self. Indeed, the mythopoetic movement, which is so greatly affected by medieval and
modern myths concerning the search for the Holy Grail, and
the intervention of the Fisher King, are likewise attempts to
integrate the conflicting poles of male aggression with stereotypically feminine passivity. Jung and his mythopoetic followers
have emphasized the role of the guiding adult male mentor, the
man who has passed his so-called midlife crisis as a significant
guide in the process of such death and rebirth of the young man.
Interestingly enough, Jung had wondered whether in fact it is
the unconscious acceptance of the power of the "woman within"
that truly leads to a young man's transformation through his
mentorship. Put in other words, such a mentoring relationship
with a Special Man may really be a wo-man in disguise.

TEIRESIAS

We return to the myth of Oedipus and, in particular, to the role of the seer Teiresias in this tragedy. If you recall, Teiresias lost his capacity to see outwardly because of Hera's wrath. She and Zeus had quarreled over which gender had more pleasure in sex, and when Teiresias answered that the woman has nine times as much delight as the man, Hera blinded him. Zeus, obviously more pleased with Teiresias's verdict than she, granted him "inner sight"—a capacity for insight and prophecy. In later Greek myths, he was sometimes described as having the body and emotional perspective of a man and woman combined. Indeed, it was this androgynous self that appeared to give him the special penetrating powers to foresee the future.

Not surprisingly, it was to Teiresias that Oedipus turned for mentorship in understanding the blight that had fallen upon his country, which had left people and land alike barren. At first, Teiresias warns Oedipus that he is not yet ready to know: "O, what anguish to be wise where wisdom is a loss!" [Roche, trans., p. 35] But Oedipus is unwilling to trust his mentor figure, and pushes him for the knowledge that he knows he holds. In turn, Teiresias, indeed perhaps too quickly, accedes to Oedipus's impulsive pressure. Although he knows or should know better, he shares his information with Oedipus under pain of personal harm and states quite simply, "The rotting canker in the state is you." [Roche, trans., p. 36]

Although it still takes time for Oedipus to digest and accept what Teiresias has said, and indeed to prove it correct, Teiresias has already abandoned his role as the protective, growth-enhancing mentor. In effect, he has thrown Oedipus to the wolves of Oedipus's own conscience. We might say that Teiresias is the prototype of the second disappointing Special Man—the mentor—who, in the face of danger, abandons his duty to contain and channel the aggression of his young male protégé. Instead, he overwhelms him with a traumatic kind of self-knowledge that he is not yet ready to grasp.

The psychoanalyst Robert Michels suggests what Teiresias *should* have said to Oedipus:

> "Oedipus, calm down. You demand that I answer your questions, and I am willing to do so. But first look at what you already know, and what you hope to find out by looking further. You imagine some horrible discovery that you fear to voice. You hope that I will deny it while you dread that I will confirm it. You threaten my life, an old blind man, and seem to feel no guilt or responsibility for what you do, claiming that it is the will of the gods. What can we learn from your fears, and from the way you treat me, for if we do not start first with these things, with your world today, and learn what your questions mean and why they arise now, if we answer your questions but do not address mine, the consequences will be disastrous."
>
> [MICHELS, PP. 615–16]

A good mentor must help his charge pay attention not just to *what* he wants to know but *how* he goes about trying to learn it. Unfortunately, Teiresias, for all his wisdom, succumbed to what would now be called his "countertransference." Like Oedipus's mother, who does not fight for his life at its inception, and indeed later seduces him into actions that will only harm him, and like his father, who is frightened of his son's potential to supplant him and traumatically abuses and abandons him, Teiresias fails him. He is unable to provide the tragic understanding of his inner nature that the hero needs to be re-created as a man.

The failure of the mentor should not be surprising, given that the men who serve in this role bring to it the same limitations in insight and fathering that they bring to their biological sons. Many men experience their mentors as not being able to fully support their growth, especially as they begin to show signs of surpassing them. Professional jealousies may well resonate with more atavistic, Laius-like reactions—the protégé metamorphoses from admiring devotee to threatening competitor for all that the mentor holds dear. Further, as Levinson points out, it is characteristic for a young man to idealize his mentor. Perhaps, as with Kohut's description of fathers and sons, for development into manhood to proceed, the mentor must make himself available—to be idealized—to inspire and respect the protégé's belief in the mentor's special talents and personal qualities. At the same time, such idealization is what leads inevitably to disillusionment. Even seers such as Teiresias can lose their temper, and with it their capacity to guide; and Laius, too, came to grief because he put too much store in oracular prophecies.

The mentor figure reconceives the seeds of masculine and feminine needs—the unmet yearnings for a Special Man, and a Special Woman. He may buoy the young man with a feeling of greater confidence and strength, with a sense of having come more fully into his manhood. Yet, if this opportunity is lost, the trauma suffered with a man's first Special Man may be reconfirmed. He may continue to seek out new mentors and repeatedly be failed again. It is, as with fathers, destined to be an unrequited love. But the hope that breathes life into the search for a Special Man can itself be sustaining. Our experience is that men can sometimes take pieces of different mentors who individually fall short of what a man needs, but who together foster a greater sense of his feeling whole. Further, as a man becomes more aware of the unrealistic expectations he has of a mentor, he may be able to accept with more grace what he can have and mourn what he can not.

MALE FRIENDSHIPS

It is not that friends necessarily ever touch. . . . We are drawn by [the other man's] wit, the set of his eyes that makes us think we are seen. We are drawn by his apparent gentleness, his directness, his valor. We are drawn by his energy, a male force we share and that reinforces ours just when the world in time seemed to have flattened us out all together. Past the shaggy-beast exterior, the threatening otherness that is also our own physical self, we find a heart that beats with ours, a brain that chimes with ours, and understanding that includes the same masculinity that is, too often, a burden in this life.

[S. MILLER, *MEN AND FRIENDSHIP*, PP. 12–13]

Male friendships are echoes of Special Men from earlier in life, as well as intensely felt relations with their own adult stamp. They are a favorite theme in American literature and film—Huckleberry Finn and Jim, Ishmael and Queequeg, Natty Bumppo and Chingachgook, Butch Cassidy and the Sundance Kid, and "Dances with wolves" and "Wind in his hair." Michael Farrell has observed that recurrent themes include two men of different races who move away from women into dangerous environments. In such wildernesses men's resourcefulness and loyalty to each other are tested and strengthened by a series of challenges, which culminate in an act of violence. Farrell believes that the central fantasy is that male brothers can find fulfillment outside of relationships with women and the nuclear family. There is an escapist and even a misogynous impulse motivating such romanticization of male friendship, which is precisely what concerns many women about Robert Bly's glorification of male bonding. But we believe that another key element in male friendship is proving one's manhood through rites of passage (discussed in Chapter 5).

Some psychologists and sociologists, including Daniel Levinson, have claimed that in the real world most men have no close male friends. But much of the research does not support this. Michael Farrell and S. Rosenberg found in a 1981 study in Boston that 80 percent of their group had male friends that they saw regularly. A study done in 1972 in Detroit by E. Laumann reported that over two-thirds of the men said they were close to other men. It does appear, however, that when men marry, they see their male friends less frequently, that this trend continues until midlife, and that the arrival of children accelerates this decline. It is only with retirement that men's involvement with friends builds again. Men are interested in and capable of friendship with other men, but these ties are supplanted by family duties. Perhaps this is why men feel that, like fictional heroes, they have to leave women and family for the wilderness in order to get together, and why this theme of going off to enact rituals with other men is a central theme in the men's movement.

For women, intimacy and friendship appear to involve sharing their feelings and innermost concerns; for most men, it is the experience of a challenge or task that bonds them together without words. When women greet each other they often hug and kiss, while men shake hands or slap each other on the back in an affectionate manner that simultaneously evokes the competitive aggression of the playing field. These differences may be related to gender differences in how children play from early schoolyard days: boys engage in more rough-and-tumble play with an orientation toward competition and dominance, while girls' play involves cooperative fantasy, flexibility, and a concern for each other's feelings. Interestingly, little girls try but find it difficult to influence boys to join in cross-gender groups. Eleanor Maccoby concludes that girls' rebuffs by boys and their aversion to boys' ways of playing serves to segregate girls from boys and reinforces gender differences. Further, much of the social structures in which boys relate—Boy Scouts, Little League, YMCA, high school sports—are competitive and goal-oriented, and stress skill acquisition and winning more than intimacy.[2]

When Yale University psychologist Elizabeth Aries constructed discussion groups of college-age men and women she found some notable examples in the all-male versus all-female groups. While males tend to reveal very little about themselves, women did the opposite. In the male groups there was a considerable "hazing" or testing period, in which a stable dominance hierarchy was created. This, of course, speaks to the typical "style" of male friendships, in which doing replaces feeling, and a shared sense of closeness ensues through mutual interests and unquestioned acceptance. As Drury Sherrod puts it, ". . . men seek not intimacy but companionship, not disclosure but commitment . . . men infer intimacy simply because they are friends."

[2]There is general agreement that gender differences in styles of relating begin very early. However, some researchers believe that these differences are not attributable primarily to peer-group interactions but to differential treatment of boys and girls in their families and to cultural messages about gender.

HOMOPHOBIA

Our sense is that men seek out close male friends for the same reason that women seek out their friends: to share an intimate part of the self with a Special Man, who is neither a parent, mentor, nor blood relative. Many theorists have suggested that men avoid too much intimacy with their male friends for fear of experiencing "passive longings" or intense or tender love that they associate with homosexuality. It is also said that such closeness threatens men's gender identity because it evokes memories of undifferentiated merger with mother. Men must not share their feelings in front of another man because they are ashamed to be thought of as "acting like a woman." These concerns may account for the reason portrayals of male bonding are often interracial, from Huckleberry Finn and Jim all the way up to Mel Gibson and Danny Glover; however fervently men may wish to connect, there must be a clearly defined barrier. Only if men are sure they can remain differentiated is it safe to be close. They must also be depicted as facing great dangers. In this way their anxiety about intimacy is masked by an external threat and their need to depend on each other is camouflaged as necessity.

But men fear such attachments not solely because they are anxious about losing their penises or being feminized but because they stir up feelings that feel too intense. They may need to deny their love for other men out of fear of sustaining the same hurt that they remember in their earliest relationships— their being pushed out of mother's warm nest and not being caught by a caring father. The long shadow of this trauma falls upon male friendships just as it does on their mentors.

LAST CHANCES

It is poignant to see a grown man notice his father age and realize that his last chance to connect with him is slipping away.

When we ask a male patient, "Is this the way you want it to end?" he often is brought to tears and is stirred to new efforts to relate to his father. In many cases, such deathbed attempts to "convert" a father fall far short of what the man feels he needs. For example, one man in his forties, who felt he had just recently matured enough to approach his father in a new way, became enraged at his elderly father, whose deafness reminded him of his lifelong inability to really listen.

A successful young lawyer in his thirties sought psychotherapeutic help as a result of his difficulty in sustaining relationships with women. One of the major themes in his sessions was how much he had felt pushed around by his mother and unsupported by his scientific, aloof father. Bart recalled how his father would blame him instead of supporting him against his mother. He had grown up with several sisters and felt that his father was his only male potential ally. He not only felt uncared for by both parents but disillusioned in his father's capacity to "be a man."

During the late phase of the treatment, Bart's father developed metastatic cancer. Typical of his family style, Bart at first denied the severity of the illness and avoided getting the facts that would allow for an appropriate emotional response. The therapist encouraged Bart to speak to his father's doctor and as a result Bart found out that his father had little time left to live. Aware that his father also knew this, Bart pondered whether to travel home several thousand miles to have a last conversation. The impending final separation shocked him, but he continued to deny the emotional meaning that his father held for him. "He was never there for me, so why should I care for him now? Of course, I would like to be helpful, but he doesn't mean that much to me. He never has, really, and there's no reason for me to feel pushed."

As the therapist supported Bart's sense that he didn't *have to* care about his father (thereby not reenacting his being pushed around by mother), a new side emerged. Bart began to weep openly about how hurt he had felt. He decided that, despite himself, he still cared very much for his father and he went home to see him.

When Bart returned from his visit home, no miracle had occurred. He said that he had had a deeper conversation than usual but one that still felt incomplete. However, he felt that he had done what was right, that he had done it because *he* wanted to, and that he had embraced his father as strongly as this man would accept. "It was better than I thought it would be," he said. "He just couldn't do any more." For the first time he felt that compromise was possible.

After Bart's father died, he talked about a fantasy he had held ever since he was eight years old of having an older brother who could guide him. Such a reparative relationship with a Special Man had never occurred until now. The relationship with his therapist had been doubly curative: it allowed him to acknowledge his need for his father and to feel the real guidance from a peer-mentor that he had never before received. He began to feel more intimate with his wife and to contemplate having children of his own.

FOR MOST MEN it is impossible to effect what Grace Paley called "enormous changes at the last moment." It can be extremely difficult for them even to try to talk about feelings with their fathers, in part because of the taboo against directness. They fear yet another rejection or disappointment. Many worry about their father's own vulnerability and fear that he won't be able to tolerate confrontation or openness. Some remain forever caught in their longings and complaints, never becoming the men they wish they could be. Others, like Bart, are able to mourn their fathers and move on. For practically all of us, our relationships with Special Men remain not quite frozen, but awkward and out of synch. As Lance Morrow describes it:

> "Our two gazes, when we get together, are fixed not upon each other, but upon some third object, some third reality, usually politics or journalism. It works. We can be together. We can take a certain warmth from each other—take it side-long, almost—while outwardly fastening upon some harmless business between us. It is a form of emotional triangulation and distancing, very Japanese, I came to think,

in its exquisite evasiveness. Or maybe merely clumsily masculine, a way of loving each other without saying so, or even
directly feeling it."

SO IT IS that boys become older, bigger, stronger, but not
necessarily feel like men. They may leave behind the Special
Men and Special Women of childhood; still, they search for
replacements to set old wrongs right. As we shall see, they also
find ways to affirm their masculinity through arduous and risky
ventures. They will make great sacrifices to fulfill their duty and
to earn respect. For being a man is both burden and privilege, as
any fallen hero can attest.

5

▼

AUTHORITY AND RESPECT

Conventional wisdom holds that "hell hath no fury like a woman scorned." Yet more often it is the anger of men that gets out of control. Women are rightly concerned about how anger is many men's only expressed emotion, how destructive men can be, and about how women often are the targets for their rage. Such anger also emerges in competition between men and in the often vicious attempts to seize power, possessions, and prestige on the corporate battlefield, in the bedroom, on the playing field, or in outright bloodshed.

If we are to understand men and their power struggles and the spirit of aggression that often accompanies them, we must try to understand what power, anger, honor, and shame mean to men. We must search for their roots in biology and in men's development. We must also study men in different cultures and in the present-day struggles in which modern men are engaged. But the story of angry clashes, of power achieved and lost, of authority that is rightful or corrupt is an ancient one. In this chapter and the next, we will look to Homer's men as well as the men of our time for deeper understandings of this less gentle side of men.

THE WRATH OF ACHILLES

The *Iliad* depicts larger-than-life tales of honor and glory. Written in the eighth century B.C., it looks nostalgically on a long-past heroic age when men struggled for the immortality of remembered valor, while gods helped them conquer and then abandoned them to death. The poet invites us to savor the sights of battle, the rush of combat, such that even gruesome scenes acquire more than a patina of sensuality. But in essence it is a poignant story of both savage and delicate emotions. In Homer we see clearly two men's preoccupations with honor and the hurtful consequences of rage uncontrolled. In its portrayal of the underside of valor—damaged manhood and shame—it points toward a re-creation of masculinity in our time through mourning and the acceptance of loss and human vulnerability.

Although entitled the *Iliad* (meaning a poem about Ilium, or Troy), the poet begins the lengthy ballad with an incantation to the muse concerning the central focus of the work—Achilles' narcissistic rage, and its consequences for both his comrades and his enemies:

> *Anger be now your song, immortal one,*
> *Akhilleus' anger doomed and ruinous,*
> *that caused the Akhaians loss on bitter loss*
> *and crowded brave souls into the underbloom,*
> *leaving so many dead men . . .*
> [FITZGERALD, TRANS., BOOK 1, LL. 1–5]

Ostensibly about the ten-year Trojan War, this bloody conflict provides the stage to explore the inner workings of one great warrior—Achilles. Described most briefly, Achilles, acting on prophetic advice, calls the other lords of battle to a tribunal. He urges Agamemnon, the king, to relinquish some of the booty gained as tribute in his victories, because it appears to be bringing a plague upon his own peoples. Specifically, he wants Agamemnon to appease the gods by releasing a priest's daughter from slavery. Perhaps feeling that his authority has been doubly challenged by Achilles—first by his calling the council, and second by his request that Agamemnon give up his share of the spoils—he first refuses. Then he relents by threatening, angrily, to replace his loss by taking one of the other chieftains' war prizes. Achilles assumes the worst—that Agamemnon means to take his own hard-won booty—and pushes the king into a showdown in which the king asserts his right to take from Achilles the beautiful slave girl Briseus.

This selfish abuse of royal authority and unconcern for Achilles' honor stirs this temperamental warrior to feel overwhelming shame and reactive rage:

> *See how the Lord of the great plains, Agamemnon,*
> *humiliated me! He has my prize,*
> *by his own whim for himself . . .*
> [FITZGERALD, TRANS., BOOK 1, LL. 411–13]

Achilles struggles with whether to kill Agamemnon on the spot or "hold his rage in check and give it time." [Book 1, l. 225]. With divine intervention, he is able to forswear the sword, but his tongue is not so easily restrained. Insults are hurled, with Achilles accusing Agamemnon of cowardly weakness and Agamemnon in turn accusing Achilles of blind ambition and the wish to "Lord it over everyone, hold power over everyone, give orders to the rest of us." [Book 1, ll. 338–40] Able to stave off immediate violence, but unable to contemplate his feelings without action, Achilles threatens to withdraw from the war so that Agamemnon will be chastened by the devastation to his ranks that will ensue without Achilles' support ("you will eat your heart out, raging with remorse for this dishonor done by you . . ." [Book 1, ll. 289–91]

Agamemnon takes Achilles' slave and Achilles withdraws from the battle, leaving the Greeks at the Trojans' mercy. The gods choose sides, and the fate of the warriors is sealed.

As the Greeks are pressed hard by the Trojans, Agamemnon realizes his mistake and sends emissaries to Achilles with a generous offer of riches and his own daughter in marriage. Achilles, still nursing his wounded pride, spurns them, even when proffered by his surrogate father, who helped raise him as a child:

> *I will not share one word of counsel with him,*
> *nor will I act with him; he robbed me blind,*
> *broke faith with me:* he gets no second chance
> to play me for a fool. Once is enough.
> *To hell with him . . .*
>
> [FITZGERALD, TRANS., BOOK 9,
> LL. 456–59; EMPHASIS OURS]

Once more we see a man determined that he will never be shamed again. To be once shamed is to be forever on guard. Homer suggests that there is another reason for Achilles' reluctance to return to battle. Offered by the gods the choice of a short life crowned with immortal glory or a long life without great deeds, Achilles had previously chosen to be a great warrior. But his self-imposed inaction has led to existential questions:

> *I say no wealth is worth my life! Not all they claim*
> *was stored in the depths of Troy, that city built on riches . . .*
> *Cattle and fat sheep can all be had for the raiding,*
> *tripods all for the trading, and tawny-headed stallions.*
> *But a man's life breath cannot come back again—*
> *no raiders in force, no trading brings it back,*
> *once it slips through a man's clenched teeth.*
>
> [FAGLES, TRANS., BOOK 9, LL. 488–97]

Achilles' men are moved to support their comrades and he allows his beloved friend Patroclus to join the fray, indeed urges him to do so in Achilles' own armor. As the audiences—ancient and modern—hearing the poet speak are soon aware, Patroclus faces certain death at the hands of Hector.

When Achilles learns of the death of Patroclus and that Hector has taken his armor:

> *A black cloud of grief came shrouding over Achilles.*
> *Both hands clawing the ground for soot and filth,*

he poured it over his head, fouled his handsome face
and black ashes settled onto his fresh clean war-shirt.
Overpowered in all his power, he sprawled in the dust.
Achilles lay there, fallen . . .
tearing his hair, defiling it with his own hands.
[FAGLES, TRANS., BOOK 18, LL. 24–30]

Achilles' grief at losing his most loved comrade is doubled by his guilt that his withdrawal from the battle ensured the death. However, while rueful about its consequences, the warrior knows only rage and destruction:

. . . let strife and rancor
perish from the lives of gods and men,
with anger that envenoms even the wise
and is sweeter than slow-dripping honey,
clouding the hearts of men like smoke: just so
the marshal of the army, Agamemnon,
moved me to anger. But we'll let that go,
though I'm still sore at heart; it is all past,
and I have quelled my passion as I must.
Now I must go to look for the destroyer
of my great friend. I shall confront the dark
drear spirit of death at any hour Zeus
and the other gods may wish to make an end.
[FITZGERALD, TRANS., BOOK 18,
LL. 123–34]

Achilles understands the addictive appeal of rage, or what we might less poetically describe as the rush of adrenaline. For some men, while their anger may be sparked in reaction to wounded pride, something deeply savage in their nature may be roused from its primeval slumber and then be difficult to put to rest. Further, as Seth Schein points out in *The Mortal Hero*, Achilles has not forgiven Agamemnon—rather, he has transferred his rage and wish to avenge his wounded honor to Hector, and in doing so, becomes even more savage:

*So as the great Achilles rampaged on, his sharp-hoofed stallions
trampled shields and corpses, axle under his chariot splashed
with blood, blood on the handrails sweeping round the car,
sprays of blood shooting up from the stallions' hoofs and
churning, whirling rims—and the son of Peleus
charioteering on to seize his glory, bloody filth
splattering both strong arms, Achilles' invincible arms—*

[FAGLES, TRANS., BOOK 20, LL. 563–69]

Before his honor was sullied by Agamemnon, Achilles would
often spare a defeated warrior's life and would honor the dead's
remains in accord with the chivalry of battle. But now he has no
compassion, and even after he has killed Hector, he is tempted to
"slaughter you and eat you raw." [Fitzgerald, trans., Book 22,
l. 413] He drags Hector's body behind his chariot, seeking in
vain to cleanse his own soul though the debasement of another.
In Achilles' hell of shame there can be no forgiveness.

AN ANCIENT MYTH OR
A MODERN PARABLE?

Though the weapons are archaic, the human dramas portrayed make the *Iliad* much more than an arcane tome, dusty
with the passage of time. Can we not see Achilles and Agamemnon among our present corporation CEOs: Digital's Ken Olsen
and a slew of vice presidents who engaged in battle and who
were, each in turn, forced to leave the field; or Thomas Pyle,
the brilliant CEO of Harvard Community Health Plan, who
built it from a small family into a citadel and then was toppled
by his tribunal of doctor executives for his arrogant and person-
alized aggrandizement and for not sharing power with his chieftains. Do we not see it in retrospect in the Kennedy/Khrushchev
confrontation in Cuba? What at the time was trumpeted as a
profile in courage in retrospect may have been an ego-driven
rattling of sabers rather than a responsible negotiation from

strength. Did we not see it in the Persian Gulf in the macho posturing of President Bush and Saddam Hussein, each of them needing to prove that neither country, neither *man* would lose face? Beneath the chivalrous language of the *Iliad* and the blood-less euphemisms of Pentagon-speak is the same football-field, warrior mentality of "I'll kick his ass."

Through anger—the final common pathway for all their feel-ings—men express their vulnerability and powerlessness in their search for authority. Anger has always been the favorite son of men's limited family of emotions. It is the stepchild of men's vulnerability and powerlessness in search of legitimate author-ity. Its true parentage remains too shameful to face—hence, the poorly defined response of rage, by which men hope to gain respect.

MEN, WOMEN, AND POWER

Men seek power. They are uncomfortable in positions of relative weakness and need to feel "on top." What is seldom appreciated is that men may seek power as a substitute for a more confident feeling of authority.

Authority differs from other forms of power. By authority we mean a legitimatized or negotiated form of leadership, and with it a mature sense of responsibility. It is a particular power that has a social purpose and meaning and that commands respect. In our democratic societies it is a delegated sense of responsibility that brings with it a balance sheet between the utilization of strength, force, privilege, or role on the one hand, and responsibili-ties of protection, support, feedback, and accountability on the other. We believe that most men have a deep personal need to be respected and would like to wield power that is agreed to, not extorted. They want power justified by competence, not simply "because I said so." In the words of Judith Jordan and Jean Baker Miller, they want power to *accomplish* things, to implement personal change, not power *over* other people. Yet in the absence of such authority, and the understanding of its meaning, men often feel threatened and express their darker sides: they boss, they devalue in order to feel superior, and they abuse and hurt. In response to such men, women are faced with propping them up, enduring their mistreatment, or leaving.

For the vast majority of men who struggle with feelings of powerlessness but are capable of change, the challenge is two-fold, and in both aspects, men need the sensitivity and support of women. First, men need to learn to cultivate sources of authority and not settle for shows of mere power. For example, men have commonly abdicated their authority in the family through their absence and by allowing women to run the house-hold while periodically insisting that they are still Head of the Household. When fathers take control inconsistently, in a loud voice, or in abrupt ways that are out of synch with the delicate balances built up by day-to-day familiarity, they wind up being feared rather than being respected. To reclaim authority and respect men need to know their own selves better, learn how to collaborate with other men and women, and find ways "to make their mark" without harming others.

Most men see power as a scarce commodity that they have to compete with other men and, increasingly, with women, to command. In the new power equation with women, men often fear that women's empowerment means that they will have less power. This narrow, win/lose definition of power makes men fearful, mistrustful of closeness, aggressive, and, often, abhor-rent to women. It also prevents them from considering how shared power could enhance both partners' freedom.

As the psychiatrist Edward Shapiro points out, a fundamental aspect of leadership is to define a group task and to act in accord with that task. In the aftermath of the women's movement, men are confused about their role and the task that gives it meaning. They are reacting to the new voice of women when they should be developing their own new voice. Only by taking leadership in setting the agenda of gender can men speak again with authority. This new male authority will be power not to which women silently acquiesce but with which they can join in mutual respect.

The second task for men is to develop a greater tolerance for being receptive or passive, orientations that are usually labeled as "weak." These are traits generally assigned to women in our society because men are too ashamed to acknowledge them. Men are sometimes afraid of or don't enjoy exercising power. Yet unlike women, many of whom also avoid powerful positions, men have had to hide this trait and compensate for their feelings of "cowardice" by expressing the darker traits we have mentioned. Paradoxically, it is when men can acknowledge, bear, and put into perspective[1] these so-called feminine traits in themselves that they are more capable of asserting themselves in healthy and positive ways. Men need to learn how to *share* power with other men and with women. They also need to experiment with being interdependent with men and with women rather than either repudiating their own needs in a macho form of protectionism or covertly trying to get women to take care of them, as though they remained children in their mother's arms.

Men tend to be more aggressive and express anger more easily than women in our society. Like most folk wisdom, this simple truth hides a great deal of complexity. For Achilles, and for his modern counterparts, anger is a protective screen behind which lurk more meaningful and complex mixtures of sadness, love, fellowship, and joy.

Many women suspect that when it comes to questions of power and aggression between the genders, "men really just don't get it!" This expression became a pointed commentary during the Clarence Thomas/Anita Hill Supreme Court hearings, and in the "date-rape" trial of William Kennedy Smith. Whatever one's belief in the credibility of the complex characters involved, what was most striking was our cultural confusion about harassment, force, and sexual attraction. Many men have

---

[1] The phrase "to acknowledge, bear, and put into perspective" is adapted from the late psychiatrist Elvin Semrad's dictum for psychotherapy. He may well have been thinking of what men specifically need to do in order to mature fully.

a difficult time understanding that the issue in sexual harassment is not sexual and in date rape is not the date. In other words, it is the misuse of power through harassment or force through rape that frightens women and confuses men. On the other hand, men also feel that women "really just don't get it." The positive facets of male aggression may be particularly difficult to recognize in an era when women have revealed these aspects of men to be so often damaging and abusive to them.

THE WARRIOR MENTALITY

To Achilles, only honor, courage, and the demonstration of physical prowess count. Only by pursuing these heroic goals can he affirm himself, and this is best done by killing other heroes in one-to-one combat and obtaining their armor as a trophy. Even the defeated warrior can achieve greatness, for if he fought without cowardice he, no less than his conqueror, has placed honor above death. Indeed, the fallen hero may be especially honored—he has defied his fate at the hands of a superior foe, and also basks in the reflected glory of his conqueror. Like the sinner who is dispatched from this life at the moment of prayer, his ending sanctifies all that has gone before. But in contrast to Judeo-Christian notions, the fallen hero's reward is not an afterlife but the immortality of song.

The warrior mentality embraces fully the *cult of autonomy*— the hero must achieve greatness and face his death alone. While he may fight in defense of his kin, the ultimate duty he owes is to personal excellence. This attitude also requires a denial of anything "feminine." There is little room for fear, reflection, connection, or doubt. In exchange, the warrior gains an unambiguous pathway to manhood: kill or be killed, his masculinity will be "in the can."

As John Keegan has described in *The Face of Battle*, these same values were in force during the Middle Ages, such as at the battle of Agincourt, in 1415: "To meet a similarly equipped

opponent was the occasion for which the armoured soldier
trained perhaps every day of his life from the onset of manhood.
To meet and beat him was a triumph, the highest form which
self-expression could take in the medieval nobleman's way of
life." [p. 110]

By 1815, at Waterloo, due to the advanced nature of weap-
onry, honor in warfare was no longer a matter of single combat
and obtaining trophies. Yet the demonstration of courage was
still enough to keep men from running away in battle. As Keegan points out, "Honour, so absolutely concrete in Homer, was
for the British officer of 1815 an almost wholly abstract ideal,
a matter of comportment, of exposure to risk, of acceptance of
death if it should come, of private satisfaction—if it should
not—at having fulfilled an unwritten code." [p. 194]

A hundred years later, at the Somme and dozens of other
World War I battlefields, men were ready to go to their deaths
by the hundreds of thousands, killed by men they could not
even see.

In *Fire in the Belly*, Sam Keen points out that part of being
a man is to have the life of a warrior. It is his sense that in
many cultures the main purpose of inititation rights for males
is to turn them into soldiers. Men are taught to avoid, to eschew anything feminine, and to become stoic, unfeeling, and
militaristic: "The neophyte learns to disdain woman's ways,
to eject the sensuous knowledge of the body he learned kines-
thetically from his mother and to deny all that is 'feminine'
and soft in himself." [Keen, p. 29] Boys, and later men, Keen
argues, are socialized toward action, warfare, and conquering,
rather than feeling, reflection, and connection. "Nothing
shapes, and forms, and molds us so much as society's demand
that we become specialists in the use of power and violence."
[p. 37] For Keen, men have achieved a warrior psyche, and
have been "culturally designed with conquest, killing, or dying
in mind." [p. 38] As a result of such cultural designation and
gender socialization men acquire, in Keen's scheme, a host of
limiting psychological defenses. They come to admire toughness
and aggression, strive for status, adopt a pose of self-sufficiency
and emotional stoicism, and shun all things feminine.

While the price men pay for the warrior mentality is a life of Type A anxiety, posttraumatic stress, and emotional estrangement from the women they love, the cost of not being so trained, Keen points out, is an even greater sense of humiliation or degradation: men who are too sensitive or compassionate to fight grow up feeling that they are sissies who have failed the test of manhood. As S. L. A. Marshall, in *Men Against Fire*, observes:

> Whenever one surveys the forces of the battlefield, it is to see that fear is general among men, but to observe further that men commonly are loath that their fear will be expressed in specific acts which their comrades will recognize as cowardice. The majority are unwilling to take extraordinary risks and do not aspire to a hero's role, but they are equally unwilling that they should be considered the least worthy among those present. . . . When a soldier is known . . . to the men who are around him, he has . . . reason to fear losing the one thing that he is likely to value more highly than life— his reputation as a man among other men.
>
> [MARSHALL, PP. 144–53]

Those who do become warriors can become "missing in action." Like Vietnam veterans, men who survive the peacetime battles required of a warrior are traumatized and lost. One meaning of America's preoccupation with the MIAs of Vietnam is that they are a poignant symbol for the damaged manhood of our generation. We cannot rest while we wonder if Achilles still drags Hector's body behind his chariot or Odysseus remains a captive, yearning to come home.

THE BIG IMPOSSIBLE

David Gilmore, in his review of scores of cultures studied by anthropologists, ranging from preindustrial Western cultures to Micronesia and Africa, concludes that while biological maleness may be a predestined phenomenon, *manhood* is a culturally created concept and a fragile achievement:

> In particular, there is a constantly recurring notion that real manhood is different from simple anatomical maleness, that it is not a natural condition that comes about spontaneously through biological maturation, but rather is a *precarious or artificial state that boys must win against powerful odds.* This recurrent notion that manhood is problematic, a critical threshold that boys must pass through testing, is found at all levels of sociocultural development regardless of what other alternative roles are recognized. It is found amongst the simplest hunters and fishermen, amongst peasants and sophisticated urbanized people; it is found in all continents and environments. It is found among both warrior peoples and those who have never killed in anger.
>
> [GILMORE, P. 11, ITALICS OURS]

Gilmore finds that, while girls and women may also be judged by exacting standards, the achievement of femaleness is less precarious. Rarely is their status as a "woman" up for grabs. The sheer number and the chilling effect of negative terms utilized for men who do not act in a "manly way" according to our societal imperatives—"sissy," "effeminate," a "wimp,"or a "fag"—is proof of Gilmore's argument. The cultural push to "become a man" even occurs in egalitarian, peaceful societies. For example, the Kung! bushmen are sometimes called the "harmless people" because of their gentleness and cooperative spirit; still, to become a bushman, boys must pass a special test of skill and endurance.

One American Indian group calls the ritual changes required to become a man the "Big Impossible," a fitting metaphor for the slippery slope on which manhood must be achieved.

> Among most of the peoples anthropologists are familiar with, true manhood is a precious and elusive status beyond mere maleness, a hortatory image that men and boys aspire to and that their culture demanded of them as a metaphor of belonging. Although this stressed or embattled quality varies in intensity . . . true manhood . . . *frequently shows an inner insecurity that needs dramatic proof.* Its vindication is doubtful, resting on rigid codes of decisive action in many spheres of life: as husband, father, lover, provider, warrior. A restricted status, there are always men *who fail the test.*
>
> [GILMORE, P. 17, ITALICS OURS]

Michael Herzfeld, in his study of a small village on the island of Crete, found that men engage in a constant struggle to gain a precarious sense of manhood. It is not sufficient to "be a good man"—one must "be good *at* being a man." That is, only by dramatic deeds that "speak for themselves" can one maintain one's reputation among other men.

In ritual "rites of passage," originally documented by Van Gennep, the father or elder male mentors cajole, push, brutalize, or nurture boys into the roles of manhood. Significantly, such rites almost always include the separation of young boys from their early attachment to women, and particularly from their mothers. For example, as Gilbert Herdt reports in *Guardians of the Flutes*, the initiation rites of the Sambia of New Guinea begin when boys are seven to ten years old and include oral ingestion of older boys' semen and painful bleeding by sticking grass reeds up the nose. While such actions seek to mark the boy as emphatically *not* a woman, curiously they incorporate basic feminine biologic functions that men lack: the bleeding is a counterpart to menstruation and semen is ingested instead of mother's milk. These acts betray men's primal fear of being women and the willingness to endure trauma in order to ensure separation from them.

In the *Odyssey*, Telemachus leaves his mother and childhood home and braves danger to seek the advice of older male mentors—Nestor and Menelaus. He then undergoes a physical initiation prescribed by his father—the slaying of the suitors—

during which he is slightly wounded. (Scarification is a common feature of initiation rites.) His last act in the *Odyssey* is to put to death twelve female servants who had been unfaithful to his father, perhaps demonstrating his triumph over the feminine influences of his youth.

Gilmore argues that bedrock "deep structures" of masculinity are necessary in all cultures to prevent reconnecting with mother. The fiercely demarcated rites of passage are a stern reminder to the perpetual little boy within that he can never be welcomed back to mother's nurturing arms.

We believe that it is not the fear of such a regression but the dread of uncovering *the trauma of having been so abruptly pulled away* that leads so many little boys and, later, men to reenact their early hurt and pain, such as by loving and leaving women and seeking sponsorship from male mentors who inevitably disappoint. Being blocked from the early trauma, they are unable to heal the wound of a lost mother, which in our society occurs without the active guidance of a benign father. If ever the boy or adult man yearns for or ventures too close to mother's world, he feels ashamed.

So much of a man's sense of hidden vulnerability and avoidance of shame is linked to his not wanting to be seen as too dependent upon women—Momma's little boy—and therefore not passing the test of a true man. And so in our search for some of the roots of men's overstepping for power out of a fear that they will not be accorded true authority and respect, we must go back to the pain of separation from the cocoon of a loving maternal embrace.

SHAME, SHAME, SHAME...

In Chapter 2, we mentioned how one of our patients, who was anxious about starting a new relationship after a failed marriage, thought of a nursery rhyme—"Fool me once, shame on you; Fool me twice, shame on me"—and began sobbing. It is this sense of public vulnerability, of being exposed as a failure and a fool, that is at the root of men's terrible fear of being shamed.

Historically, women have been seen as particularly prone to the affect of shame and men to that of guilt, reflecting the female gender's greater inwardness and the male's proclivity to action. Yet it is painfully clear that men will go to great lengths to avoid shame, and as we shall show, often those lengths involve what psychologists and psychiatrists call reaction formation, or the attempt to turn something into its opposite. Men often transform the signal of shame into anger to forestall a vulnerability within, and a public exposure of insufficiency without.

One such man, desperate to maintain a façade of social "success" as proof of his manhood, was admitted to a private psychiatric hospital for forensic evaluation. Seth had confessed to repeated crimes of check forgery and embezzlement.

What particularly confused the authorities was how brazenly Seth had engaged in repetitive crimes, at which he was bound to be caught. A full evaluation revealed that this sophisticated, middle-aged business man, who in his early years had been quite successful, continued to fear failure, as his fathers and brothers both had failed in their middle years.

When some economic setbacks did ensue, Seth felt so humiliated and frightened that the loss of a portion of his fortune would lead to the loss of his wife and family's love that he took flight into fancy: he wrote checks for amounts he could not afford and forged other people's signature so as to create the illusion of economic prosperity that in reality he no longer enjoyed.

Although a faint voice told him that he would eventually get caught, Seth's wish to postpone the discovery that his success was a sham drove him irresistibly to steal what he could not legitimately obtain. When Seth was seen in the hospital, he was clearly depressed and remorseful. Even so, he said he probably would do the same thing again, if he had to, because the public disgrace of failure was more powerful and humiliating than the consequences of his crimes.

Although this is an extreme example, it highlights the darker side of men's need to be responsible and the dangers of running from shame. In the final book of the *Iliad*, when the gods are lamenting Achilles' savagery, Apollo observes:

> *Achilles has lost all pity! No shame in the man,*
> *shame that does great harm or drives men on to good.*
> [FAGLES, TRANS., BOOK 24, LL. 52–53]

The Greeks ascribed to the gods great antipathy to men's overweening pride, which they called hubris. Recall, for instance, that Oedipus was struck down as a lesson on the dangers of blind arrogance. The "good" that Apollo says that shame drives men to may indeed be its tempering influence on pride. Shame humbles by reminding us of our fallibility, of our essential humanness and therefore vulnerability to the innermost twists of our own knife. At his worst, the man without shame can engage in all manner of shameless acts, unhampered by the restraining influence of how he appears through others' eyes. The psychologist Steven Krugman has written that shame is a signal warning of a loss of the self's integrity. Whether as a check on an arrogant man's hubris or as a spur to a mistreated man to assert his dignity, men ignore this signal at their peril.

Seth, the embezzler, illustrates only one of the many transformations of shame. Andrew Morrison argues that shame is the primary emotion that underlies most psychological adaptations. For example, depression can be seen as a response to the injury caused the self by shame, contempt is a projection of our own shame onto others, and rage may be a self-restorative attempt to expel unbearable feelings of shame. Many men turn to gambling, to womanizing, to overwork, and to alcohol and other drugs to dull themselves to shame. Indeed, it is also very like the wrath of Achilles and the destructive ways he, too, had to protect his honor. Steven Krugman suggests that men's violence may be a last-ditch attempt to defend against feelings of shame. Men's dread of shame engenders a stubborn denial of reality that cares nothing for consequences.

Judy Jordan, a feminist scholar and our colleague at McLean Hospital, has suggested that shame is not solely an internal psychological experience of inadequacy, but rather a painful sense of being unloved by others. She points out that shame is more than the underside of narcissistic pride; it is a "felt sense of unworthiness . . . deep sense of unlovability, with the ongoing awareness of how much one wants to connect with others . . . one feels unworthy of love . . . because one is defective or flawed in some essential way." [Jordan (1989) p. 16]

Similarly, Jean Baker Miller speaks of shame as "condemned isolation . . . being locked out of the possibility of connection." [J. B Miller, quoted in Jordan (1989) p. 16]

This dimension of shame is illustrated by one patient's description of his loss of face. He said that shame is something like the sense of passing an old friend on a street corner, and of stopping to wave and say hello. You feel your hand extended and then the other person walks by with hardly a response. You blush, pretend that you hadn't waved, and look around to see if anyone noticed that you looked pathetic.

We suggested earlier that while little girls are allowed to continue to identify with their mothers, little boys between the ages of three and five begin to recognize that they are different. The sense of being a "we" is fractured by this growing sense of otherness. Little boys and their mothers feel great pressure to push away so they don't end up as "Momma's boys." Without an involved father, boys are left feeling a loss that cannot be acknowledged. As Steven Krugman points out, these and other secret feelings of need for support and reassurance lead men to shy away from other males to avoid self-disclosure. Like the man who tried to wave to an old friend, they are left with a shameful sense of failed connection.

SEARCHING FOR LEGITIMATE AUTHORITY

Plagued by a feeling of being defective and unlovable, and shamed by their need of other people to affirm them, men resort to seizing power. While they wish they could acquire authority in legitimate ways, it is often wrested from other men or expressed as power over women. Jean Baker Miller distinguishes between power as "forced strength or influence" and power as "the capacity to produce a change." Because men feel unable to produce a change, they feel impotent and powerless. Since they feel too much shame about acknowledging their interdependence with others, they turn to force.

As James Redfield, the noted Greek scholar, observes, "A community has need for a dominant figure; the existence of a single paramount of authority limits conflict, guarantees solidarity, and enables the community to function." [Redfield, p. 85] However, legitimate authority requires that the leader renounce selfish gain and narcissistic needs. Even more than Achilles in the role of greatest warrior, the acceptance of self-sacrifice is part of the king's role. Agamemnon's inability to compromise[2] is a tragic error and a perversion of his responsibilities as king:

> Agamemnon suffers from the paradox of authority: authority often seems to confer power to do everything except what the person possessing it wants for himself. As Agamemnon says later, with rather touching openness, he kept the girl because he liked her. . . . But precisely because he is king, Agamemnon is not allowed to follow his own inclinations; he has more power than other men but less freedom. This paradox has puzzled wiser men than Agamemnon.
>
> [REDFIELD, P. 88]

A central theme of the 1960s protest movement and of the flower-child ethos of that time was a mistrust of authority. People were urged to "Kill the pig" and "Don't trust anyone over thirty." Oliver Stone's conspiracy theory of John F. Kennedy's assassination is straight out of the sixties zeitgeist that those in power are corrupt, dangerous, and opposed to change. Whether due to devastating reality, to wounded cynicism about

---

[2]Bernard Knox has pointed out that even Agamemnon's offer of gifts to Achilles is not accompanied by an apology, and this contributes to Achilles continuing sense of grievance.

politics after the death of Kennedy- and King-style idealism, or
to tranference of anger from absent fathers to surrogate fathers in
institutional life, authority had more the association of Orwell's
1984 (the date now a nostalgic marker of how much older we've
become) than of the old-fashioned policeman who helps lost
children find their way home. The legacy of this mistrust of
authority is that grown-up men of the sixties generation have
had difficulty integrating the exercise of authority as a valued
aspect of masculinity. Already concerned about following in
their father's footsteps, these men are highly vulnerable to
women's legitimate and often incisive attacks on men's abuse
of power, leading them to feel ashamed of any exercise of power
or to reject defensively what women have to say.

In his early twenties, John Parkman had burned his draft card
and heeded the call to "turn on, tune in, drop out." At forty-
five, he had a wife, two teenage kids, a BMW, and a successful
law practice. Although he had first worked as a public defender
after graduating from law school, he had moved on to corporate
law. Then, soon after accepting a government position with
enhanced responsibilities and prestige, he became depressed. In
a series of meetings with him, it emerged that he was deeply
troubled by the realization that he had become much of what
he had despised in his youth. During his law career he had
refused a number of promotions, ostensibly because he wanted
to preserve a family life, but in retrospect he had felt uncomfortable with any position of authority. He also was disappointed
that as a father he could be harsh and uncompromising and he
wondered if after all he was "a wolf in sheep's clothing."

AGGRESSIVENESS VERSUS
ASSERTIVENESS

Until recently, concern about violence, whether committed
by individuals or organized by the state, has obscured the fact
that the problem is primarily due to acts committed by *men,*

both against other men and against women. The Surgeon General reported in June 1992, that violence is the leading cause of injury to women age fifteen to forty-four.

Some argue that men's aggression and hunger for power are driven by testosterone. In hamsters, rats, and rhesus monkeys testosterone levels (or androgen levels in general) are correlated with greater aggressive activity in males, although animal models are too simplistic to explain human development. Broadly, hormones affect development at two points. First, *in utero*, androgens act to differentiate the female fetus into a male, possibly including divergent brain development. Second, at puberty androgens activate potentialities for secondary sexual characteristics, and perhaps lead to further divergence of basic emotional and behavioral characteristics. One recent finding of interest is that it is not the absolute level of testosterone in the bloodstream that determines expression of anger, but its day-to-day *variability* in both girls and boys. Further, the problem of male violence perpetrated on women is less one of excess "masculinity" than its felt lack: Battering, raping, and murdering women are the last resort of insecure, desperate men who have found no other ways to express anger or to rescue their pride. Indeed, no matter what biology predisposes, men still have the responsibility to manage their violent impulses.

The psychoanalytic researcher Gerald Stechler and his colleagues have theorized that from early years aggressiveness and assertiveness are distinct modes of engaging with the world that for some boys may later coalesce with their identity and for some girls diverge from it. Little boys may engage in power struggles or violent aggressive activities as a distorted form of asserting their sense of self. In contrast, the need of little girls to maintain their close connection with mother may lead them to fear any assertion as an aggressive act because it means breaking this tie. In adult life, women often have a difficult time being assertive for fear it is aggression, and men have a difficult time inhibiting aggression for fear they will lose their assertiveness. For men, they would rather have angry, hurtful control struggles that alienate them from other men and from women than to risk the shame of passivity. Their credo becomes "Do it to others so that they won't do it to you." Small wonder that men, like Agamemnon, more often engage in forceful, dominating displays of power and seldom achieve the respectful control necessary to be seen worthy of legitimate authority.

THE VULNERABILITY OF MEN: ACHILLES' HEEL

It is commonly believed that women are the "weaker sex" and that men can "take it." But the notion that men are destined by biology to be tougher than women may turn out to have been a self-soothing cultural lullaby to avoid the painful recognition of its mirror opposite: male vulnerability. Both in myth and in modern epidemiology men are seen more realistically as possessing the equivalent of Achilles' heel.

Achilles' mother was a goddess, but his father was mortal, and the product of such hybrid unions was always mortal as well. According to legend, his mother sought to make him impervious to wounds by dipping the infant in the river Styx, leaving only the heel by which she held him as his single vulnerable point. There is another charming story about how she tried to protect her son. It had been foretold that Achilles would either live a long but unremarkable life or go to Troy, win glory, and be cut down in his youth. Hoping to prolong his life, she spirited the boy away from the gathering expedition to Troy and took him to an island, disguised as a girl. However, Odysseus learned of his whereabouts, and by leaving armor in the women's chambers, uncovered that he was a boy by the interest young Achilles showed in it. (Evidently, the ancient Greeks knew a fair amount about early gender development.)

According to myth, Paris's arrow mortally wounds Achilles on his vulnerable heel, and it is this critical tendon in the foot that still immortalizes Achilles' name. Its severing can prematurely terminate a great athlete's career and as men age it becomes more vulnerable to tearing. Once again the symbol of wounded feet appears as a clue to a man's true origins. In this myth, it symbolizes a mother's vain attempts to hold onto and protect her son, even at the cost of turning him into a girl. She cannot avert his destiny of violence and vulnerability.

In the *Iliad*, Homer does not mention the legend of Achilles' heel, although he must have been aware of it. Instead, he portrays Achilles' anguish about the mortal price he knows he will pay for his glory. All warriors face the same stark choice, but Achilles knows specifically that once he kills Hector, his own death will swiftly follow. His hybrid parentage further underscores the paradox of his godlike powers coexisting with fatal human vulnerability.

Modern epidemiologic findings suggest that it is not by chance that Achilles' mortal parent is the male. While it is not yet clear whether men are constitutionally more aggressive than women, they may be constitutionally more vulnerable. We know, for example, that the male sex hormone testosterone is important in strenthening male muscles, but is an equally significant threat to men's hearts. Testosterone triggers production of low-density lipoprotein (LDL), the so-called bad cholesterol that clogs vital blood vessels, while female hormones appear to stimulate the liver to create "good cholesterol" and elastic blood vessels. The result is that males have twice the risk of coronary artery disease than females do. Male hormones promote the growth of long bones while female hormones tend to stop growth at puberty, with males on average being 10 percent taller than females. Stress hormones, which may aid in combat situations by providing for stronger heart contractions and faster blood clotting, also produce higher blood pressure.

Practically from the moment of conception, males have a more tenuous foothold on life than females—males are more likely to undergo complications during labor and delivery and have more birth defects. Male children also suffer from more sex-linked genetic abnormalities than females and have higher rates of behavior disorders and learning disabilities. In the United States the average man dies seven years earlier than the average woman, rates of death are higher for men than women of all ages, and due to the frequency of violent deaths in men between the ages of fifteen and twenty-four, men die at three times the rate of women. Historically, men's death rates from lung cancer have been six times greater than those of women, and twice as high for cirrhosis of the liver and heart disease.[3] Indeed, the seeming health liability incurred by virtue of being born male has led the researcher J. Harrison to suggest that the Surgeon General should issue an advisory: "Warning: masculinity may be dangerous to your health." Regrettably, as the prevalence of male violent acts toward women makes clear, masculinity is also dangerous to *women*'s health.

Still, much of the "biological" vulnerability of males cannot be traced to genetic differences alone. The psychologist Joseph Pleck, among other theorists, believes that men are ground down trying to live up to an inhuman standard of manhood, or what he calls "sex role strain." David and Brannon describe four features of this stereotyped male role. One factor is what they call the "give 'em hell" stance of violence and daring. The injunction to become a "sturdy oak" refers to men's stoicism and the inability to share pain or to grieve. The necessity to be a "big wheel" is the need to achieve status and power at any cost, and the fourth and most traumatizing they call "No sissy stuff"—the condemnation of anything even vaguely feminine. These commandments encase men in an emotional straitjacket as isolating and corrosive to the body and soul as a prisoner's solitary confinement. The remorseless, private keeper of this legion of cultural prisoners is each man's shame.

Put most simply, worn down by the effort not to appear limp-wristed, many men turn up lame.

---

[3] See Eisler and Blalock, 1991. Note that as women's cigarette smoking has increased, the gender gap in death rates due to lung cancer and other tobacco-related diseases has narrowed.

THE "MACHO" DREAM OF
FLORAL ARRANGEMENT

One such casualty of "sex role strain" that one of us treated was a working-class man in his middle thirties. Joe was suffering from repeated bouts of drinking and the ravages it had caused to his body and self-respect when he was admitted to the hospital following a serious suicide attempt.

The youngest of three brothers, Joe had always felt isolated, alienated, and very much like the "runt" of the litter. He believed he could never quite compete with his father, or his brothers, who were both older than he, and physically stronger. Although he was closer to his mother and a maternal aunt, his connection to them was guilty and furtive since he feared such nurturing would brand him a "sissy."

Joe entered into three extremely self-defeating and then failed marriages and fathered a number of children with each woman. Over an extended period of time he became more and more depressed about his capacity "to be the kind of person I really wanted to be." He said that he came face-to-face with his own despair most strongly when he almost struck his youngest son, whom he cared a great deal about, and for whom he was now a single parent. In his son's pain and sense of betrayal Joe saw his own suppressed yearning for support, about which he had felt so much shame. At first for the sake of his son, but gradually also for himself, he agreed to see a therapist.

In therapy it became clear that during late adolescence and young adulthood Joe had shown very clear proclivities and talent in floral arrangement, but out of fear that this was not an acceptable field for a man, he gave up numerous opportunities for achievement. Instead he turned to odd jobs and self-employment schemes that repeatedly failed. The "real men" of the family—his fathers and brothers—had been unsuccessful construction contractors and alcoholics. As Joe felt increasing freedom to diverge from such family loyalties, he began to contemplate the possibility of moving into the field of landscaping, a compromise between the stereotypically male outdoor activities of his family and the delicate arrangement of flowers of his inner self.

GRIEF, MOURNING, AND THE TRANSFORMATION OF RAGE

The beauty of the *Iliad* and its meaning come from the transformation of the godlike yet vulnerable mortal hero Achilles. Through grieving Achilles turns from preoccupations with shame, honor, and rageful war to mortality and fellowship.

Achilles had postponed the burial of his beloved friend Patroclus until he had killed Hector, ostensibly to defend both their honor, but also because he could not yet face the finality of loss. Now, at the ritual cremation of Patroclus's body on the funeral pyre, Achilles' anger gives way to open grief:

> As a father weeps when he burns his son's bones,
> dead on his wedding day,
> and his death has plunged his parents in despair . . .
> so Achilles wept as he burned his dear friend's bones,
> dragging himself around the pyre, choked with sobs.
>
> [FAGLES, TRANS., BOOK 23, LL. 254–58]

Yet even now, with the reawakening of tenderness and concern, Achilles is still unable to make peace with himself. He continues to drag the dead body of Hector around in the dust and refuses it burial. Like men today who must split off and project into women and into other men the shameful, vulnerable parts of themselves, he cannot face the fact that the dishonored body of the dead warrior is also himself.[4]

In the final book of the *Iliad*, Hector's father, King Priam, comes to Achilles to beg for the right to bury his son ("I put to

---

[4]In *The Poetics of Manhood*, Michael Herzfeld points out that for men in a rural society on Crete the deaths of male relatives are still experienced as "wounds to the self."

my lips the hands of the man who killed my son" [Fagles, Trans., l. 591]). Priam asks Achilles to think of his own father and find pity. Moved by the old man's incantation of a father's love for his son, Achilles joins his enemy in the open expression of grief and mourning:

> *Those words stirred within Achilles a deep desire*
> *to grieve for his own father. Taking the old man's hand*
> *he gently moved him back. And overpowered by memory*
> *both men gave way to grief. Priam wept freely*
> *for man-killing Hector, throbbing, crouching*
> *before Achilles' feet as Achilles wept himself,*
> *now for his father, now for Patroclus once again,*
> *and their sobbing rose and fell throughout the house.*
>
> [FAGLES, TRANS., BOOK 24, LL. 592–99]

And so the struggle over power and glory becomes tempered by the reality of death. Achilles has undergone a rite of passage in which he has recognized that rage cannot prevent and indeed inevitably leads to loss, and that honor without compassion has no lasting value. His enemy is no longer the other, for both he and Hector, Priam and Patroclus share the same fate. Through shared mourning he relinquishes his rage and is brought back to a fellowship with other men in which honor and sacrifice become affirmations rather than a defensive posture.

As Bennett Simon, the noted psychoanalyst and Greek scholar, has pointed out:

> . . . Homer has elaborated the complex picture of what is needed to resolve the turmoil and sorrow of the human heart. *Action* alone does not suffice; discharge of emotions is not enough. The acceptance of a common humanity and a common mortality begins to achieve some therapeutic affect. At first it only allows Priam and Achilles to mourn at the same time, separately, each for his own sorrows. But the realization that each can empathize with the other brings them closer and allows for something more than pity to surface. Finally, both the disease called the "wrath of Achilles" and

the implacable grief of Priam are brought to some resolution by a profound realization not only that each can be in the other's place, but that each has within him parts of all others: man and woman, mother and father, parent and child, sister and brother, friend and foe, beast and human.

[SIMON (1988), P. 76]

The Greek tragic cycle, as in Sophocles' *Oedipus the King*, follows a simple progression from what the early Greeks called hubris and *atē,* to nemesis. Freely translated, in the jargon of our time, hubris consists of grandiose "self-pumping," the kind of narcissistic sense of specialness that leads to *atē,* or a blindness that overtakes rational judgment. The combination of such overblown grandiosity and idealization of the self, with its consequent intolerance for shame and the denial of limitations (including death) leads to the inevitable tragic outcome or consequence—nemesis.

Heinz Kohut has described the developmental sequence by which the grandiose dreams of childhood either evolve into the mature idealization of adulthood or remain stagnated in a world of fantasied omnipotence. In the chapter on Special Men we noted how boys need to idealize their fathers as a way station toward feeling that being a man is both admirable and possible. Other opportunities present themselves through a man's life for hero worship, and the *Iliad*'s exaltation of the warrior resonates with both ancient and modern men's need to perform heroic deeds vicariously.

The Homeric poem was really a communal activity, told by the reciter to large groups who engaged in a collective process of identification with the heroic characters and with their transformation. We can imagine them still, after a feast, gathered by torchlight to hear the poet's song. They each know how the story begins and how it ends, but they listen, rapt, as if hearing the story for the first time. In the language of psychotherapy, the audience—ancient or modern—first shares the idealized view of the hero. Later we recognize the limitations of the heroic code, mourn our boyhood dreams, and learn to honor our capacities for empathy, sadness, and vulnerability. For all of Homer's appreciation of the tragic limitations of the warrior's code, the *Iliad* is not an antiwar poem. Anger can be indulged to dangerous excess—as Achilles admits, it "is sweeter than slow-dripping honey, clouding the hearts of men like smoke." [Fitzgerald, Trans., Book 18, ll. 125–26] Yet the courage to face all perils, even to die, is still a manly virtue. As we shall soon see, men are also capable of such sacrifice in heeding a more communal duty than Achilles owed to himself. So, in a myriad of ways, we hope the men of today find themselves in the heroes of the past. Their fall and the balanced recognition of the hero and heel, and Achilles' heel in all of us may be the beginning of a new form of authority and respect for men.

6

▼

DUTY: WORK AND FAMILY

A man is bound and dedicated to duty. If he does not fulfill certain narrowly defined obligations to work and family—"the man of the house," "the breadwinner," "the dutiful husband," "the dutiful son"—he does not feel like a man. Whatever he may want or actually do, he must answer to the voice that tells him what he ought to do.

At times saddled with, at others privileged by, such responsibilities, he has paid a price for the prerogatives of manhood. Being a dutiful worker, husband, and father are all essential to masculinity, but each alone is limiting. By trying too earnestly to live within a social role, men may lose their personal meaning.

For example, Allan, a man in his mid-forties, was trying to reconstruct his early family life in psychotherapy. As he sorted through cartons of memorabilia that had been packed up after his parents' deaths several years before, he found an extremely poignant photograph of himself sitting with a violin. He was obviously posed—sitting stark upright, struggling to smile, but looking pained and uncomfortable. The false self and the vulnerability Allan saw in the picture reminded him of the pressure he had felt to live up to the demands of his parents. There had been no space for his own emotions and dreams. In many ways he felt that he was still trapped with the violin—never quite learning the instrument well and never quite achieving the love he always sought.

Increasing numbers of men are feeling disenchanted with what David Gilmore has called the three injunctions of "real" manhood: impregnator, protector, and provider. For example, as more women have entered professions formerly restricted to men, and as they demand more of men than economic support, men's love affair with work has acquired some unattractive wrinkles. They are realizing, as Senator Paul Tsongas put it, that "no man on his death bed ever said 'I wish I had spent more time with my work.' " But the hearth is hardly a refuge from demands of self-imposed or socially required duty. For one thing, women are no longer able or willing to accept being 1950s–style homemakers. In that era, only 28 percent of married women with children age six to seventeen were in the paid work force; by 1991 this figure had risen to 70 percent, and even 50 percent of those mothers with children under age six worked outside the home. Women are asking and often *telling* men to take on more of the burden of what Arlie Hochschild has called "the second shift." The challenge that working mothers have long faced of reconciling career with family is now a dilemma for men. It is complicated by men's hostility toward women for usurping their traditional role as provider and for unconsciously wanting men to remain in it.

The women's movement has challenged traditional roles, but research studies suggest that more change has occurred in men's and women's professed beliefs than in what they actually do. During the 1960s, husbands put in an average of one hour each day of child care and housework, compared to over seven hours a day for housewives and four to five hours a day for employed wives. Husbands increased their contribution by only six minutes a day when their wives worked. A 1985 study by Bradley Googins of the Boston University School of Social Work found that married mothers worked an average of eighty-five hours a week on job, homemaking, and child care, compared with sixty-six hours for married fathers. This discrepancy begins to hint at men's still limited role in the home. In a 1986 study of married couples, Dana Hiller found that most agreed that child care should be a shared responsibility, but that less than one-half actually practiced this. Of the more than half who said they expected to share housekeeping chores, only one-third of the husbands shared even two tasks equally—dishwashing and shopping. More recent studies suggest that there has been slight movement toward greater equality: Juster and Stafford report a 20 percent increase between 1965 and 1981 in the amount of family work that husbands do, but according to a 1989 study by Douthitt, it remains only a third of what wives do. The traditional division of labor and the expectation that the man be the primary breadwinner remain strong, even among women.

Challenging gender stereotypes makes both sexes anxious and it is unclear if our children's marriages will look more like our own or our parents'. For now, men are ripsawed by old and new expectations. The glacial pace by which men take on more "women's work" obscures the bedrock stress that most men feel as they seek to define and live up to the duties emblematic of manhood.

LOYALTIES

Loyalties are only clear when abstract. In the real world of relationships, we are often faced with conflicting claims, with ambiguous loyalties. We feel pulled by a powerful set of obligations of which we are only dimly aware. Stephen Toulmin, of the University of Chicago, points out that irresolvable or ambiguous loyalties often reflect social and historical situations. He was referring to the ethical dilemmas consequent upon rapid changes in health care organization, but the same might apply to marital loyalties in this age of gender strain.

In *The Seven Basic Quarrels of Marriage* one of us commented:

> The first promise in the marriage ceremony is a promise of loyalty and love—a call on two profound sentiments, one almost as mysterious as the other. We seldom realize what

an accumulation of loyalties we bring with us to a marriage
and how much of a gamble it is trying to unite them under
the arch of the new commitment.

[P. 54]

The accumulation of loyalties that a man and a woman brings
to a marriage includes loyalties to their roots—what they absorb
from their families growing up, learn in school, and acquire
from the "close-touch world" around them as they grow up.
Much of these loyalties are "invisible"—they are encoded in
nonverbal styles and habits of thinking and feeling that are as
much a part of us as right- or left-handedness. Each partner
unwittingly recruits the other to re-create the cherished parts of
their original family and to make up for what it lacked.

Our experience in treating couples is that people seldom
appreciate how the loyalty they expect from their partner inevitably conflicts with cherished allegiances to the past. Many of
these allegiances are cast in the molds of gender. Consciously,
a man may not want to emulate his father's slavelike devotion
to work at the expense of family; but to deviate from this role
may still feel like a betrayal. And so his duty to work and family
are tangled in a web of feeling, much of which may be invisible.
As Harry Levinson has pointed out, a man forms unconscious
"contracts" at work and in the family that anchor him securely
when the equation of give and get is balanced. But in times of
organizational stress and change, when work roles are being
radically redefined, a man may feel robbed not only of his job
but of his identity.

HECTOR

As with his slayer, Achilles, Hector's bravery and fierceness
are celebrated in the *Iliad* as worthy of a warrior. He, too, is
driven to defend his honor, though the certain cost be his death
in battle:

▼

. . . But I should die of shame
before our Trojan men and noblewomen
if like a coward I avoided battle,
nor am I moved to. Long ago I learned
how to be brave, how to go forward always
and to contend for honor, Father's and mine

[FITZGERALD, TRANS., BOOK 6,
LL. 514–19]

Unlike Achilles, Hector obeys the call of a higher form of duty than that of the hero's pursuit of glory—he is sworn to protect his city, the Trojan people, and, most of all, his wife and child. We might think of Hector as representing the transition from a culture of shame to a culture of guilt in that shame is a simple, innate emotion that emanates from concerns about the self, while guilt is a complex, socially acquired sense that is rooted in relationships.

The *Iliad* and the *Odyssey* depict the experience of shame at times as the public humiliation of the self, as in Achilles' shaming by Agamemnon, and at others as the failure or potential failure of a man to fulfill his duty to his community, as with Hector. When we compare Homer's men to men today we need to keep in mind, as Hermann Frankel (quoted in Simon, 1978) has pointed out, that Homeric man was not viewed as a private or closed being but as an "open force field." For example, inner conflict is depicted as an interaction between a man's separate parts (limbs, strength, spirit) or between a man and a god. Thus, the depiction of shame in Homer might be thought of as intermediate between the modern gender-based positions— male theorists' description of shame as an *internal* feeling of inadequacy and female theorists' as a loss of *interpersonal* connection.

In the *Iliad* the word *aidos* is used to express Hector's sense of obligation to community and family. As Seth Schein points out, while *aidos* has been translated as "shame" or "respect," it encompasses both the inner call to duty as well as the need to live up to the expectations of others. According to James Redfield: "Aidos is . . . an emotion provoked by the perception of one's place in the social structure and of the obligations which accompany that place. . . . [It is] felt toward persons in the exercise of their social roles."

There is a poignant, very personal cast to Hector's *aidos*. His tragedy is not just that he must die to uphold his honor, but that in answering the call to defend his city he knows that he will abandon his family. As Hector tells his wife, Andromache, when she begs him not to leave the tower of Troy to return to battle:

> *Honor—for in my heart and soul I know*
> *a day will come when ancient Ilion falls,*
> *when Priam and the folk of Priam perish.*
> *Not by the Trojans' anguish on that day*
> *am I so overborne in mind—the pain*
> *of Hecuba herself, or Priam king,*
> *or of my brothers, many valorous*
> *who will have fallen in dust before our enemies—*
> *as by your own grief, when some armed Akhaian*
> *takes you in tears, your free life stripped away . . .*
> *And seeing you in tears, a man may say:*
> *'There is the wife of Hektor, who fought best*
> *of Trojan horsemen when they fought at Troy.'*
> [FITZGERALD, TRANS., BOOK 6,
> LL. 520–40]

Like many men today, whose duty to work and to family effectively bereaves their wives and children through their absence, Hector faced a moral dilemma.

MORAL DILEMMAS

Men are struggling to do the right thing, but they are faced with moral dilemmas that require choosing between two forms of duty. Compromise is difficult because loyalties feel so absolute and much remains unconscious. How can one compromise on something that feels so central to our values, to the core of our self? Further, many of the misunderstandings between men and women derive from their different approaches to moral decisions. These approaches are as ancient as Greek philosophy.

Epictetus held that some things are clearly virtues and others are clearly vices and to be good means to embrace the virtues. This is an absolute notion of morality. The other tradition, exemplified by Epicurus, holds that what is good and moral is defined by whatever gets you closer to a desirable end. His is a teleological, pragmatic theory. When Abraham wrestled with whether to obey God's command to slay his son, he was laboring under the strict definition of morality that if the father tells you to do something, you must do it. Kant's view that a moral act is defined by the fact that you do something because it is your duty is based on absolute obedience to law rather than to a person. Absolute versus relative; mandated by a personal authority versus guided by an abstract principle—these distinctions have long preoccupied moral philosophers. So, too, has the question of whether men's moral sense differs from that of women.

Sigmund Freud saw in Oedipus's tragic fall the origins of morality and justice. He believed that we vicariously enjoy his transgressions and applaud the moral that crimes against the nuclear family ultimately do not pay. Being good thus derives from feared punishment by the paternal authority. Since only boys have a tangible organ to lose through father's retribution, Freud felt that girls were under a weaker imperative to internalize prohibitions and had a less developed moral sense.

Lawrence Kohlberg's typology of moral development starts with the fear of punishment by taking note that boys and girls mature into a moral code based not on feared consequences but on reciprocity and equality. Through succesively more complex social roles, people learn to walk in each other's shoes and to be guided by universal principles of justice rather than by self-interest, feelings, or individual circumstance. While not overtly subscribing to Freud's notion of women's moral inferiority,

Kohlberg's original theory was based entirely on studies of men. His assumption was that men's psychology applies equally to women. However, when women were judged by Kohlberg's moral categories, most received less mature scores than men.

Carol Gilligan, in *In a Different Voice*, took issue with this cognitive version of female defectiveness. Based on her own research, she agreed that women's moral orientation is indeed different from men's but, she emphasized, not inherently less mature. While accepting the validity of Freud's and Kohlberg's ethic of fairness and justice for *men*, she suggested that women are guided less by abstract principles than by an ethic of care and responsibility based on special relationships. For women, the appeal to abstract principle loses touch with real-life connection and can justify indifference. Rather than being something to mature beyond, women's reliance on feeling and involvement in particular situations is the essence of their moral stance.

Gilligan felt that these different perspectives on morality might explain some of the difficulties men and women have in understanding each other:

> . . . men and women may speak different languages that they assume are the same, using similar words to encode disparate experiences of self and social relationships. Because these languages share an overlapping moral vocabulary, they contain a propensity for systematic mistranslation, creating misunderstandings which impede communication and limit the potential for cooperation and care in relationships.
>
> [P. 173]

For example, men and women ascribe different meanings to caring for each other: women conceive of it as sharing confidences, listening, and emotional understanding, while men take care from a distance, by providing for material things and sharing through doing. In one couple, it became clear that the woman's notion of loyalty owed to each other was to always put the partner first, while the man's primary injunction was to not deliberately cause the other harm. These different perspectives led to major fights between them, especially before the underlying assumptions were clarified. Such misunderstandings may underlie many struggles over how men and women understand the duties owed to each other and to the family.

In another couple, a therapist suggested that each partner do something loving for the other person during the next week. When the couple returned for the ensuing session, the man was pleased to report that he had carried out his assignment. Surprised, his partner wanted to know what he thought he had done. It turned out that his loving act had been to wax her car.

Men's way of caring by doing is not a less developed form of love than women's caring by feeling. Each rests on an ethic of responsibility for others. At their best, both can be powerful in their tenderness.

THE SAFETY OF DISTANCE

The different moral perspectives of men and women may be based on different neurologic "hard wiring"—the cognitive tilting of men toward the left side of the brain and women toward the right. The more intuitive, feeling-based immersion in a specific situation that Gilligan describes as more typical of women's approach to moral problem-solving and men's more abstract, objective approach represent contrasting cognitive styles.

But cognitive styles may parallel and perhaps even be shaped by divergent early life experiences by which boys have learned that safety lies in removing themselves from personal involvement and girls feel pulled to remain in connection. As we have seen, the trauma boys experience by virtue of being first left by mother and then not adequately supported by father leads to a lifelong overvaluation of autonomy. It is no surprise then that a man's moral development follows his emotional path toward separation from relationships. Safety is to be found in not relying on any particular relationship but on principles that reaffirm a community that surrounds him from a safe distance. Men's moral stance likewise reflects their concern about their own and others' aggression—women fear a lack of involvement in moral matters; men seek to protect against trespass on rights.

The distance men seek is not the self-absorption of Narcissus. As David Gilmore points out, men's concern for others, their duty to care, is less direct than women's but can be full of selfless generosity and even sacrifice:

> Manhood therefore is also a nurturing concept, if we define that term as giving, subventing, or other-directed. It is true that this male giving is different from, and less demonstrative and more obscure than, the female. It is less direct, less immediate, more involved with externals; the "other" involved may be society in general rather than specific persons.
>
> The form of nourishment also differs. Women nurture others directly. They do this with their bodies, with their milk and their love. This is very sacrificial and generous. But surprisingly, "real" men nurture, too, although they would perhaps not be pleased to hear it put this way. Their support is indirect and thus less easy to conceptualize. *Men nurture their society by shedding their blood, their sweat, and their semen,* by bringing home food for both child and mother, by producing children, and by dying if necessary in faraway places to provide a safe haven for their people. This, too, is nurturing in the sense of endowing or increasing. . . . To support his family, the man has to be distant, away hunting or fighting wars; to be tender, he must be tough enough to fend off enemies. To be generous, he must be selfish enough to amass goods, often by defeating other men; to be gentle, he must first be strong, even ruthless in confronting enemies; to love he must be aggressive enough to court, seduce, and "win" a wife.
>
> [PP. 229–30]

Gilmore's description of men's duty to care is as apt an epitaph for Hector as it is of a modern father, such as Mario Cuomo's portrait of his father, who cared from the safety of distance:

I knew him only as a person who worked twenty-four hours a day. We never sat down to dinner, or very rarely—on the holidays, in the later years. He never took me for a walk. He never had a man-to-man talk with me. I never saw him relaxed until, in later years, the store had to be closed on Sunday mornings after ten o'clock. . . . I think of him as being very affectionate, but I don't remember him putting his arm around me. You always had the sense that he had great feeling for you. You saw him providing for you, at enormous pain to himself. You saw him doing nothing for himself—never bought himself anything, never enjoyed himself. . . . So the overwhelming impression we got was that this man was offering us his life: he didn't have to put his arm around you.

[*THE NEW YORKER*, APRIL 9, 1984, P. 51]

SISYPHUS

Men's more abstract morality and the sense of duty expressed at a distance that emanates from it can lead to an even more attentuated personal connection. Men can lose touch with why they are laboring so much and for whom. The familiar myth of Sisyphus is the ancient prototype of such a man.

While occasionally praised for his wisdom, by most accounts Sisyphus is the most cunning of men and a master thief. It is said that he could outdo even Autolycus, who could metamorphose black unhorned beasts to white horned ones and so disguise his thefts.[1] In short, he is hardly at Kohlberg's highest stage of moral development. His transgressions included betrayal of divine secrets. For this, Zeus ordered Hades, lord of the Underworld, to place Sisyphus in chains. But Sisyphus puts Hades himself into handcuffs by suggesting that he demonstrate their use. With Hades incapacitated, no one can die, even people who

[1] As Michael Herzfeld has pointed out, in at least one rural society in Crete the brazen theft of animals from another powerful man has traditionally been a way to demonstrate one's manhood.

have been eaten by wild animals or beheaded. The God of War sets Hades free and delivers Sisyphus to his keeping. But Sisyphus is not yet done. He had arranged beforehand with his wife not to bury him, which in those times was a great dishonor to the dead. On reaching the Palace of Hades, he complains, "As an unburied person, I have no right to be here. My presence here is most irregular. Let me go back to the mortal world and avenge the neglect shown to me. I can arrange for my proper burial and return in three days." Once back home, he breaks his promise to return. He is brought back to Hades by force.

Sisyphus is not only compelled to remain in Hades—he is given exemplary punishment. The Judges of the Dead show him an immense block of stone and order him to roll it to the top of a hill and then down the other side. The last joke is on Sisyphus, for he can never succeed in completing his task. As Homer relates in the *Odyssey*:

> . . . *He was suffering strong pains,*
> *and with both arms embracing the monstrous stone, struggling*
> *with hands and feet alike, he would try to push the stone upward*
> *to the crest of the hill, but when it was on the point of going*
> *over the top, the force of gravity turned it backward,*
> *and the pitiless stone rolled back down to the level. He then*
> *tried once more to push it up, straining hard, and sweat ran*
> *all down his body, and over his head a cloud of dust rose.*
>
> [LATTIMORE, TRANS., BOOK 11,
> LL. 593–600]

Like Oedipus, Sisyphus attempts to escape his destiny and is punished for his hubris. Instead of blinding and banishment, repetitive, futile labor is Sisyphus's lot for all time. For many men, their reach exceeds their grasp, and work, far from a place of living out their Dream, becomes an assembly line of deadening routine, or what Albert Camus referred to as "that unspeakable penalty in which the whole being is exerted toward accomplishing nothing." We see Sisyphus as an apt metaphor for the workaholic of our time—alone, alienated, unable to escape his fate, policed by a conscience that demands unceasing work.

To Camus, Sisyphus is the absurd hero. He pictures Sisyphus watching the stone roll back down to the plain—his descent down with measured step is a breathing space in which he is superior to his fate because he is conscious of his predicament. So, too, Camus feels, can modern men escape the tyranny of meaningless toil: "At that subtle moment when man glances backward over his life, Sisyphus returning toward his rock, in that slight pivoting he contemplates that series of unrelated actions which becomes his fate, created by him, combined under his memory's eye and soon sealed by his death." [*The Myth of Sisyphus*, p. 123]

Camus's existentialism is a comforting antidote to the despair of mindless duty. It depends, however, on a man breaking free of his inner prison of duty.

THE TYRANNY OF SHOULDS

In our clinical experience of individual therapy and business consultations with men, we have found that their Sisyphus-like toil is often self-imposed. This is not to deny that many men are caught in work full of drudgery. But when the insatiable demands of duty are an internal matter as well, there is no time clock to them, no way to leave them at the job. For instance, a man whose image of himself is not in concert with the nature of his work task is not living up to his own ideal. To have no way to close this gap leads to despair.

In his book *Neurotic Styles*, David Shapiro describes how such men live under constant, self-imposed strain, a tense necessity to be always active at some kind of work, to be always trying to do something. Shapiro's portrait is of the extreme, which to clinicians would justify the diagnosis of a character disorder. Still, without pathologizing men, it may be useful to see the continuum by which many men have obsessive traits.

The compulsive's activity actually has the appearance of being pressed or motivated by something beyond the interest of the acting person. . . . [H]e acts, and indeed he feels, as though he were being pressed by some necessity or requirement which he is at pains to satisfy. In actual fact, he *is* pressed by such a necessity or requirement. It is a requirement and a pressure that he applies to himself. . . . The obsessive-compulsive person functions like his own overseer issuing commands, directives, reminders, warnings, and admonitions concerning not only what is to be done and what is not to be done, but also what is to be wanted, felt, and even thought. This is the meaning of the single most characteristic thought content of obsessive-compulsive people: "*I should.*"

One compulsive person likened his whole life to a train that was running efficiently, fast, pulling a substantial load, but on a track laid out for it.

[DAVID SHAPIRO, PP. 33–40, ITALICS OURS]

Shapiro goes on to point out how such individuals have lost a sense of self-direction, based on a coherent sense of needs and wishes. Rather than the personal impulse being a guide to action, it is seen as a potential threat to the accomplishment of work. He tells himself what he should do rather than listening to the promptings of his own heart because he cannot tolerate relinquishing control, even over his own emotions.

This is the paradox of men who have embraced autonomy to the extreme—to have to always be in control means that they are *not* in control. To the extent that the "feminine" aspects of the self—intuition and feeling—are mistrusted, they become paralyzed by indecision and are not free.

WORK AND RELATIONSHIPS

Despite men's increasing participation in the family and disenchantment with work, they are not likely to turn away from their commitment to work. Men will continue to strive, to compete, to produce. Men expect this of themselves, and despite women's wish to be more independent, their need of men to protect and provide for them remains strong. Men have long used work to bolster their self-esteem and to make up for deficiencies in relationships. One outcome is workaholism and the bondage of "shoulds." But as George Vaillant's and Daniel Levinson's landmark studies have pointed out, working is not just a defense—men have fundamental needs to achieve, to feel effective, and to live out a Dream.

Both of these studies have been criticized by women for their bias toward work as the fundamental axis of male adaptation. Vaillant's study (described in *Adaptation to Life*) was based on a sample of Harvard undergraduate students, who were interviewed at several points in their adult lives, and who were initially selected by university deans because they seemed least likely to come in contact with a counseling service—they were "able to paddle their own canoe." Not surprisingly, this sampling bias toward the extreme of the independence continuum led to a vision of men who valued intimacy far less highly than success. It is a rarefied version of the self-fulfilling prophecy.

Levinson's sample is more representative, but he, too, focused on men's Dream—the "personal myth" in which a man pursues a noble quest. The Special Woman is given an important supporting role, in contrast to Vaillant's work, where they are largely offstage, but she is still only important insofar as she facilitates a man's Dream. If she impedes it, she must be discarded, like any other nonessential life structure, so that the rocket of ambition can escape the pull of gravity and soar ever higher.

Levinson's and Vaillant's studies do not reflect the modest shift toward a more balanced, whole man, but if the pursuit of personal achievement is given a central place and relationships with women relatively neglected, this order of priorities largely reflects how men are. These studies provide a sophisticated look at the complexity of men's relationship to work, making clear that healthy adaptation is an evolutionary process. Men do not so much choose as *form* an occupation, through a series of commitments, shifts, and reformulation of their priorities. As Eliot Jacques describes, as a man matures the quality of his creativity must shift from meteorlike bursts to a more sculpted energy.

The successful man at fifty is not running around trying to prove he can still do what he did at twenty. His products are apt to be less dazzling but more polished. Those who remain wedded to youthful impulses are in fearful denial of aging— they may be smart but never become wise.

Work success is closely entwined with success in relationships, or as George Vaillant put it, "Lucky at work means lucky in love." When Vaillant's men were studied at age thirty-five and again at age fifty, those men with the worst outcomes also had marriages and friendship patterns that were barren. Ninety-four percent of the men who had achieved a solid work identity had already mastered the task of staying married for a long period of time, whereas only fourteen out of seventy men who were rated as unable to achieve intimacy with one person ever made a stable job commitment. Career success was not simply a matter of staying married, which may reflect conformity or the advantages of not having to bother with cooking and cleaning. Successful men also tended to remain with the same employer, could identify an important mentor, and had assumed responsibility for other adults (as father, mentor, etc.) Perhaps these men were conformists. But Vaillant believes that these men were successful primarily because they had sustained relationships for long periods of time and were unusually adept at taking in what other people had to offer. Such data support Erik Erikson's assertion that men who can form intimate connections earlier in life will later be productive in work as well as in interpersonal arenas, a functional capacity he called "generativity."

A WHO AND A WHAT

To have an occupation is to have an identity, to have a job is to have a place in the world, or as Harry Levinson puts it, to be "a who and a what." Traditional definitions of masculinity require that a man function as "head of the household," and both sexes remain uncomfortable when the wife earns more than the husband. Gender competition aside, a man needs to have a role; he needs to be doing something. Whether an atavistic residue of men's role as hunter and gatherer, or compensation for not being able to bear children, men's psychic economy, as with Homeric heroes, is programmed for action.

A job can relieve some of the pressures of inner duty, but a man is driven to be a specific Who and a What. He cannot rest easy unless he is working toward his aspirations. Referred to by Daniel Levinson as the Dream, and by Harry Levinson as the ego ideal, his vision of possibilities is born in the omnipotent fantasy of boyhood. In some measure, the Dream demands that the world accommodate to its expectations; to some degree, it bends in accord with experience and becomes less grandiose and more specific.

A highly successful thirty-five-year-old advertising executive would get up at five each weekday morning so that he could write short stories for two hours before getting ready for work. He said that he liked his job, and that in any event he needed the financial security that it gave to him and his family. But his love was for his writing. He had not yet had a story published and writing could be agony, but he had to do it. He said that it offered him his best chance to rise above the day-to-day, to stand apart from his earthbound duties, and perhaps to drink the ambrosia of immortality.

Without the Dream, a man is no better off than Sisyphus. But the Dream can also be a destructive tyrant, as in Arthur Miller's *Death of a Salesman*, in which Willy Loman tortures both himself and his sons with grandiose visions. Levinson believes that during the midlife transition in particular, success and failure must be assessed in more complex, life-sized terms if a man is to make peace with himself. Otherwise, as with the Special Woman, a man's dream of success can become his worst nightmare. Like Shapiro's obsessive-compulsive, he may become tortured and paralyzed by murmured shoulds and might-have-beens that he cannot silence.

FAMILY REDUX

Work also seduces men because it offers a chance to rework old relationships. Much has been written about the ways a marital relationship can be a kind of seance in which ghosts from childhood are unwittingly summoned by the re-experience of intimacy. With work, it is not intimacy that is the catalyst for reviving old conflicts; it is because, as in a marriage, so much is at stake—one's livelihood, one's future, one's dream. As Harry Levinson has pointed out, the need of the individual to look to an organization to provide things he cannot provide for himself sets up a dynamic of dependency. But these realistic ways in which an individual relies on the organization become magnified largely in unconscious ways by past longings and fears.

One's boss, "the administration," and other authority figures may be looked to for care, protection, security, for sponsoring one's private dream. At the same time, they can become the focus of suspicion, of concerns about actual or feared exploitation and betrayal. Not uncommonly, such good and bad parental surrogates can coexist, parceled out into different individuals or parts of an organization. In this way, work functions as an appendage to the psyche, helping to balance conflicting forces within the self.

Howard, a man whom we saw in consultation, had had a disastrous first marriage, during which he and his wife had owned a restaurant, originally financed largely by his wife's family. It was not clear if the business or his marriage went sour first. He was now seeking advice about whether to get remarried to a woman who owned a bookstore. Howard explained that she knew books and had the capital and he had good business sense, so he thought they would make good partners. However, a personal fight would inevitably lead to doubts about their business arrangement and an argument at work would give them cold feet about the marriage. In exploring why he seemed to pursue a pattern of combining his work and personal commitments, it emerged that Howard had grown up as the oldest son in a family that owned a cleaning business. He had always thought that he would one day inherit the business and run it as his own, but his father had sold it when the patient was in his early twenties. He felt that at least in part his father's decision was based on a lack of confidence in his oldest son, which left a stain of shame that he was compelled to try to remove.

While the intertwining of work with family issues is usually less dramatic, the nuclear family remains a subplot in any work setting to which a person has more than a casual attachment. Men are not any more prone than women to re-creating family dynamics in a work setting, but their greater investment in work has made their transferences especially powerful. They may now be particularly vulnerable in this arena insofar as organizations are now less able than in decades past to provide lifelong security and the pace of change has accelerated, at the same time that the new woman has undermined other aspects of masculinity.

PROGRAMMED FOR OBSOLESCENCE

While R. S. Pasick and others have pointed out that men are "raised to work," the environment in which they have been emotionally programmed to achieve mastery and bolster their self-esteem—the work organization—has radically changed over the last ten years. The concept of a hierarchically structured organization with top-down lines of authority, once the mainstay of *Fortune* 500 America, is quickly becoming a dinosaur. In its place are rapidly changing, educationally oriented work systems with an emphasis on circles of quality, team productivity, and an interactive managerial style.

As Americans have had to face the recent success of Japanese industry, they have also come to study and even revere such "foreign" approaches to management. The irony is that one of the major intellectual forces behind Japanese management is an American-born mathematician/physicist, Dr. W. Edwards Deming, who inspired the quality revolution in postwar Japan.

At that point, American industry turned its back, but corporate America is now moving swiftly toward such collaborative, process-oriented management. In practical terms, this means that managers are only considered useful if they are able to coach, not boss, teams of employees. The new leader must try to support interdependent work styles.

Imagine the consternation of many men inside organizations who have been socialized to be "macho," individualistic leaders and who find themselves without the skills necessary to create consensus and teamwork. The leader and dutiful follower arrangement of the general and his troops is no longer acceptable in the modern workplace. Consequently, men are often at a loss as to how to fulfill their duties. Their self-esteem and their manhood suffer and they feel betrayed.

The Boston Globe business section has proclaimed "the age of the warm, democratic executive" (March 1992) and extolled the work of Frances Hesselbein, a female manager who has been able to develop circles of colleagues to run complex organizations. Women's socialization for interpersonal connection (without a well-honed, competitive edge) makes them, in many cases, better suited candidates for leadership than many of their male colleagues. As Arnold Hiatt, the chief of Stride Rite Corporation, has said about the demise of the tough boss: "The Marlboro Man is no longer in vogue."

In the work that one of us does with senior corporation executives, we have been struck with the shift toward the need to empower their employees. Many of them who have been used to hierarchical organizations require psychological retooling to fulfill their new duties. Not only can this create gut-wrenching struggles for a rigidly autonomous male executive, but it can lead to a sense of deep betrayal: his old gender destiny is now impossible to fulfill. Women appear to be the winners in this economic war in which men feel they lack the new high-tech "firepower" of teamwork and collaboration.

MASTERY AND SUBLIMATION

Classical Freudian theory asserts that men seek to manage their aggression through work, a process known in psychoanalytic parlance as sublimation. Whether a man pounds nails on a roofing job, competes for research grants at a university, or plans hostile takeovers of multimillion-dollar companies, constructive tasks become an outlet for aggression.

Sports and sex are two other modes for its discharge, but given that most men have already invested substantial energies in both, men are unlikely to be able to do without work. For Freud, work was one of the two linchpins of a successful life, the other being love.

Work is not simply a figurative punching bag or the equivalent of a nudist camp for aggressive appetites juiced up on testosterone. The psychologist Robert White, building on the work of ego psychologists such as Ernest Hartmann, pointed out that all socially desirable acts should not be called sublimation. He believed that much of what men do in the way of acquiring skills, of developing mastery and competence, is motivated by the pleasure of feeling effective rather than by the residue of dark, instinctual drives.

We have yet to clearly parcel out aggressiveness from a wish for mastery, and it may yet turn out that there is a subtle but significant gender difference in the way that this need to accomplish tangible results is experienced. The new psychology of women has suggested that women's priority is usually to help other people grow, while men are geared toward making things and achieving. As the culture shifts toward making opportunities for women to compete and nurtures little girls' autonomy, we will learn more about whether gender differences are innate or socially mediated.

THE ATYPICAL HERO

Like Hector and Sisyphus, Odysseus, Homer's atypical hero of the *Odyssey*, is a man who struggles with his relation to duty. Odysseus has heroic traits, but he is also small in stature, cunning, and gluttonous. Homer refers to him as "a man of many resources" and "devious-devising." It was Odysseus, for instance, who thought of the ruse of the Trojan Horse. He is also intensely curious—like Oedipus, he often gets into trouble because of his desire to know. His name is variously translated as "trouble" or "the causer and victim of pain." In Homer's epic poem, this is indeed his lot.

James Joyce chose him as the prototype for his modern epic of a man's wanderings, which in *Ulysses* consist largely of interior voyages. According to Frank Budgen, Joyce stated that he chose Odysseus because he was the only good, "complete man" of literature, for in the *Odyssey* he is portrayed as a father, a son, a husband, lover, and warrior. In his many imperfections and virtues, he is a more believable character than either Hector or Achilles. He seems one of us.

As we have discussed earlier, the Homeric model of the mind represented conflicting aspects of the self as relationships with forces of nature or with gods and goddesses. At the other extreme, Joyce's novel renders all that is external as inner dialogue. C. P. Cavafy, in his poem "Ithaka," reminds us that:

> *The Laistrygonians and the Cyclops,*
> *angry Poseidon—you will not meet them*
> *unless you carry them in your soul,*
> *unless your soul raise them up before you.*

We might liken this division between external and inner worlds to the gender-based dichotomy in which women define themselves through connection and men through autonomy. In our view, neither perspective alone will suffice to understand the *Odyssey*.

THE ODYSSEY

Odysseus is a king in Ithaca with a wife and infant son when Agamemnon and Menelaus gain his reluctant consent to join them in laying siege to Troy. The Trojan dandy Paris had just run off with Menelaus's wife, the surpassingly beautiful Helen. Odysseus spends ten years as a warrior at Troy, and when the city falls, he, like the other Achaeans, boards one of the hollow ships and heads for home. It is ten more years before he returns.

During Odysseus's wanderings his curiosity and a variety of temptations, most of them personified as women, lead him and his companions into danger and make them forgetful of home. First, his men taste the honey-sweet fruit of the Lotus-eaters and they have to be dragged, weeping, back to the ships.

They sail on to the land of the Cyclops where Odysseus insists on exploring a one-eyed monster's cave. He escapes death by claiming that his name is "Nobody," so that when the Cyclops tells his friends who has put out his eye, they think his misfortune is the work of the gods and do not try to help him. Only when Odysseus boards ship again does he taunt the Cyclops by revealing his true name, an ill-advised lapse into arrogance, since the Cyclops' father is the sea god, Poseidon. For the rest of his journey, Odysseus is hounded by this angry god, who leads him off course and to shipwreck.

The dawn has just "showed again with her rosy fingers" when Odysseus and his crew, still grieving over their companions eaten by the Cyclops, cast off the anchoring cables and sail on. Aided by the precious gift of an oxskin, stuffed with the courses of all the blowing winds except the favorable West Wind, they are blown so close to home that they can see people on shore tending their fires. But while Odysseus sleeps, his companions open the oxskin bag in search of silver and gold. All the ill winds burst out and sweep them far from their country.

More hideous misfortunes await them. After all but one ship is destroyed by the Laistrygonians, they arrive on Circe's island. An advance guard drinks her potion of wine, into which she

▼

has put "malignant drugs, to make them forgetful of their own country." [Lattimore, trans., Book, 10 ll. 236] She then strikes them with a wand and turns them into swine.

For much of the *Odyssey*, Odysseus is aided by the goddess Athene. But in this instance, the god Hermes gives him a special medicine that enables him to resist Circe's porcine spells. Still, her feminine allure is sufficient to keep him as her lover for a full year until his men remind him of his duty:

> *"What ails you now? It is time to think about our own country,*
> *if truly it is ordained that you shall survive and come back*
> *to your strong-founded house and to the land of your fathers."*
>
> [LATTIMORE, TRANS., BOOK 10, LL. 472–74]

Circe agrees to help him return home, but only after he has gone to Hades and consulted with the seer Teiresias.

Teiresias tells him that in his absencee the suitors are despoiling his household and courting his wife, and that after he has returned home and killed them, he must go on yet another journey. He also offers him some advice:

> *"Glorious Odysseus, what you are after is sweet homecoming,*
> *but the god will make it hard for you. I think you will not*
> *escape the Shaker of the Earth, who holds a grudge against you*
> *in his heart, and because you blinded his dear son, hates you.*
> *But even so and still you might come back, after much suffering,*
> *if you can contain your own desire, and contain your companions . . ."*
>
> [LATTIMORE, TRANS., BOOK 11, LL. 100–105]

All will be well, he says, if "you keep your mind on homecoming" [Lattimore, trans., Book 11, l. 110] and do not harm the sacred cattle and fat sheep of Helios.

Odysseus meets many other ghosts in Hades, including Achilles, his mother, and Agamemnon. He asks his mother how she died, and she answers, ". . . shining Odysseus, it was my longing for you, your cleverness and your gentle ways, that took the sweet spirit of life from me." [Lattimore, trans., Book 11, ll. 202–3] He tries to take her in his arms but since she is a soul without flesh or bones they cannot find comfort in the embrace of mourning.

Agamemnon, whose wife and wife's lover murdered him upon his return from the Trojan War, understandably has a jaundiced view of women. He advises Odysseus not to trust any of them, including his wife, Penelope: "Tell her part of it, but let the rest be hidden in silence." [Lattimore, trans., Book 11, l. 443]

Following Circe's instructions, Odysseus stops up the ears of his men with wax and has them lash him tightly to the mast, so that they cannot be tempted by the Sirens' sweet song of knowledge. Odysseus is unable to turn the ship toward them, where the beach is littered with bones of men who never came home.

After passing two other terrifying females—Scylla (a six-headed monster who eats men alive) and Charybdis (a whirpool that can suck a whole ship into the deep)—the dwindling band makes port on the island of the sacred animals of Helios. They intend to stay only one night because of Teiresias's warnings, but the winds change and maroon them for a month. Odysseus's men slaughter the forbidden cattle and in punishment Zeus strikes their ship with a thunderbolt. All except Odysseus are killed, as he grabs hold of two timbers and ten days later washes ashore on Calypso's island.

Like Circe, Calypso is an immortal nymph who tries to enchant Odysseus into forgetting his home. He stays with her for seven years, until "his eyes . . . never wiped dry of tears, and the sweet lifetime . . . draining out of him, . . . he wept for a way home, since the nymph was no longer pleasing to him." [Lattimore, trans., Book 5, ll. 151–54] In their parting, he acknowledges to Calypso that mortal Penelope is no match for her ageless beauty, but that he longs to see his wife.

His raft is once more wrecked by Poseidon. But, directed by Athene, Odysseus floats ashore, where one last time he is tempted to marry another woman—in this instance, Nausicaa "of the white arms," who is the young daughter of King Alcinous. At last, laden with gifts, after twenty years of war and wanderings, he returns to Ithaca disguised as an old beggar.

Remembering Agamemnon's cautionary advice, Odysseus trusts no one. Cautiously he reveals his identity to his son and to a servant who recognizes him by the scar on his thigh—a childhood wound received from the tusk of a boar that he killed when he visited his mother's father, Autolycus. Telemachus becomes more manly as he helps his father to kill the suitors. Only then does Odysseus divulge his true identity to his wife. They recognize each other by the private knowledge that their bed could not be moved because one of the bedposts is the root of an olive tree around which the couple's room was built by Odysseus. The *Odyssey* concludes with Odysseus reestablished as husband, father, son, and king.

ODYSSEUS'S DUTY

Odysseus leaves home reluctantly to fulfill his duty to his countrymen. As in the case of modern men wedded to their work, having left the family it can be extraordinarily difficult to find a way back. Odysseus is not pulled home by guilt but by longing. His sense of obligation is not the onerous duty of Sisyphus. Quite simply, he is homesick. His duty is personal, not abstract; it is an internal matter, though, as with Hector, inseparably linked to those he loves. Alternating with his intense longings for homecoming is his "forgetfulness"—the sweet pleasures of the Lotus and of sharing the bed of immortal nymphs can seem preferable to an uncertain reception at home. Like many men today, the oblivion of drugs, of affairs, and of work are seductive alternatives to the struggle to find a role as husband and father. Odysseus knows from Agamemnon just

how bitter a homecoming some men can receive. We never see
Odysseus questioning whether he wants to or should return
home; he just "forgets" about it—a metaphor for unconscious
conflict. In this sense, he is completely unlike Shapiro's obsessive-compulsive man, who can never have holidays from duty.

Like Oedipus, but with a happier ending, Odysseus's destiny
is to return to his original family. To the ancient Greeks, Calypso's offer to Odysseus of immortality was a powerful seduc-
tion. Much of the *Iliad* and the *Odyssey* revolve around men's
tragic awareness of their inability to escape death. Indeed, Odysseus stayed with Calypso for seven years—like many men at
midlife who are tempted to deny death through the company
of a younger woman. But in the end Odysseus rejects her offer,
because Calypso's form of immortality is only a different kind of
death. For men immortality consists solely in doing meaningful
deeds and in the nurturing of the next generation, who will
remember these deeds. Like Adam and Eve, who chose to leave
the Garden of Eden so that they could take part in family life
and the continuity of generations, Odysseus leaves Calypso's
island for home.

We also see Odysseus struggling to rediscover his identity.
A wanderer, he has lost the social roles that give a man a place
in the world—a "who" and a "what." Often he assumes disguises and makes up stories to conceal his identity. His calling
himself "Nobody" with the Cyclops is emblematic of his predicament, which at times he turns to his advantage but is also
why he must come back to Ithaca. Like men today, the obligations of work and family, while often onerous, are what give
meaning to a man's struggles.

Odysseus, Hector, and Achilles must each affirm his manhood by doing what is right. Each must endure painful rites of
passage in his quest to become a man. But while Achilles' and
Hector's sense of honor has more to do with avoiding shame,
Odysseus is less concerned with how he looks than with finding
his rightful place in a social fabric. Odysseus wants to love and
work and do all of this with what nowadays we call "significant
others." In all of these ways, he is a hero for our times.

ODYSSEUS AND OEDIPUS

Wishes to murder the father and replace him in the mother's bed are only slightly more disguised in the *Odyssey* than in *Oedipus the King*. Odysseus's mother so dotes on him that she dies pining for his return. He gets married and has an infant son, but then sails away from his wife and mother for twenty years. Perhaps this is why Odysseus must "forget" about home, or as Freud would have put it, must repress his conflicts about women. He is drawn to and seeks to escape from numinous "Special Women," such as Circe and Calypso—powerful, maternal presences who fulfill a man's desires at the price of his freedom. Always in the shadows is the angry father—Poseidon—who tries to keep Odysseus from returning to his wife. Just as Freud described in little boys' development, our hero is caught between the wish to know, to possess, and to enjoy exactly that which he is told is forbidden and dangerous. One solution is represented in the episode of the Sirens—Odysseus has his thirst for dangerous knowledge partly gratified, but, unlike Oedipus, is prevented from acting impulsively—an apt metaphor for the goal of psychoanalysis.

As in Sophocles' *Oedipus the King*, the search for knowledge (of the unconscious) and vying with the father are dangerous. Poseidon is vengeful toward Odysseus because he has used his wooden *pole* to put out the eye*ball* of Poseidon's son. At the same time, Odysseus is both father and son—the young suitors vie with Telemachus to replace his absent father. Odysseus must return home to secure the nuclear family: the young men who vied for the mother are severely punished, and the son, whose coming of age makes him a potential rival of his father, is saved from Oedipus's fate. Instead, he joins his father in a rite of passage through which male generations unite against threats to the family. In contrast to Laius, the father's duty is to help the son who comes of age integrate into the family in a loving way.

Women in the *Odyssey* are seen by men as powerful and devious. Most are sphinxlike destroyers, such as the Sirens, Scylla, and Charybdis, or temptresses who entice men to shirk their duty. And yet, in spite of these "bad" women, Athene is Odysseus's most faithful ally, and, while Odysseus fears that he will meet the same fate as Agamemnon at the hands of a shiftless wife, Penelope ultimately proves faithful. The marriage bed that Odysseus built with his own hands cannot be moved.

In *Ulysses*, Joyce chose to represent all of Homer's "good" and "bad" images of women into the single character of Molly Bloom. Odysseus's women are likewise all facets of femininity that, as Cavafy put it, a man's own soul raises up before him. Men divide women into prostitutes and madonnas, just as women divide them into good and bad men. In pursuit of his duty, a man must both integrate these images of women and recognize that the "feminine" forces that nurture and oppose his Dream are also within himself.

THE WOUND

As we mentioned earlier, Odysseus, like Oedipus, sustained a childhood wound by which others discover his true identity. He was gored by a boar's tusk while visiting his mother's father, Autolycus. We have interpreted Oedipus's wound not as symbolic castration but as the traumatic residue of separation from mother and the lack of compensatory support by father. Odysseus's wound is also deeper than Freud's Oedipus complex. The killing of a boar was a typical heroic feat, symbolic of the young Odysseus having passed the test of manhood. But the wound also hints at the hero's vulnerability and the complexity of his roots.

Homer, like Sophocles, had to choose what mythic themes to include, and which to leave out. Only after we had been drawn to Sisyphus and Odysseus as separate representations of men's duty did we find out the secret of Odysseus's true parentage about which Homer was silent. To quote Robert Graves's story:

> . . . although Sisyphus noticed that his own herds grew
> steadily smaller, while those of Autolycus increased, he was

unable at first to convict him of theft; and therefore, one
day, engraved the inside of all his cattle's hooves with the
monogram SS, or, some say, with the words "Stolen by
Autolycus." That night Autolycus helped himself as usual,
and at dawn hoof-prints along the road provided Sisyphus
with sufficient evidence to summon neighbors in witness of
the theft. He visited Autolycus's stable, recognized his stolen
beasts by their marked hooves and, leaving his witnesses to
remonstrate with the thief, hurried around the house, entered
by the portal, and while the argument was in progress outside, seduced Autolycus's daughter, Anticleia, wife to
Laertes the Argive. *She bore him Odysseus, the manner of whose
conception is enough to account for the cunning he habitually
showed.* . . .

[GRAVES, 1960, VOL. 1, PP. 216–17, ITALICS OURS]

That is, according to this myth, Odysseus was the illegiti-
mate son of Sisyphus. As Homer has Telemachus observe in
the *Odyssey* when asked whether he is Odysseus's son, "My
mother says indeed I am his. I for my part do not know. *Nobody
really knows his own father.*" [Lattimore, trans., Book 1, ll.
215–16, italics ours]

Into each myth new life is breathed by interpretation. We
suggest that today's grown-up sons of absent fathers, who were
adrift in work that either lost its purpose or whose meaning
they could not convey to their sons, are wandering like Odysseus. Sons of "organization men" can no longer rely on the
work identities that their fathers bequeathed to them. In Edward
Shapiro's phrase, such men are "lost in familiar places." They
must make both an inner and outer journey in which duties to
self and others need to be integrated. Along the way are many
temptations and dangers—disappearing into the role of breadwinner, doing things only because one should, and losing oneself by remaining a wanderer who is neither a "who" nor a
"what."

As men today try to find themselves in the face of women's
anger, we are reminded that Odysseus's mother was the innocent victim of the fight between two men and that as a grown

man Odysseus abandoned his wife for twenty years. Can we really blame women for being angry at men and for being unable or unwilling to help us find our true selves?

At the close of the *Odyssey*, Odysseus must set out on yet another journey, whose ending we do not know. Similarly, Cavafy advises the descendants of Odysseus to

> *Ask that your way be long . . .*
> *Have Ithaka always in your mind.*
> *Your arrival there is what you are destined for.*
> *But do not in the least hurry the journey.*

It is sound advice reminiscent of Daniel Levinson's, George Vaillant's, and Erik Erikson's plea for men to regard success not as a goodness to be once and forever achieved—not as an event but as a process. It is a painful quest that begins in childhood with our first dream and ends only with our last.

7

▼

Sports: Men at Play

Men care about more than work and sex. A man lost in thought may be assessing his business prospects or enjoying a sexual fantasy, but he is just as likely to be remembering last Sunday's backhand passing shot for match point.

When we asked one woman whether she had enjoyed her recent family vacation in the Caribbean, she replied: "Every morning he went off with his father to play golf. In the afternoons, he went scuba diving or wind surfing while I stayed on the beach playing with the kids. We spend more time together when we're at home and he has to work!"

A female colleague, who is also a good friend, remarked to one of us upon learning that the weekend plan included watching football on television, "I still like you *even though you like sports.*" Though good-natured, there was an unmistakable tone of superiority, an attitude that men's preoccupation with playing and watching sports stamped them as a tad less cultured or mature than women. This rift in understanding may not be ordained by our biology but goes back at least as far as the different games that segregated groups of girls and boys play in the schoolyard.

It is not that women cannot love sports. But just as little girls and boys have distinctive play styles—one cooperative, the other roughly competitive—women and men have different orientations to sports. For example, an informal study done by one of us on the golf course demonstrated how men and women handle themselves in adversity. Most of the men cursed when they hooked a drive, got into a bad humor when they were playing poorly, and took their play extremely seriously. In contrast, the women tended to be relaxed and lighthearted. Clearly, less was at stake than for the men. Of course, there are competitive women golfers and laid-back male golfers, and increasing numbers of women are "hooked" on sports, but we believe the gender differences we have described run true to form.

Perhaps embittered by men's eagerness to choose a golf game or the Super Bowl over an intimate getaway with them, perhaps merely perplexed by a passion that they do not fully understand, women are left wondering about men's priorities. It might well seem that love of football is an atavistic lust, carried by the same Neanderthal gene as the inability to remember birthdays or to do the laundry.

PLAY AND RELATIONSHIPS

Men's absorption in play often takes them away from relationships. For example, in one couple, the wife had encouraged her husband to develop friendships with other men but then found herself a "golf widow" when her husband became increasingly consumed by efforts to reduce his handicap. A compulsive sports bettor confessed to us that even while making love to his wife he would listen to the game results by keeping a small radio underneath his pillow. When she wondered where the sounds were coming from, he denied hearing anything. On any given Sunday in the fall, many a man can be found in front of his television set watching football, happy at being able to avoid a wife, a girlfriend, or a mother.

Sports emphatically differentiate a man from the world of women. He reaffirms his manhood through the rituals that he shares exclusively with men. Developmental psychologists tell us that as he or she grows up, a child moves from play done on his own (solitary play) to play done with another child in tandem but not in interaction (parallel play) to true collaborative play. What distresses women is that so many men seem to remain little boys who, if they play with women at all, only do so in bed.

To understand what is good about masculinity as well as where it may go astray, we need to understand men at play. We believe that its place in a psychology of men has been neglected, and that its contribution to loving relationships has not been understood. After all, ethologists tell us that primate play is closely linked with social development, and in childhood almost all relationships are mediated through play. In the new hierarchy of healthy relationships, in which feminine styles of relating are held out as a model for what men should aspire to, we may have lost an appreciation for the subtle, indigenous ways that men are intimate. Play, and sports in particular, need not take men away from relationships; they lead men toward rough friendships with other men with their own physical vocabulary, their own disciplines of love.

THE PASSION OF SPORTS

If we are to uncover and celebrate distinctly male values, both sexes have much to learn from men at play. As Showell Styles has remarked, sports are "useless, like poetry, and dangerous, like lovemaking." In part, the appeal of sports is aesthetic, for whose appreciation the artist is most richly equipped. Curiously, there is a rich literary tradition of sportswriting, particularly connected with baseball, but relatively few of its insights have made their way into the discussion about gender. For this reason, many of the illustrations we will draw upon in this chapter come from poets and writers.

Men struggle to prove that they are men, yet, paradoxically, also want to remain little boys. Whether through bowling or playing softball, rooting for a sports team, or playing cards with the guys, men need to play. Through sports, and play in all its organized and spontaneous forms, men find respite from the demands of inner duty and of women and they maintain a nostalgic link to boyhood. They offer what the sociologist Allen Guttman has called "emotional time out." Yet sports have many different meanings. For the serious tennis player, it can be a place to show his superiority. For the weekend golfer, it may be a chance to spend time with friends in a place where time slows down. For the aging marathon runner, it may symbolize a struggle against the effects of time. For the pickup basketball player, it is a way of having physical contact with other men that does not threaten him. For the diehard baseball fan, the yearly unrequited dream of his team winning the World Series (a fulfillment not enjoyed by us Red Sox fans born after 1918) provides a bittersweet, intoxicating brew of pain, forgetfulness, and insane hope that is eagerly quaffed every spring. One thing is clear: so much passion means more than a casual love.

> There was no moment like it, and anyone who had ever played high school football could still recall it with perfect clarity, that emotional peak, that time in life when all energy was concentrated on a single point and everything was crystal clear. Whatever happened afterward, whatever success, or failure, or happiness, or horror, it could not be forgotten.
>
> [BISSINGER, P. 319]

While some psychoanalysts grumble that sports, at bottom, are motivated by helplessness and the counterphobic need for mastery,[1] notions of sublimation and the shadow play of instinctual forces hardly do them justice. Sports are not a side show for the captive display of tamed versions of sex and aggression. For one thing, they provide an aesthetic, total engagement of the senses. As the psychiatrist and former Harvard football team captain Phillip Isenberg comments:

[1] See Daniel Dervin (in Bibliography) for a scholarly, though somewhat reductive, examination of sports from a psychoanalytic perspective.

Sports offer some remarkably intensified experiences. One becomes familiar with pressure and excitements which have a logic, timing, physical reality, and esthetic which provide a wordless confirmation of some fundamental facts. In this sense activity in sports is an unmistakable enactment of both fantasy and actuality where the contests are continual opportunities to reshape one with the other. They are also some special memories which stay alive.

[ISENBERG, PP. 6–10]

Sports psychologists refer to athletes at peak performance as being so intensely concentrated on the present moment that time seems to slow, and they are unaware of certain aspects of their surroundings and intensely focused on others. Such feelings of unusual power and heightened faculties are akin to trances, drug-induced states, or falling in love. Few if any places in their lives offer men such self-transcendent experiences. Unlike sex, which carries the risk of unpredictable involvement with women, sports can be performed alone or, if with other men, the bounds of intimacy are strictly prescribed. While a casual game of tennis or watching "Monday Night Football" does not deliver the same primeval jolt as the athlete at peak performance enjoys, the sense of being away in a special, bounded space is much the same. As with a drug, the sights, sounds, and smells associated with altered states of consciousness themselves acquire an almost magical power to evoke the original experience. In vicarious form, the armchair quarterback as well as the weekend athlete relives his own imagined or re-created moments of sports joy and glory.

THE OLYMPICS

Myth has it that Heracles came to mainland Greece from Crete with four brothers and that at Olympia he won a race with them. Henceforth it was determined that the Olympic

Games would be held every four years. Archeologists confirm that these games began to be held at this interval at the second or third full moon after the summer solstice, starting in 776 B.C. Heralds would be sent out to announce a formal truce and athletes were given a month to prepare for an event that lasted five days. Consistent with its sacred appointed time, the games were held in a sacred precinct, and no women were allowed to attend. As H. D. F. Kitto has pointed out, the Greeks made the games part of their religion. The contest, or *agon*, was an opportunity to display *arete*, or excellence, which was the most worthy offering that one could make to the gods.

By excellence the Greeks did not have in mind a specialized skill, such as bench-pressing the most weight or running faster than anyone else. True, great physical strength, agility, and speed could be godlike, but it was the *balance* of attributes that they most admired. As Kitto points out, the marathon race was a modern invention and would have been considered an anomaly by the ancient Greeks. Instead, they held races of two hundred yards and one and a half miles, a race in armor, the long jump, discus throwing, the javelin, chariot racing, boxing, and wrestling. But the most important event was the pentathlon, which was made up of a race, throwing the discus and the javelin, a jump, and wrestling. In this way, the whole man would be tested.

The victors of the games received a modest award—an olive tree branch or wreath cut from a sacred grove by a boy whose two parents were still alive—but great public adoration. When the victor returned to his home city, a small segment of the city walls would be broken to allow him to pass through, instead of opening the gates, since it was believed that with great athletes the city had no need of walls to protect it. Other public honors might include a free dinner at public expense for the rest of his life and the commissioning of a victory ode, of which Pindar is our most famous exemplar:

> *In the Pythian games*
> *you pinned four wrestlers*
> *unrelentingly, and sent*

> them home in losers' gloom;
> no pleasant laughter cheered them as they reached
> their mothers' sides; shunning ridicule,
> they took to alleys, licking losers' wounds.
>
> [*PINDAR'S ODES*, PYTHIAN 8]

While the Greeks valued how the games were played, it mattered intensely whether you won or lost. To win, by definition, meant that you were favored by the gods.

The Greek value of harmonious development of mind and body, of proportion and grace, was considered effeminate by the Romans, who glorified fighting. Instead of beauty they preferred the blood of gladiatorial contests; instead of aesthetic balance, their taste ran to excess, such as the combat of women against dwarves held by the Emperor Domitian in A.D. 90. The line between the serious and the pretend, between war games and war, was lost.

In modern sports events, which take place in arenas and coliseums not unlike their ancient precursors, the spectacles may evoke the same sense of nearness to the gods or at least a quasi-religious state of awe. As Bissinger describes in *Friday Night Lights*, "[Being a Permain football player was like] being a gladiator, like walking into the Roman Colosseum with all those thousands in the stands yelling yay or nay, all wishing they could be you down there on that field."

Whether as participant or spectator, sports create a stage for the hero: alone, triumphant, glorious. Instead of death defied, as with Achilles, the athlete braves defeat and the limits of bodily prowess.

Leon Chorbajian notes that the growth of spectator sports in the United States coincides with the closing of the American frontier and the emergence of the industrial age. Having fewer opportunities in work and leisure to express rugged masculinity, frustrated men have turned to sports. Spectator sports may well be the last natural preserve for the hero, whom nine-to-five jobs and women's insightful criticism threaten with extinction. Perhaps, at their worst, sports become an aphrodisiac for flagging masculine egos, a self-soothing, repetitive ritual as perverse and lonely as the imaginary Universal Baseball Association of Robert Coover's Henry Waugh. But they may also be a man's best chance to dare to be a hero and, like Achilles, through pain transform himself.

TRANSFORMATIONS

> The spectators jump up from their seats and shout, some wave their hands, some their garments, some leap from the ground, and some grapple with their neighbors for joy; for these really amazing deeds make it impossible for the spectators to contain themselves. Is there anyone so without feeling as not to applaud this athlete?
>
> [PHILOSTRATUS, 2ND CENTURY, A.D.
> (ARTHUR FAIRBANKS, TRANS., P. 151)]

This description of the spectators at Olympia could just as well be of fans at Boston Garden or Fenway Park, or at any of thousands of professional, college, or high school arenas. Men, who anywhere else would suppress their feelings, unabashedly voice rage, exultation, epithets, and pleas for deliverance and exchange "high fives" with strangers.

One baseball fan told us how odd this emotional bond to a sports team seemed to him:

> After watching a particularly tough loss, I sometimes feel foolish about how upset I am. Who are these guys whose winning and losing I'm so invested in? I don't know them from Adam, and if I did, I'd think as many of them were jerks as on the team I want them so much to beat. I doubt they'd want me as a close friend either. The funny thing is, it really doesn't matter. Deep down, a voice tells me that I'm just trying to make myself not care, like a guy who discovers his girlfriend has cheated on him and he's trying to convince himself that her mouth is too small or she doesn't cook very well.

Like love, and perhaps like family, the bonds men feel to their teams are powerful, irrational, and somehow necessary.

Heinz Kohut would call these odd love relationships "self-objects," by which he means the experience of another person as if it were a part of the self. Through idealization of sports heroes with whom he becomes identified, the individual feels uplifted by their strength and by their triumphs. In contrast to women, who perhaps more easily than men feel powerful empathic resonances with other individuals in pain, men are drawn to identifications with a team and with struggle. It would be a mistake to call men unrelated; it is a different kind of relatedness than that of women.

The late commissioner of baseball and Renaissance scholar A. Bartlett Giamatti referred to baseball as creating "a reservoir of transformation." He pointed out that through sports we experience the lightening of cares, the common is made into the uncommon, and individuals are transformed into a sense of community. In this same sense, "self-objects" are wished-for transformations of the self—to be graceful, young, and strong; to be a hero; to merely be carefree. In pathological narcissism, self-objects are *required* to sustain a damaged self. As with a brace on a blown-out knee, the support helps but the vulnerability remains. Without meaning to saddle men with pathological labels, we believe that the average man relies on narcissistic-like means to repair his psyche—hence his exaltation in sports victories and his devastation in defeat:

> In the aftermath of a win there was no place more giddy than the locker room, the players whooping and hollering, readying themselves for the spoils of victory with strokes of the comb as meticulous as brush strokes by Michelangelo and gobs of Lagerfeld aftershave as pungent as the smell of ripened Juicy Fruit. They would leave the field house and waiting outside for them would be a haze of boosters and parents and Pepettes and cheerleaders. The faces of the parents and boosters would be etched with the same stunning kind of pride you might see in a hospital delivery room . . . but in the aftermath of a loss the field house emptied quietly and quickly, as if the place was cursed and it was somehow shameful to be there at all.
>
> [BISSINGER, PP. 233–34]

Grandiosity may be expressed in the pursuit of perfect form as well as victory. As Pindar put it,

> *From one who lends his passion to perfection,*
> *sparing neither pains nor means,*
> *and gains a sought-for goal we should*
> *withhold no praise or*
> *compliments . . .*
>
> [*PINDAR'S ODES*, ISTHMIAN 1]

Sports provides a vehicle for indulging the wish for perfection, or as Giamatti put it, to "kill the snake of error" in our lives. It offers the longed-for promise of redemption from narcissistic wounds. One can, perhaps, after all be special, by virtue of great talent displayed, odds overcome, or because victory has filled our sails with god-sent gifts. The bodybuilder is the most dramatic demonstration of how the quest to perfect the body can become idolatry, but it is not uncommon for other athletes to be as fussy about their bodies as any woman about her figure.

But sports is not just about hero worship and Walter Mitty–like fantasies of glory. As Giamatti points out, transformation can occur merely by participating:

> That aspiration is to be taken out of the self. It is to be for a moment in touch, because common pleasure is so intense, with a joy that cannot be described . . . a moment when we are free of all constraint of all kinds, when pure energy and pure order create an instant of complete coherence. In that instant, pulled to our feet, we are pulled out of ourselves. We feel what we saw, become what we perceived.
>
> It is a moment when something not modern but ancient, primitive—primordial—takes over. It is a sensation not merely of winning, for the lesson of life is that you cannot win, no matter how hard you work, but of fully playing.
>
> [GIAMATTI, PP. 34–35]

Whether through investing a piece of oneself in an idealized other or by losing the self in a transcendent experience, the boundaries of the self are enlarged. Some have called this the regeneration of the self; others refer to it as making the self over. Both point to a profound, dynamic change.

The poet Donald Hall, who shares with Giamatti an intellectual's love of baseball, has an artist's appreciation for the transforming effect of sports:

> I watch the intense and concentrated pushing of the self past the self's limits. It is like writing poems, or what writing poems ought to be if you are going to last as a poet, you have to bring everything to the poem that you have ever learned, as to the painting if you are a painter or to the swing of the bat if you are hitter, and everything that you could ever do. You have to push up to the limit, and then past the limit.
>
> [HALL, P. 22]

The common thread through all these transformations is that sports offers hope. Since all of life, as one sports fan has remarked, is "5 to 2, against," we are buoyed by the possibility that, just once, we will overcome. As the New York Mets pitcher Tug McGraw exhorted his teammates and fans during their championship season, "You gotta believe."

The psychologist Rick Michael has pointed out that hope is a delicate balance, standing between unrealistic expectations and pessimism. Sports provides fields and ringside seats to play with this balance, to risk disappointment, and to accommodate our fondest wishes with reality in a safe place where the saving grace is "there's always next year."

NOSTALGIA

The hope that sports evokes is an echo of our boyhood. It reminds us of when we were young and all seemed fresh and possible. In playing, we remember. We remember the home-run hit in the last punchball game of school in June of fourth grade, we remember the touchdown pass caught just off the ground and the way we faked two defenders out of their jockstraps and drove for the score. Such private sports highlight "films" are what Michael Novak has called "permanent interior pictures." Our bodies also remember. Though crusted with newer, less welcome pains of age, our muscles, when called upon to stretch that extra inch, remind us of other carefree times when we were lost in play. These memories and sensations are part of other small and large rituals that link us to our childhood. The middle-aged man who is charged with excitement for baseball's "opening day" or for his alma mater's football game against its archrival has little habits that are inseparably linked to his past and to the game—reading the sports section in the morning, wearing a special scarf, meeting up with friends. Nostalgia is forever preserved by tradition, by the sense of being part of something that has endured over time. As Phillip Isenberg describes his experience of Harvard football, it links the generations of men in a brotherhood of established truths and values— manliness, generosity, fairness, and self-sacrifice.

As Donald Hall puts it, "Everyone needs to find some place in life where the child can walk," [Hall, p. 2] such as in a game; here the adult's ambiguous successes and costly failures can be left behind for conflict that is never concealed and outcomes certain but of no consequence.

The nostalgic hope of sports is inseparably linked with a bittersweet awareness of time's passing. The cycle of seasons in which each sport has an assigned place is a calendar of a man's life that reminds him of his past as it offers promise of renewal. As Thomas Wolfe wrote about baseball:

> [It is] really a part of the whole weather of our lives, of the thing that it is our own, of the whole fabric, the million memories of America. For example, in the memory of almost everyone of us, is there anything that can evoke spring—the first fine days of April—better than the sound of the ball smacking into the pocket of the big mitt, the sound of the bat as it hits the horsehide: for me, at any rate,

and I am being literal and not rhetorical—almost everything I know about spring is in it—the first leaf, the jonquil, the maple tree, the smell of grass upon your hands and knees, the coming into flower of April. And is there anything that can tell more about an American summer than, say, the smell of the wooden bleachers in a small town baseball park, that resinous, sultry and exciting smell of old dry wood?

[THOMAS WOLFE, IN GUTTMAN,
FROM RITUAL TO RECORD, P. 101]

Perhaps better than any other American sport, baseball embodies remembered past and future hope. On the one hand, it is saturated with tradition and records. Each act is accounted for and measured against the yardstick of our own performances and of past heroes. Yet each spring, every player begins with an unblemished average of .000. The two stock characters of every spring training—the aging veteran and the rookie—who both struggle to make the team, are like Kohut's "self-objects": they are the living standard-bearers of our own fond hopes.

"YOU WOULD OF KISSED THEM"

The nostalgia of sports is also through their connecting us to the Special Men of our past. As Donald Hall describes:

Baseball is fathers and sons. . . . Baseball is the generations, looping backward and forever and with a million apparitions of sticks and balls, cricket and rounders, and the games the Iroquois played in Connecticut before the English came. Baseball is fathers and sons playing catch, lazy and murderous, wild and controlled, the profound archaic song of birth, growth, age, and death. This diamond encloses what we are. . . .

Baseball connects American males with each other, not only through bleacher friendships and neighbor loyalties, not only through barroom fights, but, most importantly, through generations. When you are small, you may not discuss politics or union dues or profit margins with your father's cigar-smoking friends when your father has gone out for a six-pack, but you may discuss baseball.

[HALL, PP. 30, 49–50]

For men sports provide a form of brotherhood for which women have no true equivalent. It is not surprising that women often do not appreciate men's love of sports and underestimate men's relatedness since, as in the ancient Olympics, they are usually barred from men's private world of play.

While there are sports of individual achievement, men's connections to other men are nowhere so palpable and unashamedly acknowledged as in The Team. Through it a man experiences an intense sense of belonging, of community, even of love, that he may never find anywhere else. Sports is a rite of passage. To know how to throw a spiral in football, to be able to withstand the stinging pain of a baseball caught against the thin layer of cowhide covering the palm, to stand in the batter's box when a fast ball is thrown "high and tight" are all rituals of manhood. In belonging to the team, one belongs to the world of men. In not being part of these rites, one's manhood becomes suspect— the nonathlete faces a difficult journey of finding other pathways to affirm his masculinity. Further, The Team can exact a tyrannical allegiance, which also leaves long-lasting legacies of bitter resentment of authority and shame at the surrendering of one's identity.

As in other rites of passage, mentors may impede or facilitate the boy's journey into the world of men: The Coach. We remember our own coaches with a vividness and bittersweet affection that points up their role in our growth: Mr. Boyers, who, when the fifth-grade star athlete complained about the clumsy jostlings of other boys during a basketball game, told him to be patient with them since they had not developed as rapidly as he; Mr. Bertrand, the high school football coach who, during a tackling drill when one boy was shaken up told him to "walk it off," only to find later that he had broken his collar bone; and "Scrappy Al," who during baseball practice instilled the virtues of "hustle" and "heads up" play.

The Coach not only teaches skills, which in themselves are intrinsic to becoming a man, but more important he inspires a respect for himself, for the group, and for its task. At his worst, he uses shame and intimidation to exhort boys to "play with pain" and to "not be a girl." At his best, he fosters a respect for discipline—both for the external authority who at first creates its standards and later for the internalized form that maintains itself—will, determination, self-sacrifice. As with the father earlier in a boy's life, at best he makes himself available as a hero to be idealized. He does not have to be liked as long as he is worthy of authority, which he earns by focusing, defining, and protecting the group's task and by his fairness. As with any group process, each individual's self-esteem becomes enhanced by a cohesive group in which individual goals are subordinated to the good of the whole. The Team, mentored by The Coach, tempers the male imperative of autonomy. The truly mature coach can watch his charges come together and "act as one." He wants The Team to make things happen such that he himself becomes irrelevant. In this way, like the good father, The Coach helps a boy to grow up not in isolation but in connection.

As we have said earlier, it is crucial to an understanding of men to realize that *their most loving experiences take place in a group where the task is clear and where feelings are subordinated to that task.* Men share with each other less by talking about feelings than by sharing a task. This is not a homophobic solution or an embryonic form of intimacy but part of the deep structure of masculinity. These forms of love are closely linked with authority in which ambivalence has been mastered enough so that tenderness and aggression can coexist. This has major implications for the misunderstandings that arise between men and women when women feel that men are defective in the capacity for intimacy one-to-one, and men can find no acceptable outlets for their aggressiveness. Stripped of the forms of sports that channel and limit aggression between men, with women men abuse, overpower, devalue, or shamefully withdraw.

Daniel Dervin points out that the athlete often talks to himself in a voice that may be benevolent or caustic, and that is reminiscent of coaches or other mentor figures. One young man admitted to us that the torrent of self-criticism unleashed by a poor tennis performance was such that he could feel suicidal. An older man revealed that in his thirties he had to break several golf clubs each season in order to exorcise his inner accusatory demons. Such permanent interior dialogues suggest the personal role that athletic relationships have in shaping a man's growth and the way that sports remain an arena for wrestling with the harsh spectators men carry within.

In describing his feelings toward his minor-league baseball team that was competing for a championship, one man in his thirties recalled:"I looked around the infield and I thought that I really didn't know them but I felt such tenderness—the kind of closeness men feel from wanting the same thing so much even if they never get it."

In Mark Harris's novel *Bang the Drum Slowly*, another ballplayer expressed his love this way:

> ". . . you felt warm toward them, and you looked at them, and them at you, and you were both alive, and you might as well said, 'Ain't it something? Being alive, I mean! Ain't it really a great thing at that?' and if they would of been a girl you would of kissed them, though you never said such a thing out loud but only went on about your business."

American men may slap each other on the back or give each other special handshakes. They may hug, but they almost never kiss, and as Harris suggests, almost equal to this taboo is the injunction not to talk about loving feelings. We see here just how far men have come from the world of women with its joy in talking about the nuances of relationship. Perhaps men are not only declaring their world as distinct from women's and therefore emblematic of masculinity by its differentness. Through The Team and the silent rituals of sports *they have less need to talk about their connections.*

WAR WITHOUT DEATH

Anthropologic studies of sport suggest that the agony of defeat in some ancient cultures was literally sacrificial death. Aggression is now blocked from its terminal goal, but in boxing, football, and hockey its brutality is no less naked:

> It was the whole reason he played football, for those hits, for those acts of physical violence that made him tingle and feel wonderful, for those quintessential shots that made him smile from ear to ear and earned him claps on the back from his teammates when he drove some defensive lineman to the sidelines and pinned him right on his butt. He knew he was an asshole when he played, but he figured it was better to be, as he saw it, an "asshole playin' football rather than in real life."
>
> [BISSINGER, P. 13]

For men, whether driven by testosterone or cultural imperative, the struggle to express aggression in socially acceptable forms has its own rules and rhythms, its own aesthetic in each sport. Both the aggression and the limits are intrinsic to these forms of play. The Coach ideally carries on the early father's role of sanctioning and teaching the boundaries of aggression. On the one hand, boys are taught to be aggressive, to play hard, but uncontrolled violence can hurt the team and is contrary to the rules of fair play that are honored almost on a par with winning. Sports become a male rite of passage in that they test the boy's capacity to take risks by exposing himself to humiliation and physical pain. To compete successfully, a boy or man must master fear.

In sports there are clear winners and losers—kill or be killed—except these are wars (usually) without death. In endless repetition, the struggle goes on to ensure that one's opponent will be shamed, not oneself. The goal is not to inflict bodily pain but emotional hurt. As with many forms of play, old traumas may be reenacted, except that the roles are reversed.

Instead of being shamed, as the young boy was by his parents
for not wanting to separate from mother, he takes the active
role shaming others.

Sports are a martial art, for men's aggression is not just
siphoned off; it is perfected. The famous observation about
Napoleon's defeat by the British is that it was prepared for on
the playing fields of Eton and Harrow. Further, there may be
more than a hint of enjoyment in the defeat of others and a
glorification of violence and struggle. Men's darker traits include a lust for blood and its sublimated versions—total domination of an opponent or the enjoyment of inflicted pain.

In sports, where the taboo against men's touching each other
is relaxed, love and hate, violence and tenderness are often hard
to distinguish, as D. H. Lawrence's description in *Women in
Love* suggests:

> So they wrestled swiftly, rapturously, intent and mindless
> at last, two essential white figures working into a tighter,
> closer oneness of struggle, with a strange, octopus-like knot-
> ting and flashing of limbs in the subdued light of the room;
> a tense white knot of flesh gripped in silence between the
> walls of old brown books. Now and again came a sharp gasp
> of breath, or a sound like a sigh, then the rapid thudding of
> movement on the thickly-carpeted floor, then the strange
> sound of flesh escaping under flesh. Often, in the white inter-
> laced knot of violent living being that swayed silently, there
> was no head to be seen, only the swift, tight limbs, the solid
> white backs, the physical junction of two bodies clinched
> into oneness.
>
> [*WOMEN IN LOVE*, PP. 274–75]

Through playing, aggression can be transformed into love.
Perhaps, once sufficient anger has been expressed and differentiation firmly achieved through different uniforms and team identities, a move toward each other can safely occur without
threatening men's fragile autonomy. One's opponent may be
recognized as worthy of respect, even admiration. Some observ-

ers have suggested that the elaborate rituals of male sports are necessary to mediate the dangerous aggression and love between men. It may be that these rituals are just as necessary for men in relation to women, and that lacking the social structures that sports provide, men are more confused about how to deal with their impulses, which emerge more often in lust and violence, fight or flight, rather than in a playful space of mingled aggression and love.

THE LOSS OF OMNIPOTENCE

Homer introduces games once in each of his two epics. In the *Odyssey*, when Odysseus's host, King Alcinous, notices him grieve as a singer tells the story of Troy, he suggests that the men engage in athletic contests. In the *Iliad*, after Achilles has burned the body of Patroclus on the funeral pyre and made many sacrifices to him, he seats the troops around him and sets out prizes for which they can compete. On both occasions, sports are intended to console a man over a loss, to renew a man's joy in living. In fact, the origin of all the great Greek games (Pythian, Olympian, Isthmian, and Nemean) was after funerals of great heroes.

We have suggested that it is the hero's capacity to grieve that transforms him. Sports can be a refuge from the sadnesses of the world; they may distract a man with a glass menagerie of inconsequential fantasy. If sports were only about hero fantasies of glorious victory and shaming one's opponents, then they would merely help a man to avoid facing his vulnerability. They would not transform. But sports are also about loss.

In the evening after the Red Sox sustained their most hideous loss ever in Game Six of the 1986 World Series (by losing on Bill Buckner's error after being one strike away from the championship), callers phoned into the radio sports programs to moan, to vent their rage, to build modern funeral pyres of grief. The depth of feeling and the openness with which men expressed their sense of loss was cathartic. Fortune had cruelly played with their dreams. If in the greater scheme of life's misfortunes, such public mourning over a game might seem a bit childish, it did not seem so at the time. It also did not appear unmanly. Sports inevitably bring men face-to-face with loss and sanction the expression of disappointment and grief that most men would otherwise not have access to. Aristotle commented on the group catharsis that can occur through drama or readings of epic poems. Sports, too, provide a community of men, who, even if in the anonymity of a crowd, make both the joy of sports more intense and their disappointments seem more bearable.

To learn how to deal with defeat is to come to terms with loss and shame. One learns, as A. E. Housman put it, that glory "withers quicker than the rose." Unfortunately, fathers and mentors may often fail to teach sons about bearing loss. It becomes something feared and catastrophic and no pride develops in doing one's personal best or in learning to bear defeat. Like Achilles, they wrap themselves in a fragile cloak of honor. For example, each year in the Super Bowl athletes talk about how "getting to the show" means nothing, that only "winning it all" counts. To end the season on a loss, even after a season full of victories, means that the entire off-season will be spent getting over a bitter disappointment. Obviously, there is something amiss. These attitudes help explain the vulnerability of athletes at all levels to abusing their bodies with steroids and numbing drugs. When limits cannot be faced, Icarus keeps on striving to reach the sun.

Sports are about the recognition of limits. As Phillip Isenberg points out, it teaches that you have to live within the limits of the game and of your body, to realize your *relative* talents. It is a good teacher about limits because, unlike in much of life, in sports the limits are so obvious and the consequences for ignoring them are tangible and immediate.

Inevitably, a man's dream of omnipotence is interrupted by injury and aging. He realizes that he will join the ranks of what A. E. Housman called:

Runners whom renown outran
And the name died before the man.

[``TO AN ATHLETE DYING
YOUNG,'' LL. 19–20]

In sports one also cannot help realizing the limiting effect of chance. No matter what one's talents, no matter how unfair it might be, one loses. As one Boston sportswriter referred to Carl Yastrzemski ignominiously popping out with the tying run on in the 1978 playoff game against the Yankees, "God must have been out shelling a peanut." As Pindar observed:

. . . but even for competitors the dole of chance can
not be known until the very end:
it grants now this, now that.
The best man does not always win and may
be tripped by his inferior's ability.

[*PINDAR'S ODES*, ISTHMIAN 4]

In another ode, he cautions:

The one who wins without great strain
seems to make fools of others
and fortify his life with well-made plans;
but men are not the agents of their fate: chance
alone holds some on high and pushes others down.

[PYTHIAN 8]

Sports can be merely a diversion, but the more a man invests of himself, either through his own performance or as a spectator through his surrogates, the more serious play becomes. He cannot help being moved by his victories and defeats, and ultimately being humbled.

CHILDLIKE OR CHILDISH

Women sometimes find it endearing when men act like little boys—it can be a welcome change from the invulnerable stance men usually assume. But then there is the beloved husband who pouts and stalks around when frustrated. Women are all too familiar with the ways men pull rank (as the economic provider or "head of the household") because, like spoiled children, they have to get their way.

The challenge for men is to retain their boyish spirit and to leave their childish ways behind. Men need a measure of privacy in their play, which women may be able to accept if men sometimes invite them into their "clubhouse." While men playing at sports will always look like little boys, the adult equivalents of boys' games are not functionally the same. There is nostalgia in sports and elements of escape, but there is also a here-and-now aesthetic with its own forms of love.

Sigmund Freud and Robert Waelder both observed that sometimes children will repeatedly play out traumatic experiences in order to master them. For example, Freud described how a young boy would make a toy disappear and reappear so as to work through his feelings about separating from his mother. Play provides an arena for psychological mastery because it is a relatively safe place, freed of consequences and where scripts can be rewritten in accord with one's need. The repetition compulsion may in part explain the devotion that men have to sports. But, as Erik Erikson has pointed out, play is also a vehicle for renewal, communication, practice of growing faculties, and self-expression.

Men can get stuck in a variety of ways that may make it seem that sports are largely forms of immaturity: they can turn to sports to provide them with oblivion, they can get caught up in an idealized world; and they can easily allow winning to seem more important than the process of play. They can make the perfection of their body or their skills a form of worship without a soul. Perhaps worst is the danger of losing touch with the original magical, transforming potential of sports. Allen Guttman has argued that in modern sports pursuit of the record has replaced ritual:

> When qualitative distinctions fade and lose their force, we turn to quantitative ones. When we can no longer distinguish the sacred from the profane or even the good from the bad, we content ourselves with minute discriminations between the batting average of the .308 and the .307 hitter. Once the gods have vanished from Mount Olympus or from Dante's Paradise, we can no longer win to appease them or to save our souls, but we can set a new record. It is a uniquely modern form of immortality.
>
> [GUTTMAN (1978), PP. 54–55]

We believe that despite the tawdry patina of profit, the glorification of meaningless achievements, and the sacrilege of artificial turf and "trash sports," the gods still occasionally attend certain athletic events. Religiosity, in both its best and worst incarnations, still adheres to sports. As with any potent social form, it becomes what we make of it. It is well to remember that the ancient Greeks venerated sports but always appreciated the need for balance. It was the whole man that competed, and sports had a place no more and no less important than the intellect.

In our own time, we may need to remind ourselves of the way that sports both uplift and humble us, indeed how they embody the tragic vision of fallen heroes:

> And he, who in his youth
> secures a fine advantage,
> gathers hope and flies
> on wings of manly action,
> disdaining cost. Men's happiness is early-
> ripened fruit that falls to earth
> from shakings of adversity
> Men are day-bound. What is a man? what is
> he not? Man is a shadow's dream. But when divine

advantage comes, men gain a radiance and a richer
life.

[*PINDAR'S ODES*, PYTHIAN 8]

   The radiance and the shadow's dream—both are parts of men
that the contest helps to reveal. So, too, do sports teach how
love and aggression can be contained in relationships that may
not only survive rough intimacies but can be enhanced by them.
As in an Olympic truce, sports provide a neutral ground—a
potential space in which the jagged pieces of men's rough-hewn
nature can be softened or reassembled in creative transformations. Sports offer a chance to reshape and renew. Further, the
spirit of play, which may get lost in the cult of victory, of
competition, and of record-seeking is what we believe men need
to cultivate to keep sports in proper perspective with the rest of
life's pleasures and misfortunes. It is essential to that other very
fragile and confusing form of physical relationship called making love.

8

▼

LOVE AND LUST

In our time of gender confusion, sex is the most dangerous act between a man and a woman, not only because of AIDS, but because they each have to risk their fragile sense of self. It is hard to admit that you need someone about whom you understand so little and fear so much. In the increasingly heated gender wars, sex is a kind of Olympic truce in which combatants agree to suspend enmities for muted strife and play. And yet, though men and women may share in acts that promise mutual pleasure, the bedroom, too, is often a battlefield where the worst damage is done by silent falsehoods and misinterpretation.

Some sex researchers have estimated that half of American marriages are affected by sexual problems. In 1953 Alfred Kinsey found that almost half of all married men and one-fourth of married women had engaged in at least one extramarital affair by age forty. Thirty years later, Philip Blumstein and Pepper Schwartz, in *American Couples*, reported that of couples married ten or more years 30 percent of the men and 20 percent of the women were not monogamous. For a culture whose ideal of marriage is sexual fidelity and which is less and less tolerant of transgressions (as evidenced by the response to Gary Hart and Bill Clinton), these figures show a wide gap between what marriage promises sexually and what it delivers. Perhaps the most disturbing statistic is Shere Hite's claim that 50 percent of the women she interviewed in 1976 said that they faked having orgasms. This is sad evidence of the inability of women to speak honestly with men and of men to be strong enough to hear it. It suggests the degree of falseness that surrounds an act that is supposed to require the fullest disclosure.

Women feel pressure from men to have sex. They often hear from men that they are not getting enough sex or enough good sex. Women are baffled and put off by the way men demand sex even in the absence of tender feelings. Men turn to sex as the least risky and most dependable way to find connection— to get love. A still controversial research finding is that the anterior portions of the hypothalamus, an area of the brain associated with sexual behavior, is larger in heterosexual men than in either women or homosexual men. It seems that evolution may have devised an excellent way to perpetuate the torture of the human species by arranging for men and women to have differing thresholds for the amounts of love, sex, and commitment that they desire.

Gender politics have always complicated sexual politics. Not many decades ago, the lack of concern about women's needs was paralleled by an ignorance about their sexuality. Then, in the paternalistic fifties and sixties, women were understood to have sexual desires but men were held responsible for satisfying them. Sex manuals of that era exhorted men to exercise ejaculatory control. With the advent of feminism and women's claim for empowerment, sexual gratification came to be viewed not just as women's right but as their co-responsibility. Women were encouraged to learn how to pleasure themselves. While potentially lightening men's burden, feminism has also played into men's deepest fears—less able to ignore or to control women, they must now reckon with demands that they feel ill-equipped to respond to. The bill for all the fake orgasms is now being presented for collection.

In some of the middle-aged couples we see, for example, the women are increasingly vocal about what they do and don't like. A woman who used to consent to her partner's request for fellatio and anal intercourse revealed that she felt degraded by these acts. Unaware of the thorns of hostility that often accompanied his proferrings of love, her husband was bewildered and hurt by her overdue indictment of their most intimate moments. In another couple, the wife revealed only after several years that her partner's penile implant bothered her because it felt different and it "wasn't real." For women to be more honest with themselves and with men is necessary for their own sakes and ultimately will benefit both sexes. But in the short run, the delicate apparatuses between men's legs and ears are taking a beating. As Otto Kernberg has suggested, the professional development of women threatens many men, reactivating their envy and resentment of women. It dangerously intensifies the level of hostility within intimate relationships.

REAL MEN'S SEXUAL PROBLEMS

The most common complaint of men who enter sex therapy is too infrequent intercourse. They also worry a lot about their partners' inability to have orgasms. In other words, when there are sexual problems, the man's most likely focus is on the woman. But not too far beneath the surface lie concerns about his own sexual adequacy. He worries about whether he is large enough, whether he can achieve an erection, and whether he ejaculates too soon. The proportion of men who present themselves to sex therapists with specific sexual dysfunction is quite low. No doubt some men are reluctant to see a professional, but we still believe that the degree of preoccupation with these concerns is far in excess of the frequency with which symptoms of impotence and premature ejaculation occur. The *fear* of being sexually inadequate, of being shamed, is what often leads even "real men" to armor themselves in ways that themselves are dysfunctional—they become spectators, lose touch with their bodies, and develop a false self.

Masters and Johnson used the term "spectatoring" to describe the dysfunctional way that men or women can stand apart from the sexual act, observing rather than participating, judging rather than experiencing. Not surprisingly, if you are thinking, it is harder to feel, and further, thinking leads to worrying, which itself interferes with sexual pleasure. Men's preoccupation with their sexual adequacy often leads them to become spectators of their own and their partners' sexual performance. They carry an internal applause meter that measures how aroused their partners become, how long they can have intercourse without ejaculating, how many women they can have sex with, and how many times they can have sex in a night. By turning sex into a competitive Olympic event men are more likely to fall prey to impotence and, even more commonly, to become sexually dissatisfied. They may set off on a search for ever more desirable mates and novel stimulation without realizing that the most limiting factor on their pleasure is being out of touch with their *own* bodies.

Men, like women, are not immune to prohibitions against having sexual pleasure that were learned early in life. But with the cultural imperative for men to be sexually aggressive, they are apt to act the part of the Don Juan while severing their feelings from their actions. Sexual aliveness is further constrained by the disavowal of need and vulnerability that men must adopt in order to feel or appear autonomous. This leads to a split between heart and penis, such as Sam Keen has described.

Sex makes people put on disguises. As one of us has written elsewhere:

> Adopting a false self usually begins in adolescence, when the apparent sexual response of a person is often no more than a pose. Adolescent boys and girls are likely to begin sex either as a way of getting rid of nervous tension, or as a way of showing they belong to their peer group, or from the stimulus of dreams manufactured by the commercial culture. Judith Jordan notes that women in their teens or early twenties may actually want a love affair—an emotionally satisfying bond—but end up behaving as a sexual object because that seems to be the only chance to connect with boys. It is

no news, on the other hand, that boys create a false self and play the romantic lover when their intentions are purely physical—or show bravado when they are most insecure.

[BETCHER AND MACAULEY, P. 184]

The result of all of this posturing is that men lose the capacity to feel anything other than the most intense sensation—orgasm. But without psychic release, sex becomes only tension reduction, which must be compulsively sought. They become frozen in the pose of self-sufficiency in which needs must be asserted as demands and control must constantly vie with pleasure.

Ironically, the emphasis on men becoming more sensitive can itself be subsumed under a false self. The man who played the Don Juan becomes the man who plays the wounded, vulnerable lover. It is far more difficult to address, individually and as a culture, the problem of men's false self that clings to them like a second skin. This is the dilemma inherent in strictly behavioral prescriptions to sexual problems. As effective as Masters and Johnson's sex therapy is with orgasmic dysfunction and premature ejaculation, by focusing exclusively on technique rather than character they may unwittingly *promote* a false self.

The other most pervasive sexual dysfunction of "real men" is the use of sex to solve any problem, from hair loss to loss of income. Men seek sex when they are anxious, angry, sad, and lonely because they think they are only horny. They use sex to combat depression, to demonstrate their potency, and to repair their self-esteem. Women, too, piggy-back all manner of non-sexual needs on sex, and, in truth, as with other basic needs, it is impossible to segregate sex from all the other motivations that drive men and women together. Because of men's lack of familiarity with their own needs and their difficulty putting words to feelings, sex becomes the stage to silently enact *all* their unresolved conflicts. While women may at times justly feel that they are used by men as puppets in their dramas, men, too, are marionettes, jerked around by the strings of their unacknowledged fears and yearnings.

SEX AS POWER AND
VULNERABILITY

Much of men's fears and yearnings revolve around power. As we have seen in the *Iliad* and the *Odyssey*, and in the myths of Narcissus and of Oedipus, women's sexuality has a tremendous hold over men. The essential plot of the *Iliad* turns on competition between two men over possession of a woman—first, Helen, and then Briseus. Women may be slaves to men but men are also in thrall to women. It is face-saving for men to conceive of their lack of control as a result of gonadal impulses rather than as a need for personal connection to a maternal figure. But as Oedipus's cautionary tale demonstrates, exposure of this need results in public humiliation. Men are caught in a dialectic in which sexual relations are a prime vehicle for asserting power but through which their failure to achieve control (as with Meneleus's loss of Helen and Achilles' loss of Briseus) expose their shameful vulnerability.

Freud has so keenly sensitized western culture to the domination of erotic impulses in our dream life and over our behavior, that we may now be at risk for underestimating the degree to which power, rather than desire, governs sexual and other relations between men and women. Feminist theory has rightly asserted that men's sexual violence toward women is more about power than eroticism, although Camille Paglia, in *Sexual Personae*, has argued that male sexuality and aggression are inherently fused.

Long before Freud, in the second century, C.E., Artemidoros traveled through Greece listening to peoples' dreams. He devised a method of dream analysis in which, as John Winkler points out, the primary concerns of the dreamer were not sexual desires, but a calculus of profit and loss—whether the dreamer would come into money, whether a project would be successful, or whether he would recover from an illness. It was not that sexual imagery in dreams was irrelevant, but that it signified something about the dreamer's future public standing which, in ancient Greek society, was more important. To Artemidoros the meaningful choreography of sexual behavior centered around dominance and submission—whether one was phallically penetrated, and with whom. Curiously, gender and kinship, such as if a man had sexual relations with another man or with his mother, mattered less than the social status of the other person and the way intercourse occurred:

> To penetrate one's brother, whether older or younger, is good for the dreamer; for he will be above his brother and will look down on him.
> . . . he who is on bad terms with his mother will resume friendly relations with her, because of the intercourse, for it is called "friendship." . . . To have sex with one's mother on her knees is bad: it signifies a great lack because of the mother's immobility.
>
> [WINKLER, TRANS., BOOK 1, PP. 212–14]

In short, sexual relations in Artemidoros's time, and perhaps to a great extent for men today, are a means by which power and status are gained or lost. Both for Artemidoros and for Freud sexual relations are a royal road to hidden meaning. While the ancient Greek searched for indicators of social status, post-Freudian man looks for keys to the psychological self.

IN SEARCH OF THE TRUE SELF

In *Demian*, Herman Hesse laments, "I wanted only to try to live in accord with the promptings which came from my true self. Why was that so very difficult?" Even professional observers of human conduct disagree about how to find the true sexual self. George Goethals has pointed out that Erikson, for all his efforts to incorporate interpersonal flexibility into human development, was still prey to some of the heavy-handed determinism characteristic of Freud's work. Erikson felt that the boy's relationship with the first Special Woman—mother—laid the foundation for trust, which was the psychological DNA of identity formation. In turn, for Erikson, identity is essential for mature sexual relationships:

> For where an assured sense of identity is missing, even friendships and affairs become desperate attempts at delineating the fuzzy outlines of identity by mutual narcissistic mirroring: to fall in love then often means to fall on top of one's mirror image, hurting oneself and damaging the mirror. During lovemaking or in sexual fantasies, a loosening of sexual identity threatens: it even becomes unclear whether sexual excitement is experienced by the individual or by his partner . . . The ego thus loses its flexible capacity for abandoning itself to sexual and affectual sensations, in a fusion with another individual who is both partner to the sensation and guarantor of one's continuing identity: fusion with another becomes identity loss.
>
> [ERIKSON (1959), P. 125]

In contrast, Harry Stack Sullivan argued that the need to have sexual satisfaction and the need to be intimate derive from parallel lines of experience. There is no necessarily close connection between lust and love. Further, Sullivan felt that the basis for intimacy was not learned in relation to the first Special Woman or indeed to any Special Woman at all, but through friendships with other boys. In the play and comradeship of best friends, of The Team, boys learn how to collaborate, which for Sullivan is the vital ingredient in adult intimacy. In adolescence, boys must learn how to integrate what they know about collaboration with a person of the same gender into a relationship with the opposite gender. As Goethals points out, Sullivan sees young adulthood as the integration of intimacy and lust while Erikson views it as the reshaping of a capacity for intimacy initiated at the earliest stage of life. They agree that it is not by virtue of being able to be sexually intimate that true intimacy becomes possible but rather that mature sexuality depends on the capacity to be intimate.

According to the British object relations theorist, W. R. D.

Fairbairn, Freud put the cart before the horse when he postulated that relationships are merely a means for satisfying instinctual urges. Fairbairn insisted that sensual pleasure is a signpost directing an individual toward the pathways of love. That is, sex is a means and intimacy is the end, not the other way around.

Yet the difference between Erikson and Sullivan mirrors the gender difference between men and women about sex. Is it not women who so often lament to a man that they need to feel close in order to have sex, and is it not men who feel that women have the cart before the horse and that they need to have sex in order feel close? In the days before male chauvinism was recognized as such, Professor Henry Higgins wondered in *My Fair Lady* "Why can't a woman be more like a man?" While it may not now be politically correct for a man to give vent to such sentiments, Sullivan's theory that young men must struggle with translating the first intimacies learned from other boys to a language appropriate to women gives some poignancy to such impossible wishes. To honor women's insistence on not being treated as if they were defective men does not mean that men can be treated as if they were defective women.

As we have discussed, men may have to prove over and over again that they are not women, and this need accentuates innate gender differences into a hypermasculine caricature. Freud felt that men fear intimacy due to the remembered threat of castration by their father for wanting their mothers. Karen Horney suggested that it is actually the boy's failure to win his mother's sexual love that leaves a lifelong scar and that adolescent boys are retraumatized in adolescence by their often ineffective pursuit of women, whose less insistent sex drive makes them appear indifferent. Such constellations of fear and longing may lead to a fear of dependency on any one woman, an avoidance of things feminine, and an unrequited search for love. In the compulsive ways that men sometimes turn to sex and turn away from intimacy, they may be running away from the shameful wounds of childhood and in so doing strengthening a false self of feigned autonomy.

Men's compulsive need for sexual encounters with women may also be driven by their dread of loving a man, which in this culture is constrained by a morbid fear of homosexuality. In ancient Greece, homosexual contacts between adult male citizens and young boys were sanctioned as part of the initiation into manhood, and clearly met intense needs not satisfied by heterosexual relations. But sexual relations between adult men were never publicly tolerated: homosexuality had to be contained within a heterosexual adaptation, and the possibility of erotic love between equals was excluded.[1] The poems of Sappho provide some evidence that erotic love between adult women may have been more accepted, pointing up once again that since antiquity women have been encouraged to love freely, while men can only have controlled sex.

SEX AS SEANCE AND FICTION

As much as men may try to hide parts of themselves through sex, their disguises are not difficult to penetrate. Inevitably, the opportunity for intimacy evokes longed-for ways of being. Ghosts of one's ancient and childhood pasts are summoned up, as in a seance, in hopes of commemorating what was good and setting straight what was not. As psychiatrist David Scharff puts it, good sex reminds us of the nurturing good parent and disappointing sex of failures with Special Women and Special Men of our past. These associations heighten the pleasures and pains of attempted unions beyond their present-day context. In a sense, then, what may appear to be a man's penchant for relatively meaningless sexual relationships is really his attempt to manage feelings that are quite deep. These feelings are not typically expressed in words but in action and through internal fantasy. While often belied by other acts that distance, a man's wish to have intercourse may at times be the only way that he can allow himself to need and to have the need for contact fulfilled and *to repair through a sexualized reunion the traumatic loss of mother*. Perhaps because sex can be experienced as an insistent

[1] See K. J. Dover, *Greek Homosexuality* (1989).

internal pressure, need can be misinterpreted as a biological imperative and so not shame a man *who is not supposed to have needs.*

Men's sexual fantasies are their attempts to rewrite and psychologically master the scripts of their development such that pain is turned into pleasure, trauma to triumph. As Robert Stoller has written:

> Sexual excitement depends on a scenario. The person to be aroused is the writer, who has been at work on the story line since childhood. The story is an adventure in which the hero runs risks that must be escaped. Disguised as fiction, it is an autobiography in which are hidden crucial intrapsychic conflicts and screen memories of actual events, and the resolution of these elements into a happy ending, celebrated by orgasm.
>
> [STOLLER (1976), P. 908]

In less felicitous circumstances, a man or woman may have to engage repetitively in acts or fantasies that rob them of the present. Lawrence Durrell captures this predicament in his novel *Justine*, in which a man struggles with his own and his lover's phantoms:

> She told me and left me raging with a jealousy I struggled to hide—but a jealousy of an entirely novel sort. Its object was a man who though still alive, *no longer existed.* . . . [S]he had been raped by one of her relations. . . . I thought I had penetrated to the heart of The Check: from this time forward she could obtain no satisfaction in love unless she mentally recreated these incidents and re-enacted them. For her we, her lovers, had become only mental substitutes for this first childish act—so that love, as a sort of masturbation, took on all the colours of neurasthenia; she was suffering from an imagination dying of anaemia, for she could not appropriate to herself the love she felt she needed, for her satisfactions derived from the crepuscular corners of a life she was no longer living. This was passionately interesting. But what

was even more amusing was that I felt this blow to my *amour propre* as a man exactly as if she had confessed to an act of deliberate unfaithfulness. What! Every time she lay in my arms she could find no satisfaction save through this memory? In a way, then, I could not possess her: had never done so. I was merely a dummy.

. . . But here too I was sufficiently detached to observe how much love feeds upon jealousy, for as a woman out of my reach yet in my arms, she became ten times more desirable, more necessary.

[DURRELL, PP. 64–65]

Here there is no happy ending, no turning of trauma to triumph, yet the hope that one can free another or be freed from the dead hand of the past lives on.

THE BIG IMPOSSIBLE REVISITED

Some men's voracious appetite for pornography testifies to their need to feed their psychic cravings for restitutive stories. Much as dreams are often wish fulfillments, the function of sexual fantasy is to help repair the traumatized and fragile self. Just as a man's identification with sports heroes can help a deflated self regain stature in its own eyes, so can sexual fantasy repopulate a man's inner world with characters and scenarios to rescue his image as a fallen hero.

The primary character around which most pornographic films revolve is The Penis. As immortalized in the Clarence Thomas/Anita Hill hearings, Long Dong Silver, or his equivalent, is huge, ever hard, ever ready, and worshiped by numerous women. Men are depicted as in control—of their emotions and of women—while women are slaves to men and to their own sexual appetite. The only real sign of life in men is seen in the one essential scene in X-rated movies—the "come shot"— which is the final testimony to the man's virility.

This male fantasy is, as Coen puts it "the perfect world

without any nos." Women are always ready, willing, and able
to serve men's sexual needs, or if offering initial resistance,
they are overcome. Relationships are highly superficial, even
impersonal. Very commonly, a man has his way with several
women and is also permitted to watch lesbian sex. Homosexual
contact between men is not depicted.

Such caricatures of male sexuality may be unfair to men, just
as they are to women. Indeed, many men say that they do
not find such pornography stimulating, although it is not clear
whether it is the wooden predictability they dislike or the nature
of the relationship with women. Eroticism, like art, is a child
of good metaphor—nuance, subtlety, surprise, a layering of
meanings. But the repetitive portrayal of stock themes in pornography suggests that they play to the fears and wishes that
most men have at some level of consciousness. Men need to feel
that they are sexual supermen precisely because they feel so
vulnerable to failure and ridicule. They must be in control because they feel that their hold on themselves and on women is
so tenuous.

To some degree women's role in these male power-redemp-
tion dramas is a matter of their lower power position in the
culture—as the concubine, Briseus, was to Achilles and Agamemnon, they are pawns in the game of male egos, their power
only a matter of what men assign. But the vengeance with
which women are stripped of power and individuality in these
sexual fantasies suggests that the motivation is, in fact, revenge—no woman can be permitted to be Special because dependency once meant pain and shame. Mother's and every other
Special Woman's power must be denied and exorcised through
rites of sexual domination that lie hidden even in the most
innocent and tender connections that a man makes with a
woman. As Ethel Person puts it:

> Control over his penis and through it over the outside
> world become high priority for the boy. Sexuality becomes
> imbued with issues of control and dominance. . . . Men at-
> tempt to assuage their sexual self-doubts through active sex-
> uality (or fantasies of it) in which control over the penis is

sought through sexual mastery and control over the sexual
object. In his wishful fantasies the male reverses his self-
doubts and anxieties by endowing his penis with supernatural
powers that he once attributed to his all-powerful father. . . .

The impulse to solve problems of control and power
through sexual domination grows out of the conviction that
only possession and domination will guarantee fulfillment
and give surcease to the endless wheel of desire, to preserve
a precarious sense of self. The cultural milieu tends to glorify
such domination, takes its apparent strength at face value,
and minimizes its compensatory functions.

[PERSON (1986), PP. 21–22]

If this compensation is necessary because mother was once
too important and then lost, it is also necessary because a man
turned to a father who failed to provide him with models of
masculinity that were truly solid and strong. He identifies with
comic-book-like images of superheroes because the internal
scaffolding of male firmness and authority is missing. All he has
left is to act the part of a strong man and induce women to act
as if they believe it.

In this time of women's gathering strength, men's fragile
potency is further threatened by women, who, unsure of their
new stance, may at times be too aggressive, or by women whose
firm sense of self reminds a man of what he himself lacks. Add
to this women's demand that men be more vulnerable, open to
feelings, and share in housework and childcare—things that he
has been brought up to feel were unmanly—and he may feel as
though he has to become "the big impossible" lover—impossibly big, impossibly gentle, impossibly manly.

EROTIC FORMS OF HATRED

According to Helen Singer Kaplan, the well-known sex therapist, anger is the final common pathway that blocks sexual
desire and sexual performance. Though commonly associated

with sexual feelings because of the negative experiences that are often linked to early sexual development, anger is not erotic. In couples we see in our practices, bitter conflicts outside the bedroom often do make for a nonexistent or troubled sex life within it. As one woman said in relation to how it felt to her to have sex in the context of her volatile marriage, "It feels like we're not making love, we're making hate." Even in the absence of overt hostility, negative thoughts, either stemming from recent interactions with the spouse or remote causes from the past, turn off sexual desire. In Kaplan's words:

> Most patients tend to suppress their desire by evoking negative thoughts or by allowing spontaneously emerging negative thoughts to intrude when they have a sexual opportunity. They have learned to put themselves into negative emotional states by selectively focusing their attention on a perception or thought or by retrieving some memory or by allowing an association to emerge that carries a negative emotional valence. In this manner they make themselves angry, fearful, or distracted, and so tap into the natural physiologic inhibitory mechanisms which suppress sexual desire. . . . If you are angry at someone . . . you hold onto the psychic distance your anger creates [and] retrieve memories of past injustices.
>
> [KAPLAN (1979), PP. 83–89]

In contrast, Robert Stoller asserts that hostility, either overt or hidden, actually generates sexual excitement. The partner becomes a fetish who is dehumanized and then endowed with certain attributes of a person from one's past on whom one needs to be revenged. She is recruited into a role in a sexual drama directed by a man's unconscious. As Janet Malcolm has astutely pointed out, Freud's notion that even children are sexually aware is not nearly as disturbing as his thesis that at the heart of our feelings toward those we hold most dear is hatred.

How is Stoller's view to be reconciled with Kaplan's? Here again is a gender difference—men's sexuality is linked with anger more than women's. In the Sexual Fantasy Project at the

Columbia Psychoanalytic Center, Ethel Person reports that 11 percent of the men interviewed said they had fantasies of torturing a sex partner, 20 percent of whipping or beating a partner, and 44 percent admitted to fantasies of forcing someone to submit to sexual acts. By comparison, none of the women interviewed admitted to sexual torture fantasies, only 1 percent said that they enjoyed the thought of whipping or beating, and 10 percent fantasized about the use of force. Person believes that male sexuality is not inherently aggressive but that hostile fantasies are compensatory for feelings of inadequacy. Whether one blames testosterone, the nuclear family, or the structure of Western culture, men clearly are struggling to manage a whole lot of aggression. To what extent it serves the relationship or harnesses men and women into sexless or loveless unions is at the heart of eroticism.

COURTLY AND
NOT SO COURTLY LOVE

In the thirteenth century, the tradition of courtly love glorified unrequited passion for another man's wife. Such passion without consummation was one of the central themes of the Romantic poets and novelists a few centuries later. In 1896, Alice B. Stockham's *Karezza*, a popular marriage manual of the time, recommended psychological instead of physical consummation: "Given abundant time and mutual reciprocity, the [sexual] interchange becomes satisfactory and complete without crisis by either party. In the course of an hour, the physical tension subsides, the spiritual exaltation increases, and not uncommonly visions of a transcendent life are seen and consciousness of new powers experienced."

Sigmund Freud was well aware that barriers which blocked the sexual instinct from direct gratification heightened lust. Yet clearly the integration of love with lust requires something of a balance. Elsewhere one of us has written:

Our genitals and our psyches are inextricably linked by the seductive thread of taboo. We are constantly in a tug of war with our conscience—this tension can keep our impulses too tightly reined in, but it also provides much psychic release when we suddenly give in. Our fascination with the forbidden and the out of reach is not just a matter of our unresolved incestual wishes. *Every* secret carries within it the wish to conceal but also the captive wish to reveal. The tension between self-restraint and raw impulse is the taut instrument of our greatest pleasure, which needs constantly to be fine-tuned.

[BETCHER (1987), PP. 148–49]

Otto Kernberg has suggested that sexual passion arises from the "crossing of boundaries," by which he means bridging parts of the self that are separated by conflictually determined limits. Boundary crossing may involve the defiance of oedipal prohibitions as well as self-transcendence, and in healthy relationships is accompanied, paradoxically, by the formation of a new boundary that encloses the intimate, secret world of the couple. Kernberg believes that the liberation of aggression is inherent in intimate relationships because of what we have referred to as their seancelike property of calling forth repressed constellations from infancy and childhood. Inherent, too, in such wrestling matches with old ghosts and the defiance of old prohibitions is a sense of risk and danger. If it cannot be contained within a marriage or other intimate relation, it will be sought outside of it.

A man that one of us treated engaged in a series of highly intense, sexualized adventures, including dangerous excursions to parts of town known for violence and trips to foreign countries with severe political unrest. He needed to stimulate himself to relieve the inner deadness he felt because he had closed off all the pain of his childhood hurt and abandonment. He was able to maintain a dedicated intellectual connection in his marriage but it was devoid of any sexual excitement.

In the movie *Casanova 70*, Marcello Mastroianni plays a man who is only attracted to women whose conquest is dangerous. After a series of comic escapades courting other men's wives and evading their jealous husbands, he finally is able to get married. The only problem is that each night he must navigate from the bathroom to his bedroom by walking along a narrow window ledge high above the street.

Though both of these examples may seem extreme, seeking erotic stimulation through controlled risk may be intrinsic to men's sexuality. It may help explain the appeal of an extramarital affair or falling in love, for example, each of which constitutes a limited form of adventure. Robert Stoller describes how an erotic situation or "story"—whether remaining a fantasy or enacted in real life—is created:

> One function of a story written by oneself is to insure that the danger in mystery is transformed from an unknown that one cannot control to a danger controlled by the scenarist knowing he was in charge and wrote mystery into his own script. . . . The problem when constructing an erotic day-dream is how to maintain a sense of risk in the story while at the same time minimizing the risk. So one writes in safety factors that reduce danger to the illusion of danger. . . . It follows that these mechanisms (risk, illusion, mystery) will not only be present in the choice of objects one uses in making daydreams but also of those picked in the real world.
>
> [STOLLER (1976), PP. 906–07]

If there is too much danger, a man may become anxious and unable to perform sexually; if too little, he may lack desire. This may help explain why both Helen Singer Kaplan and Robert Stoller can both be right about the relation of hostility to eroticism—as with risk, there may be an optimal level that entices a man into sexual intimacies. How is it that this balance can be maintained, and in particular, how can men's aggressiveness in pleasure-seeking serve an intimate relationship and enhance both men's and women's sexual satisfaction?

A PLAYFUL BRIDGE
BETWEEN LOVE AND LUST

The ancient Greeks personified love in two ways—as Aphrodite, a surpassingly beautiful and lusty goddess, and as Eros, a mischievous boy with golden wings whose arrows can turn Stoic philosophers into dirty old men. While Eros's playfulness at times provokes more sober deities, who grumble about his irresponsibility, his magic is as powerful as it is capricious. The British object relations theorist Michael Balint saw this classical dichotomy as corresponding to a fundamental division between two kind of sexual gratification—"fore-pleasure" and "end-pleasure" (or orgasm). But what most intrigues us is that Grecian mythology should consider *playfulness* and boyish mischief intrinsic to romantic love.

Martin Buber distinguished between "I-Thou" and "I-It" relationships, which in sexual terms we would characterize as relations predominated by mutual awareness of each other's needs and self-transcendence compared to those in which the partner is largely a fetish, a dehumanized object used in the service of one's own pleasure. It is the rare individual who is able to fully transcend him or her self and who has no need to seek revenge for old traumas. Instead, most of us move back and forth between I-Thou and I-It relations. Lust starts in our deepest fantasy world, while love is driven by a yearning for fusion. If we are fortunate, as the poet Octavio Paz puts it, love reveals reality to desire. Along the way we must find ways to weave into our adult relations elements of our past that we need to commemorate or exorcise. We must walk a tightrope between present and past, between a self-centered focus on our own pleasure and an empathic awareness of our partner's needs. Play is our balancing bar.

In research conducted with young adult couples, one of us has found that intimate playfulness can provide a bridge between love and lust. Like lust, the spontaneous impulse to play begins deep in the memories and meanings of the individual. But, unlike lust, it is not stereotypically driven. Play is flexible, un-

predictable, creative. Playing is a reconnoitering of the unknown borders of two psyches, whose contours can become
reassuringly familiar only through the experience of mutual
vulnerability and nonjudgmental responsiveness. Through
playing we learn how to approach another person's more intimate self.

By intimate play we do not mean relatively formalized, rule-
bound recreational play, such as board games, sports, or danc-
ing, but rather the more idiosyncratic forms of playfulness that
evolve over time in a couple, such as private nicknames, shared
jokes and fantasies, and mock-fighting. Most of all, it is an
attitude, rather than a specific activity. For example:

> Richard and Laura are both lawyers. Their jobs are de-
> manding and, while exciting, require long hours and hard
> work. When they get home after a long day in court and at
> the office, letters still have to be drafted and cases have to be
> read. Even on weekends they find it hard to avoid meeting
> associates or potential clients. As a result, Richard and Laura
> began taking "special vacations," which have evolved into
> an annual event.
>
> The vacation is treated like an illicit affair. They tell no
> one where they are going and always go out of state, where
> they will not know anyone. They dress up in the evenings,
> eat out at expensive restaurants, indulge each other in roman-
> tic play, and enjoy a lot of creative sex. They keep to them-
> selves and rebuff attempts by other vacationing couples to
> get to know them. These vacations are so out of the ordinary
> for them that at the end of each one they jokingly say to one
> another, "Well, back to your husband," and "Back to your
> wife." Throughout the year Richard and Laura plan the next
> vacation elaborately and refer to it with a secretive, illicit air.
>
> [BETCHER (1981), P. 3]

In this fashion, the erotic ingredients of risk, illusion, nov-
elty, and mystery can become part of a committed love relationship rather than having to be split off from it. While men's
preferred modes of play are sports, we believe that their love of

one form of play may be translated into another, more intimate kind.

One of the things that men and women seek in an intimate relationship is a partner with whom they can feel free to reveal normally suppressed behavior, someone who can accept their being weak, childlike, and dependent because they can see these qualities as parts of themselves. They seek multiple pathways of being able to connect with each other. Foreplay is a metaphor for such wishes and a couple's success or failure in meeting each other's foreplay needs is a mirror of the relationship. In playful sexual relations each partner can at times use the other as a doll, enacting their own scenarios, whose hostility, in Stoller's words, becomes "subdued and graced by tolerance."

As with sports, men can look to sex as a score card, a chance to set records that will allay their self-doubts, or as ritual, in which, at its best, they lose themselves in play.

EROS AND PSYCHE

As men struggle to confirm their manhood in sex and yet retain their playful, boyish side, how is this integration of spontaneity with responsibility to be achieved? The fate of Eros in Greek myth offers one solution. According to Apuleius, Aphrodite was jealous of the mortal beauty of Psyche, so she orders Eros to cause her to fall in love with the most vile man he can find. Ever unreliable, Eros neglects his charge and falls in love with Psyche himself. Through a series of mishaps they are separated, with grave consequences for earthly love. As a talkative bird relates: " 'The result is,' screamed the gull, 'that Pleasure, Grace, and Wit have disappeared from the earth and everything there has become ugly, dull, and slovenly. Nobody bothers any longer about his wife, his friends, or his children; and the whole system of human love is in such complete disorder that it is now considered disgusting for anyone to show even natural affection.' " [Robert Graves (1951), pp. 122–23]

Aphrodite is enraged at Eros's disregard of her order, and she even considers having her natural enemy, Sobriety, clip Eros's wings once and for all. Eros throws himself on Jupiter's (Zeus's) mercy and Jupiter addresses the council of all Heavens:

> "Right honourable gods and goddesses . . . you all know the young fellow over there whom I have brought up from boyhood and whose passionate nature must, in my opinion, be curbed in some way or other. It is enough to remind you of the daily complaints that come in of his provoking someone or other of adultery or a similar crime. Well, I have decided that we must stop the young rascal from doing anything of the sort again by fastening the fetters of marriage securely upon him. He has found and seduced a pretty girl called Psyche, and my sentence is that he must have her, hold her, possess her, and cherish her from this time forth and evermore."
>
> [GRAVES (1951), PP. 141–42]

Well aware of the potential of unlimited playfulness for muddling human sexual relations as well as their dreariness without it, the Greek vision incorporated play into marriage, suggesting, perhaps, that each is enriched by the other.

9

▼

MEN AS FATHERS

Two young men are waiting for their wives to register in the hospital's labor and delivery department. In the casual intimacy of strangers, they reveal to each other their hopes for their first child. One says that he desperately wants a boy; the other, just as fervently, wants it *not* to be a boy.

Such wishes and fears reveal much about how men approach parenting. Men care about children and want to be important in their children's lives. It is hard, though, for many men to feel confident about becoming a father, especially if their images of their own fathers are foreboding or indistinct. For many men, becoming a father is like falling in love for the first time. His hard-earned autonomy is shaken by a powerful need for another person and a need to be needed. He feels ill-equipped to handle this new relationship, and while filled with hope he is quick to protect himself against disappointment. Just as men must learn how they need women, they must also learn how they need children.

As the child is father of the man, so, too, may the man be given the opportunity to be father to the child. In this endless cycle men receive their greatest second chance: to repair the damage caused by the premature loss of their earliest connections and so create a new legacy of male nurturance for generations to come.

Becoming a father—not merely the biological act of impreg-
nating—but the psychological acceptance of the caretaking role
within a family—is one of the most significant developmental
turning points of adult life. Poorly understood, and until recently given scant attention by researchers, this developmental
way station is both an opportunity and a crisis. The new father
remembers his own father—for better, and frequently for
worse—and he may learn from his own child a way to be a truly
different kind of man. As the family therapist Frank Pittman
suggests: "If a man, even a fatherless father, will let himself
learn from child-raising rather than just trying to control or
perfect his children, they can carry him through all of the stages
of human development from the other side and help make him
aware of how men and women develop, how masculinity and
femininity are taught and learned, and help him become a complete human being." [Pittman, 1992, p. 83]

In Chapter 4 we mentioned that the psychoanalyst, Heinz
Kohut has spoken of children's need for two chances to be
parented—a mirroring responsiveness and a protective nurturance. In this way, even the developmentally fated but traumatic
separation from mother can be assuaged by a loving connection
to a father. Without the safe harbor of father's love, the little
boy may turn into a man who has difficulty with any form of
deep intimacy.

Kohut, like many psychoanalytic thinkers, has overlooked
the opportunities for healing connections in later adult life. Just
as loving another adult man or woman is a chance to improve
upon one's early relationship with mother and father, fathering,
too, is a second chance. By taking care of his own son or
daughter a man may repair the hurt to his little-boy self, and in
so doing feel more intimately connected to the Special Woman
in his life. Although much has been written about the loss of
marital satisfaction in parenting, fathering may also provide a
bridge from his protective island of aloneness and help a man
to come back in from the cold.

The subtle nature of fathering as a second opportunity for
intimate connection is highlighted when men—for better or
worse—father in a second marriage. In this age of majority

remarriage, the parenting of two families in the same life cycle is no longer unusual. In a touchingly open editorial in *The New York Times* on Father's Day in 1991, one of the editors wrote about his experience of the "second round" of fatherhood. His first attempt had been "in the old-fashioned way—as a benevolent bystander." He and his family used to joke about the fact that he never changed a diaper. The day his wife was due to deliver, he dropped his wife off at the hospital and the doctor shooed him off to work. The birth was made known to him over the telephone. In retrospect, he realized that those years of fatherhood "seemed largely a void broken by a few sporadic memories." Indeed, his now-adult son, when asked what he remembered of his early experiences of his daddy, replied, "It was pathetically little." The father felt he had known his son least as a child—and loved him most as a young man.

Yet after divorce, remarriage, and the creation of a new family, our editor was willing to approach fatherhood by "tuning in, not out." This time, both he and his new wife had a career and older children to contend with and his new children were twins who had been born premature. He wrote, "As they struggled for breath and life in the intensive-care nursery, he came every day to root them on, cradle them in the crook of an arm, or deliver a vial of breast milk." Daily, their bonds grew stronger and he found that the more involved he became the more he learned the skills he required. Although he still feels at times that he is not as good a parent as he had wished to be and "no Mr. Mom," he is having fun and as his daughters approached their fourth birthday, he was enraptured by their beauty, their brilliance, and their individuality. Father's Day has taken on a new meaning: "For weeks now the girls have been preparing his Father's Day cards, and making sure they are in his favorite color. There will be no special trip to the zoo or the lake; it is not necessary. For this new and better age, Father's Day is not an annual event. It occurs daily."

Such attempts at becoming "involved" with their children are made by first-time as well as second-time fathers. In so

doing, they may escape the fate of Narcissus—searching endlessly for the mirror reflection of their own selves—or the plight
described by Aristophanes—wandering aimlessly without finding their lost halves.

We are clearly describing a very different kind of hero, whose
deeds are not immortalized in poets' song but written in the
sands where children build their castles. In a beautiful short
story by Amy Hempel about a father spending the day alone
with his two children, this notion of fathering is summed up by
the title: "Today Will Be a Quiet Day."

> They had already said good-night some minutes earlier
> when the boy and girl heard their father's voice in the dark.
> "Kids, I just remembered—I have some good news and
> some bad news. Which do you want first?"
> It was his daughter who spoke. "Let's get it over with,"
> she said. "Let's get the bad news over with."
> The father smiled. They are all right, he decided. My kids
> are as right as this rain. He smiled at the exact spots he knew
> their heads were turned to his, and doubted he would ever
> feel—not better, but *more* than he did now.
> "I lied," he said. "There is no bad news."
>
> [P. 129]

Fathering brings an undefinable "more" to men, and in this
sense, "There is no bad news." Unfortunately, there is a lot of
bad news about fathers past and about the difficulty men have
in becoming and staying involved with their families.

FALLEN FATHERS

Much like the best-sellers of our day, classical literature and
myth are replete with tales of "bad" fathers. The story of Oedipus highlights the cowardly attempt at infanticide of his father,

Laius. Frightened by the prophecy that his son will grow up to murder him, he takes preventive action by crippling his legs and exposing him on a mountainside. The tragic consequences for the family and for generations to come are the theme of Sophocles' plays, which we believe Freud misinterpreted as being merely the stuff of sons' unconscious fantasies.

Cronus, the father of Zeus, was said to have devoured all of his own children as soon as they left their mother's womb because he, too, was informed that he was destined to have his kingdom overthrown by his own son.

Tantalus, sometimes seen as the son of Zeus, was an intimate friend of the gods and freely admitted to their table. However, he abused their divine favor by killing his own son and serving him as a meal to the gods as a test of their powers of observation. For this heinous act he received the punishment in the underworld that explains his name. He sat endlessly in a pool of water that receded from him whenever he tried to drink from it, and simultaneously lay beneath beautiful fruit branches that were always kept just out of his reach. From this poignant story of a man so close to fulfillment that he could almost taste and touch it, yet condemned never to achieving it, we derive the word "tantalize." What could be a more fitting homily for modern fathers, who, in their own failure to take care of their sons and daughters, are condemned to live out their lives within their family but not part of it, fulfillment tantalizingly out of reach?

In a poignant passage of the *Iliad*, Homer describes how Hector, a heroic man of war, attempts to embrace his infant son:

> . . . *Hektor held out his arms*
> *to take his baby. But the child squirmed round*
> *on the nurse's bosom and began to wail*
> *terrified by his father's great war helmet—*
> *the flashing bronze, the crest with horse plume*
> *tossed like a living thing at everything at every nod.*
> *His father began laughing, and his mother*
> *laughed as well, then from his handsome head*

Hektor lifted off his helmet and bent
to place it, bright with sunlight, on the ground.
When he had kissed his child and swung him high
to dandle him, he said this prayer:
"O Zeus
and all immortals, may this child, my son,
become like me a prince among the Trojans.
Let him be strong and brave and rule in power
and Ilion; then someday men will say
'This fellow is far better than his father' "
[FITZGERALD, TRANS., BOOK 6,
LL. 541–57]

It is only when a man can take off his armoring that he can hold his child. By tempering his warrior spirit, he can lovingly wish *for* rather than fear being surpassed *by* his son. This enlarged capacity to feel more than rage and shame is akin to Achilles' transformation through grief. It is the type of rage turned into sadness that Robert Bly has described as a necessity for men. They must open themselves up to feelings in order to parent: ". . . who is the man locked inside the oakwomb? / A dangerous man; and there is a grief man . . ." [Bly, *Selected Poems*, p. 125]

In the biblical traditions of fathers and their children, we have noted the ambivalent connections between men. The struggles between Cain and Abel and their father-god, the binding of Isaac and Abraham's devotion to his god, the squabbling between Jacob and Esau for their father, Jacob's blessing—all represent the highly charged, rageful connections between fathers and their children. Yet throughout these stories there is a common thread—one call and one response that echo through the generations. God, the father, or the father to the son, calls out: "Where are you?" And the son answers in the ancient Hebrew, "*Henani*," or "Here I am."

Where indeed are the fathers of today, where should they be in relation to the family, and are they answering their children's cry for their fathers with a firm but tender "Here I am"?

A SHORT HISTORY OF AMERICAN FATHERHOOD

For those of us who came of age after World War II and the years surrounding the Kennedy presidency, a larger-than-life image of fathers looms. These were the days of Ozzie and Harriet and when Father Knew Best. Father was a distant "organization man" who joined us at dinner and to whom the whole family paid homage by never questioning his authority. He was a distant protector and provider and sometime disciplinarian. He could be placed upon a pedestal and seen as heroic through the distorting lenses of wish and distance. But now the fall of this idol has invited an equally unfair shower of invective. The "heroic" father of the fifties and sixties has become the *pater familias* of a dysfunctional, abusive, paternalistic, codependent family. And so the idealizing of father has led to a persecution of "bad" men.

Men's feet of clay must be seen within a realistic historical context of fathering to understand how male roles have been shaped by social forces within and outside the family.

John Demos, the social historian, has pointed out in an essay on the history of fatherhood that in Colonial times fathers were teachers who were woven into the fabric of domestic and productive life. Since most fathers were either tradesmen or farmers, home and work were integrally combined and their children worked closely with them day-to-day. With the industrial movement of the nineteenth and early twentieth century, fathers disappeared. Advice books on parenting and all aspects of family life were directed specifically toward mothers. Fathers became the distant toilers in the land of work, now far from the hearth of parenting. This was the beginning of what Alexander Mitscherlich described as the society without a father, in which fathers were vague shadows, alienated from wives and children. He became the idealized, omniscient authority or the "boogy man" who arrived too little and too late to give emotional sustenance. We unconsciously created an ideal hero for his children, perhaps especially for his sons—a distant, mysterious figure who could not come in from the cold. Behind all the bluster of patriarchal bellowings, this father who knew best was often bested by his wife and his children and was depicted in the media of his day as an incompetent bumbler and imposter. For while fathers appeared to be revered, their lack of meaningful contact with family life relegated them to being a kind of beneficent uncle who provided for physical needs but was essentially a visitor. Many of the men who are trying to father today grew up with just such elusive male presences. One man told us that he remembers as a young child waiting on his tricycle at the end of his block for his father's car to appear at dinnertime. He would then race him back to the house. But as the years passed, he came to know his father less and less and by college they had become strangers.

As late as the 1970s, Michael Lamb, the infant and family researcher, decried our lack of understanding of the role of fathers in the family. He described fathers as "the forgotten contributors to child development." In fact, the first research on fathers' impact on their sons and daughters was on father absence and father abuse—that is, how fathers fail as parents. Just as economic and historical forces had shifted fathers to the periphery of the family, researchers had also colluded in the unconscious myth of father as emotional eunuch.

THE RETURN OF THE FATHER

During the era of the silent father, men had been seen as septic intruders into the birthing process. But increasingly over the last fifteen years the impregnator and provider has come to be a partner with his wife from the prenatal period through delivery and onward. Research has shown that the birth of the baby and of the man as father are intertwined and that many men are "swept off their feet" by their feelings toward their newborn.

As fathers came into the arena of developmental study, it

also became clear that they were not just additional mothers—they had a unique, masculine form of play, of visual and physical stimulation, and of nurturant attachment to their children. It also struck researchers that the presence of fathers not only had a direct impact on their children's growth; it also had subtle effects on the family as a whole through their involvement with their wives as mothers. So, too, did mothers affect their children's development through their connection with their husbands and their support for them as fathers.

Almost without exception, research has shown that fathers still spend an extremely small period of the day with their children, even when they are highly involved. While fathers are spending somewhat more time than in the past, the lion's share almost always falls to the mother. Women often lament that while their husbands may participate in child care more than in the past, men still do not feel *responsible* for parenting. When a child is sick, it is expected that the wife will stay home from work or arrange for child care, and it is the woman who remembers that it's time to visit the dentist or to get the child new clothes. True, a father may do all these things, but they are rarely in the forefront of his consciousness as they are for his wife. If he does make a contribution to child care, he wants it to be recognized; the wife's efforts more likely are taken for granted.

In the movie *Boyz'n the Hood*, the mother tells her ex-husband that she appreciates that as primary parent he has done a good job teaching her son how to be a man. But then she chides him about thinking so much of himself: "All you've done is what mothers have been doing for years. You may be cute, but you're not special."

We are reminded of Odysseus's yearning to return home, a wish that embodied both his longings for his wife and for his son. Recall that Odysseus did not count on his family welcoming him back—he tested his wife and son and his father carefully before revealing his identity. In our own time, too, like Odysseus, men are attempting to reenter the family after a long absence, and reentry is rarely smooth.

THE BALANCING ACT

The Boston University Pregnancy and Parenthood project (BUPP) was a large-scale longitudinal study of approximately one hundred couples, beginning during the expectancy period of their first child and continuing through a five-year follow-up study.[1] The men were interviewed several times and observed in their home at play with their children. In addition, they filled out several standardized rating forms that were scored independently.

It turned out that successful fathering and marital satisfaction were most related to maintaining a balance between *affiliation* and *autonomy*—that is, between solid connections to significant others and self-focused achievement. These findings stood in stark contrast to a more traditional view of autonomy as opposite to affiliation.

From our perspective, autonomy refers to a view of the self as separate or distinct from others, participation in and enjoyment of activities that are carried out alone, and a sense of valuing the "separate" part of the self as important to one's self-esteem and development. Affiliation is defined as a view of oneself as connected to others in important ways, participation in and enjoyment of responsive, mutual relationships in which the individual still retains a sense of separate identity and values the "related" part of the self as important to one's development and self-esteem.

An example of a man in the research who could be scored high on both autonomy and affiliation was Greg. In speaking about his wife and children he said: "My wife is really warm, she can handle herself really well, which I really like. The marriage is

[1] The Boston University Pregnancy and Parenthood project was a longitudinal study under the direction of Francis K. Grossman. The work on father autonomy and affiliation was done by William Pollack in collaboration with Francis Grossman and his colleagues, Ellen Golding and Nikki Fedele. See Pollack, 1981, 1983; Grossman, Pollack, Golding, Fedele, 1987; Grossman, Pollack, and Golding, 1988. For details on the larger study, see Eichler, Winnickoff et al., 1980, and Pollack and Grossman, 1985.

really important to me. I also love being with my daughter. Saturday morning is our special time. But it's also important to me to have my own time—to read, to think by myself. Being alone makes me feel refreshed and more complete."

The perspective offered here is one of *complementarity*—autonomy is related to but not defined solely by participation in separate activities, and affiliation is not just a matter of engaging in relationships. Gerald Stechler and Sam Kaplan, two child psychoanalysts who built on the work of George Klein, defined the beginning sense of self in children and its later integrated form in adults as a combination of two apparently disparate aspects that must be integrated into one identity. They saw these two poles as the self being felt as an autonomous center of activity versus the self as part of a transcendent unit. They called the autonomous pole the "I" component and the more affiliate pole the "We" component. We agree with Stechler and Kaplan that the self can simultaneously be separate and part of an entity greater than itself. In our work, when we talk about autonomy we are referring to the sense of the "I" within the self and when we talk about affiliation we are referring to the sense of the "We" embedded with the independent self.

Although the autonomy-affiliation balance was important for women as well as men, men's definition of what is affiliative and what is autonomous differs radically from women's, and any attempt to measure these two concepts requires awareness of these basic differences. For example, the men in the study would often show a strong proclivity to be close to their children but would express this by physical play or teaching. Women appeared to be more comfortable in holding and hugging their children. We felt, however, that both of these types of interactions were evidence of affiliative capacities. Indeed, the children's responsiveness to these very different parenting styles corroborated this.

We need to recognize that there is a *his* autonomy and a *her* autonomy, a *his* intimacy and a *her* intimacy, to read between the lines when each seems to be speaking the same language.

The BUPP study also found that in more traditional family structures in which women were the primary parent, men shied away from competing with them. But when the mother was incapacitated fathers were able to lend support. Such complementary roles can sometimes exclude the man from emotional connection and load up his wife with too much responsibility, but they need not exile the man to an insignificant role. Many of these men were highly invested in their careers. Yet the fathers who reported that they were involved with and successful in their work (and therefore spent somewhat less time with their children) tended to be better able to support their child's autonomy and affiliation. Our findings suggest that the *quality* of the time that fathers spent with their children was what most mattered for their children's growth. One colleague of ours, an extremely busy physician, always sets aside time for breakfast with his son on Sunday mornings. It is a special "daddy-son time," never violated by anything other than extreme emergency or illness. Although there is no doubt that more hours like this spent together would be even better, both father and son feel a special bond through this breakfast club of two.

The BUPP study suggests that good fathers had learned to parent well from their own memories of parental nurturance and by observing their wives with whom they came to identify. Learning from their wives offered another chance for repair, in this case for the couple. It increases men's empathy for women's nurturing capacities and may help undo much of the old trauma that caused men to create such distance from women. When men are able to value what women do, particularly in their roles of mother, and to identify with it, it helps undo at the deepest unconscious layers the dread about being dependent upon women, of being close to them. It diminishes the defensive need to not *be* somehow like a woman.

THE CALL OF FATHERING

A man may sense atavistic promptings to be a father in the same way that women may feel a biological urge to become mothers. At least, studies of nonhuman primates suggest that a predisposition for caretaking is latent in the male, waiting to be stimulated by a child. William Redican, in a review on male parental care in monkeys and apes, has found that the range of behavior toward immature primates by nonhuman male primates is great. In addition to defending infants or the mother from predators, according to William Redican, such nonhuman primate fathers have been shown to assist with birth; to premasticate infants' food; and to carry, sleep with, groom, and play with the young. In some instances, they can become primary caretakers of orphans.

Male caretaking is most extensive in monogamous primates and depends upon the extent to which mothers or other female caretakers restrict or allow male involvement with their infants. In addition, when rhesus infants are reared by adult males in the absence of mothers, extensive attachment to the males ensues.

Our historical focus on father absence and father loss may have caused us to lose sight of how much being a caring father lies at the heart of men's psychological being. As the poet Robert Bly has written:

> . . . and slowly the kind man comes closer, loses his rage, sits
>   down at table.
> So I am proud only of those days that pass in undivided
>   tenderness,
> when you sit drawing, or making books, stapled, with
>   messages to the world,
> of coloring a man with fire coming out of his hair.
> Or we sit at a table, with small tea carefully poured.
> So we pass our time together, calm and delighted.
>
> [BLY (1986), "FOR MY SON NOAH,
> TEN YEARS OLD"]

Alan, a man interviewed in the BUPP study, said of his one-year-old daughter:

> It has been a lot of fun to watch her grow but at the same time it is a lot of responsibility. . . . I just had never been

around babies, and I didn't know. I just didn't have any idea
of what being a father was all about. . . . And I am really
attached. I find myself thinking about her at work, rushing
to the day-care center to pick her up, just because every day
she learns something new and you just want to see it and
kind of share it with her.

My personality has changed a lot. I take things a little
slower. I think about her more. I guess when you decide to
have a baby, you don't think about those things. You don't
think your life is really going to change. All of a sudden,
you've got to be somebody's *father*! It is different, but it's
fun.

Neil, an adjunct professor at a university in Boston, spoke
about his intimate connection with his young son. His wife is
working part-time and Neil is a first-time father who is actively
involved in child care:

One of the things that's most striking in our family is that
our son has no preference for his mother or me. Both of us
can do what he needs. . . . Often in other families the kid is
crying and Dad tries to pick him up, and that just doesn't
work. But I can soothe him just as easily, and that's because
I was very involved with him from the beginning.

Neil has shifted the nature of his work as a result of his new
role as a parent. For him, the trade-offs are worth it:

For me, being a parent has helped me get away from a
self-centeredness . . . My sense of identity feels much more
complete now. Just being a professor and researcher is pretty
shallow compared to being a parent!

[*BOSTON GLOBE MAGAZINE*, OCTOBER 27, 1991, P. 14]

We are seeing here the dynamic shift that fathering can bring
about in men's development, a shift in values and in emotional
perception that will affect all their intimate relationships. As
Robert Weiss suggests, in *Staying the Course*: "Fatherhood helps

men make sense of their lives. It helps them understand why they work [so] hard."

Perhaps, the concept of *working* at being a father and the *work* of nurturant care-giving is a good way to conceptualize what parenting may mean to men. In our generation of fathering, men have to go against the grain of their own upbringing to acquire new skills. It also may be more acceptable to men to think of this as work—an effortful, masculine endeavor with which they are familiar. Yet what is missing is a sense of play. *In fathering, men have an opportunity to join their inner sense of duty with their wish to remain little boys*—to play and work at the same time.

DUAL CAREER, DUAL PROBLEMS

Shifts in the day-to-day role of fathering are occurring at the same time as women have returned to the work force. The renewed involvement of fathers must take place in the context of a renegotiated contract between husbands and wives about their roles as parents and providers. As Rhona Rapoport and her colleagues put it:

Every family lives with a degree of imbalance, of unresolved conflict and discord over . . . issues. The tasks confronting parents today are less centered on "fitting in" to the traditional pattern of their forebears than on working out new patterns that will suit them and their situation. This involves the ability to resolve conflicts and disagreements repeatedly, and to continue to seek enjoyment even though there are residues of unresolved issues.

[RAPOPORT (1977), P. 19]

The research on dual-career couples suggests that the relationship of fathers' participation in the home to dual careers and marital happiness is complex. Many studies point to the fact that working wives are happier when their husbands help out with housework and child-rearing. More intriguing is the finding that husbands, too, are often happier in their marriages when they are active in the home, although they are concerned about the effects on their careers.

McHale and Crouter, psychologists at Pennsylvania State University, found that in dual-career families in which the mother does almost all of the housework, boys have lower self-esteem and more problems in school than boys in families who could observe their fathers doing more house chores. The researchers suggest that "what happens is that the mothers in these families are unhappy because they're doing all the work. And since the kids are predominantly involved with their mothers, they become unhappy, too."

Perceived choice is an important mediating factor in determining how dual-career marital arrangements work out: when wives feel they have a choice about working outside the home and husbands feel they can determine the extent of their involvement in child care, marriages are happier. Marital happiness also is a result of whether partners' attitudes about work and child care are consistent with what they actually do. Finally, both men and women require that there be some measure of equity, although how they conceive of this is influenced by gender: Yogev and Brett report that employed women were happier in their marriages if they felt their husbands were doing a fair share of work in the home, while husbands' marital satisfaction was related to whether they thought their wives were doing *more* than they themselves were doing!

In a study on the marital effects of parental work and child-care responsibilities, which one of us co-authored, we raised the question as to whether families in which mothers worked full-time outside the home might, ironically, run into the same kinds of problems as in "traditional" arrangements where mothers stayed at home. In the traditional marriages, couples reported in their fifties that they had "come to inhabit a very separate world" from their spouses. While their husbands had devoted themselves to their career, these women often felt "imprisoned" in their home and became depressed. As Richard Schwartz and his colleagues remarked: "Often these couples seemed not to realize that, through this specialization, they had embarked on separate trajectories in their lives. Often the sense of raising children as a mutual task, one that could bind a couple together over a lifetime, was lost early on. By the time the children were grown, the couple had drifted irrevocably apart." [Schwartz, et al., p. 4]

We wondered if the same loss of a shared task might occur in families in which mothers worked full-time, whether or not the child-rearing was taken up by the husband or delegated to a child-care worker. Interestingly, we found that it was the husbands of the part-time and not the full-time working wives who spent the most time caring for their children, suggesting that part-time working wives may provide husbands with a model that they are drawn to emulate. These husbands described mutuality as central to how their marriages worked.

ROLE STRAIN

The psychologist Joseph Pleck has suggested that "sex role strain" is a more appropriate term than "sex role identity" to describe men's struggles about gender. That is, making the grade as a man has less to do with fitting in to a culturally prescribed model than with how he handles the stress inherent in not fitting a stereotype. For instance, men are now trying to reconstruct their macho image in the light of demands on them to be nurturant caretakers of their children, and within a social context of mothering that is itself undergoing massive socioeconomic change. Often men have little emotional and practical support to buffer these stresses. For one thing, while new mothers tend to enlarge their social network by contact with other mothers, men tend to have *less* contact with other men. It is not just that male friendship may be felt as a lower priority than work and family—sadly, men are not familiar with reaching out and sharing their fathering experiences with other men.

One high-powered Los Angeles attorney and father of two young children, John Kronstadt, has struggled painfully with the tensions between "world-class career" and "world-class fathering": "The male feels not just conflicts, but intense pressures. . . . Society hasn't lowered its level of job performance, but it has raised its expectations of our roles in our children's lives." [*New York Times Magazine*, April 13, 1986, p. 48]

Many men feel caught in this maelstrom of social change regarding their fathering. One corporate executive, Russ Yarrow, has taken over a lot of child-care chores to help his wife return to work. However, he feels that this attempt at a balanced mothering/fathering alliance is often overlooked and he is angry: "I think men do just as much as women . . . Yet all the media attention is on Working Moms and Super Moms. I think the emerging issue of the nineties is the working Dad!" [*Fortune*, September 24, 1990, p. 134]

Even though men's involvement in fathering is increasing, the media and scientific literature are replete with criticism of men for not taking on more responsibility for such homework and for not tempering career ambitions in favor of family presence. Yet side by side with this demand for more father involvement is a bias that men who do take on nontraditional roles are somehow dysfunctional or effeminate. We continue to look with suspicion on a man who spends less time working than his wife, or who (heaven forbid) makes less money than she does.

Kyle Pruett, a research psychoanalyst at the Yale Child Study Center, has been studying a group of families in which the husband and wife have switched traditional roies. They have made an agreement that the father would take care of the children while the mother was primary breadwinner. Contrary to traditional fears, their children did not suffer from confused gender identity. Speaking about the now eight- to ten-year-olds, Pruett comments:

> It's not that they have conflicts about their gender identity—
> the boys are masculine and the girls are feminine, they're all
> interested in the same things their friends are. . . . But when
> they were four or five, for instance, the stage at preschool

when the girls leave the doll corner and the boys leave the block corner, these children didn't go to one or the other. The boys spent time playing with the girls in the doll corner, and the girls were building things with blocks, taking pride in their accomplishments.

[*NEWSWEEK*, MAY 28, 1990, P. 65]

In fact, Pruett felt that this nontraditional family arrangement seemed to leave the children more relaxed about their gender roles: "I saw the boys really enjoy their nurturing skills. . . . They knew what to do with the baby, they didn't see that as a girl's job, they saw it as a human job. I saw the girls have very active images of the outside world and what their mothers were doing in the workplace. . . ."

Interestingly, Pruett points out that these primary fathers did not function as "mother substitutes" but had a distinct nurturant and care-giving style. Their nurturant qualities are inherently masculine in spite of their nontraditional role. These "male mothers" are not mothers at all, but, rather, men integrating fathering into a new version of a masculine self. Pruett has argued that he has seen fathers benefit as much from taking care of the children as the children have clearly benefited from having their fathers as their caretakers: "The more involved father tends to feel differently about his own life. . . . A lot of men, if they're on the fast track, know a lot about competitive relationships, but they don't know much about intimate relationships. Children are experts in intimacy. After a while the wives in my study say, 'He's just a nicer guy.' " [*Newsweek*, May 28, 1990, p. 65]

In a recent poll done by *The Boston Globe* in November 1991, the overwhelming majority of parents named family and children as their most significant priority, ahead of personal love life, career, financial security, or leisure activities. Indeed, 81 percent of all the fathers said that the family came first. Both fathers and mothers polled found their families more satisfying than their jobs and close to 40 percent of fathers, when asked the question "If you had more free time, which of the following would you more likely do," listed at the top of their list "Spend more time with my children." And yet, while 84 percent of working mothers felt that their employers were somewhat responsive to their needs as parents *only 46 percent* of working fathers felt that their wishes to be fathers were responded to in the workplace.

A *Wall Street Journal* article (February 12, 1992) entitled "Men Find More Ways to Spend Time at Home" reported that nearly half of the sample of two hundred large company executives who were surveyed by Robert Half International stated that "managers aren't as willing to work long hours as they were five years ago." Yet it was pointed out that very few of these companies encourage workers, particularly men, to seek a flexible schedule, and so therefore "more men are finding informal ways to spend more time with their families." One mill manager who shifted his schedule to balance his wife's part-time work now cares for his infant daughter during part of the day and welcomes his six-year-old child when she comes back from school. He finds it very stressful at times but feels "*my children will know their father.*"

In addition to societal forces, men's insecurities may impede their return to the home as fathers. One study by Thomas J. DeLong and Camille Collett DeLong at Brigham Young University found that highly competent managers often feel *incompetent* in managing their relationships with their children. They quoted one man as saying: "I know exactly what to do to become CEO. It is very clear. But who sets goals for family and children?" [*Wall Street Journal*, September 12, 1991, p. 131] Work/Family Directions, a Boston consulting and research organization, has pointed out that in its surveys male managers have experienced a doubling from 1985 to 1988 of work/family conflicts, and they feel that the increase is continuing. As one executive said: "It's harder to go from being a high-level manager down to being the daddy of toddlers." One man pointed out that he needed certain reminders from his wife: "My wife would remind me, 'You're not at work right now. You're not the director here. You're a father and a husband.' " This he found a helpful form of confrontation.

In the BUPP study we found that fathers' capacity to express nurturance is directly related to their ability to call upon memories of their own fathers having been nurturant with them. These men seemed to do better overall—at their jobs as well as at home. It may be that good fathering is similar to the managerial style necessary in a modern participative organization: balancing self-starting (autonomy) and team support (affiliation) in a leadership role. It is often suggested that men need to expand their capacity for intimacy for women's sake. But autonomy is not sufficient for men's well-being; they need affiliative connection as well.

Rosalind Barnett and Nancy Marshall, at the Wellesley Center for Research on Women, have studied close to two hundred married fathers living in the suburbs of Massachusetts. The only factor that significantly correlated with the physical health of the men was their having a good relationship with their children. Significantly, there was *no* correlation between the health of these men studied and their work or marital roles.

THE GIFT OF THE MAGI

Sometimes unconscious expectations based on deeply ingrained gender roles may impede fathers from taking up their new task of parenting.

In the Boston University Pregnancy and Parenting study we found that the mother could become an inadvertent *gatekeeper*, keeping her newborn babies from her husband. This was usually subtle, such as handing the baby to the father at an inopportune moment and then saying, "Oh, dear, don't hold her like that," or "That isn't the way to change a diaper." Often the father, who already felt inadequate, would unconsciously collude by hastily giving the baby to his wife and then backing off. With men and women increasingly invading each other's traditional "turf," it is understandable that women may feel inclined to maintain some control over the household, especially over parenting. This may entail significant strain and sacrifice, particularly for career-oriented women, who are unable to draw upon their husbands to help them manage the burdens of work and home.

On the father's side, we noticed a parallel unconscious process, occurring around the birth of the newborn and into the child's first year, which we called *nest-feathering*. The new father often felt that the best way to provide for his wife and child was to work assiduously in order to gain greater income or career status—to "feather the nest" that the young fledgling and his caring maternal parent were placed in. However, what we found that most distressed women in the study was the emotional absence of their husbands during this expectancy period. So, much like the O'Henry story "The Gift of the Magi," the husband was sacrificing for the wife, and the wife for the husband, in ways that were terribly out of sync.

Our advice to these new fathers was that they spend some of their time supporting their wife and newborn by being physically and emotionally present and we suggested to their wives that they try to facilitate their husbands' learning how to take care of the newborn. We believe that men need to accept that their wifes can "mentor" them in some nurturing skills. At the same time, they also need their wives to recognize that "male" ways of parenting can be a valuable complement to mothering. The research shows that children who have the opportunity to have two healthy and different parents are more resilient in later life.

Couples should negotiate and frequently renegotiate their psychological contract of marriage and parenting. One couple became upset after the birth of their child shifted the nature of their time spent together. They sat down and made lists of their tasks and were able to detect unfair burdens that tended to sap their already depleted emotional resources. They could then redefine who should do what for whom and felt not only more productive but more supported by each other.[2]

When gatekeeping occurs it is important for the man to speak

[2]See findings reported in W.S. Pollack, "Managers as Fathers," in the *Levinson Letter*, 1991.

up for his needs as a father and for the woman to understand her unconscious feelings of precious motherhood, but to leave space for the father as well.

These "dos and don'ts" of fathering imply that while good fathering may be reparative for men, fathering itself may be repaired when necessary. One of the consequences of male-role socialization is a severe inability to identify and describe their own feelings, especially those of warmth, caring, sadness, and pain. The psychologist Ronald Levant relates this to the psychopathological disorder of *alexithymia*, a Greek word that means the inability to connect words with feelings. Levant believes that many men experience their feelings as an undifferentiated "buzz" that is vaguely unpleasant in part because it feels so unknown to them. The good news is that he found that fathers could dramatically enhance their fathering skills through videotape feedback of role plays between father and child and teaching fathers to keep a diary in which they recorded their feelings.

The success of such a psychoeducational approach suggests that good fathering need not be a rare commodity that is limited to those lucky few who had ideal fathers and mothers growing up. As with sex education, which must overcome the barrier of shame that men especially feel for not being "expert," we must find ways to speak to men in common-sense and respectful ways about fathering that demystifies it and treats it as skills that can be learned.

GOOD-ENOUGH FATHERING

The psychoanalyst Therese Benedek has used the word "fatherliness," by which she means an instinctually rooted trait that is characterized by empathic responsiveness to one's children and which she believes originates in the man's earliest memory traces of mother and father. When fully realized, with all their joys and sorrows, such parenting relationships immeasurably expand a man's appreciation of the complex value of relationships.

But we wish to define fatherliness as extending beyond the close-touch world of caring for one's own children. Just as a man's sense of duty to his family must transcend the obsessional tyranny of "shoulds," a man's fathering capacity must include a concern for others that is realized in some concrete fashion. James Redfield, in analyzing the tragic theme of the Achilles-Agamemnon feud in the *Iliad*, points to the fragility of what the Greeks conceptualized as the *polis*—the duty to care for one's community. Having lost touch with their responsibility for their people, from whom all genuine authority must flow, these "heroic" leaders were doomed to a tragic end. As Aristotle put it, "The man who is incapable of working in common, or who in his self-sufficiency has no need of others, is no part of the community, like an animal, or a god." The modern ideal, like that of the ancient Greeks, must be one of men who can temper their hubris and narcissism and make a commitment to a common good.

A father who cares only for his own son or daughter but who cares little else for others cannot possibly be inculcating a kind of reparative experience in his family and in himself that was lost for many men in premature separation from a loving connection. This capacity must go beyond selfishness, beyond a narrowly defined family loyalty. Families and family values cannot survive in isolation from the community, which, for better or worse, casts its shadow on even the most private relations of our lives. To deny how deeply our community affects our family or to ignore responsibility to care about our connections to the other private worlds nearby, which we may know only by their public face, inevitably means to lose our way. We cannot care for others in the same measure as we care for our own family, but it is important that we care.

Whether or not a man has his own children, he may become a good father through giving to neighbors, relatives, or young apprentices at work. We are referring here to a caring, mentoring role with younger people during the midlife stage of development that Erik Erikson called "generativity." It is a time when the more "feminine" aspects of the self—deep emotional expression, care-giving, nurturance, and romantic love—come to the surface and when the growing recognition of death leads to the attempt to shape a legacy.

George Vaillant, whose landmark study of the Harvard classes of 1940–1942 has followed these high-achieving men through their life cycles, sees the middle years as a time when the most well-adjusted men in his sample became more altruistic. A type of *husbanding* of relationships ensues: "It can be getting more involved with your . . . children or delighting in your [children] and encouraging them to flourish, coaching Little League, getting a church group off the ground." [*New York Times*] It is also a time when men can begin to *mentor* and express fatherliness beyond the family system. It is a way of using oneself beyond the boundaries of oneself and one's selfish needs. Dr. Robert Michels, chairman of the Psychiatry Department at Cornell Medical School, has commented: "You gain a kind of symbolic immortality by furthering a group you belong to, or cause you identify with. . . . If people are reasonably mature at middle age, they no longer experience their ideals and ambitions in a limited personal sense, but in a larger perspective. They are less concerned with their own striving, and more interested in the meaning of their lives and in *touching the lives around them*." [*New York Times*]

George Vaillant has aptly pointed out that it is hard to give something away until you have already received something yourself. You can't draw very much from a depleted reservoir. Still, we believe that all forms of fathering—biological, adoptive, and mentoring—provide men's greatest second chance. It is their second opportunity to get *and* give, to receive by giving more than they were ever able to give before, indeed, more than they ever received. In so doing, the cycles of child and father, father and child do not so much replicate themselves as generate renewed opportunities for good fathering. Duty and play can come together: as one fathers, one can experience the child within, and the growing and changing man without, with a renewed sense of self-esteem and vigor. Like Hector when he

took off his warrior shield and armoring, such men can bring
their children comfort and can genuinely pray for the greater
good of their families without any fear of narcissistic infringe-
ment or preoccupation. As one late-blooming father described
his domestic feats: "It's not a bad thing to get up in the night
and calm somebody down and get back in bed. *You feel sort of
like a hero.*" [*The Boston Globe,* June 19, 1992]

The child psychoanalyst D. W. Winnicott used the term
"good-enough mother" to refer to a *je ne sais quoi* that mothers
can trust in themselves in caring for their children. We would
like to apply the same notion to fathers. By *good-enough fathering*
we mean to encompass both the biological aspects of fatherhood, the more far-reaching aspects of fatherliness that Benedek
described, and Erikson's generativity.[3]

As in so many respects, Homer's *Odyssey* captures in an
encounter between two men a complex psychological process
occurring *within* all men. Odysseus, having returned to his
home disguised as an old beggar, is restored by the goddess,
Athene, to the prime of his manhood. When his son, Telemachus, who has witnessed this transformation, thinks him to be
a god, Odysseus answers him:

*"No, I am not a god. Why liken me to the immortals?
But I am your father, for whose sake you are always grieving
as you look for violence from others, and endure hardships."
So he spoke, and kissed his son, and the tears running
down his cheeks splashed on the ground. Until now, he was always
    unyielding.
But Telemachos, for he did not believe that this was
his father, spoke to him once again in answer, saying:
"No, you are not Odysseus my father, but some divinity
beguiles me, so that I must grieve the more, and be sorry . . .
For even now you were an old man in unseemly clothing,
but now you resemble one of the gods who hold high heaven."
Then resourceful Odysseus spoke in turn and answered him:*

[3]See F. Grossman and W. Pollack, "Good-Enough Fathering," paper presented at the National Council on Family Relations annual meeting, 1984; and
M. Diamond, 1991.

*"Telemachos, it does not become you to wonder too much
at your own father when he is here, nor doubt him. No other
Odysseus than I will ever come back to you. But here I am,
and I am as you see me, and after hardships and suffering
much I have come, in the twentieth year, back to my own
country . . ."*

[LATTIMORE, TRANS., BOOK 16, LL. 187–206]

The "old man in unseemly clothing" and "one of the gods
who hold wide heaven"—these are the historical caricatures of
fathers with which men are still saddled. Both fathers and sons
wish for godlike fathers but fear that they will only find unseemly ones. As with the two fathers in labor and delivery, one
of whom longed for a son and the other who feared to have
one, these fears and wishes are deep within all men. Fathers and
sons must come to terms with their idealizations and their bitter
disappointments to encounter each other in life-sized terms. To
be a "good-enough father" oneself and to feel that one's father
was "good enough" is to make peace with limitations, to recon-
cile, and to find a way to love. Not impossibly perfect, not
irredeemably "bad," but good enough and still trying to change.
Here is where the long and painful search for the missing father
finally can end:

*So he spoke, and sat down again, but now Telemachos
folded his great father in his arms and lamented,
shedding tears, and desire for mourning rose in both of them;
and they cried shrill in a pulsing voice, even more than the outcry
of birds, ospreys or vultures with hooked claws, whose children
were stolen away by the men of the fields, before their wings
   grew
strong; such was their pitiful cry and the tears their eyes wept.*

[LATTIMORE, TRANS., BOOK 16, LL. 213–19]

10

▼

THE RE-CREATION OF MASCULINITY

The attitude that the other sex has a fatal flaw must be replaced by a language of valued differences. This cannot happen until men truly accept the new woman as distinctly different from the "castrating bitch" they have feared in the past. It also cannot happen until men can convince themselves and women that a man's only choices are not to be a "prick" or a "wimp." We believe that a new man is ready to emerge from his seemingly hard but fragile shell. The new man will have a more flexible approach to love and work and power. He will be strong but tender and more respectful of women's needs and of his own. He will have a richer language with which to talk to women about both their needs and it will be a language that is distinctly his own.

THE LAST HERO

According to myth, Cleomedes of Astypalaea was an exceptional athlete who accidentally killed his opponent in an Olympic boxing competition. For this reason, his prize was denied to him. He returned home and, mad from grief, he pulled down a pillar that supported the roof of a school, killing sixty children. The citizens of Astypalaea began to stone him, so he took refuge inside a wooden chest in the shrine of Athena. But when the people were finally able to break open the planks, Cleomedes had disappeared. Envoys were sent to Delphi to ask for guidance. The priestess of Apollo replied: "*Last of the heroes* is Cleomedes of Astypalaea. Honor him with sacrifices as one no longer mortal." No doubt relieved to hear that he was the last hero they would have to deal with, the citizens of Astypalaea established a cult in his name, which was still being observed when Pausanias wrote about Cleomedes in the second century A.D.

Bernard Knox, in *The Heroic Temper*, points out that the story of Cleomedes exemplifies the dual nature of the Greek attitude toward the hero. On the one hand, the hero's bones are guarded and his fierce spirit admired and invoked—his ability to transcend ordinary human limitations was inspiring and was an example to be followed, especially in war.[1] But, as the story of Cleomedes makes clear, the Greeks also felt that, in peacetime and in civilized society, the hero did not make a reliable "pillar" for the community. We have seen, too, how Achilles' temper, Oedipus's hubris, and Odysseus's curiosity brought ruin on themselves, on their companions, or on their families.

In our own time, men's wanton violence is under scrutiny, their so-called narcissism and self-sufficiency under attack, and their capacity for connection to others seen as deficient. It is not women alone who have become suspicious of heroes. From a geopolitical perspective, weapons of mass destruction and the fragility of the environment make a present-day Cleomedes unacceptable.

Women's belief that there is something intrinsically wrong with masculinity corresponds to men's sense that all is not well. We do not agree that men are "wounded" or defective, or that men or women are somehow psychologically less than they should be. Men are in pain, and the inability to get at the source

---

[1] Socrates, in his own heroic (or stubborn) refusal to compromise on his philosophic principles, also invoked the spirit of Achilles.

of this pain leaves both men and women at odds and at risk. Biologically, men are vulnerable to heart disease; emotionally, they are just as vulnerable to being "heartsick," and, as any good cardiologist knows, the two maladies are related.

Dean Ornish, the well-known rehabilitation cardiologist, has helped large numbers of men and women with severe heart disease to make the radical changes in diet, exercise, and meditation that can lead to the unclogging of coronary arteries without the need to resort to bypass surgery or complex medical regimes. Dr. Ornish has commented on a major personal change that affected his capacity to become a truly successful man. A brilliant student in high school, he found in college that he was no longer the "brightest kid." Concerned that he was stupid, and struggling with a crisis of self-worth, Ornish contemplated suicide. Indeed, it was only a serendipitous contraction of mononucleosis that interrupted the self-destructive process. It was an indelible moment of personal change, so significant that he remembered it vividly over twenty years later. Ornish said, "I go back to it all the time because it was a transforming moment. I realized that the less I needed success, the less I felt stress. The less I felt about my ambitions, the more I succeeded." [*New York Times*, December 29, 1991] Not only was this insight literally lifesaving for Ornish himself, it later became the backbone of his creative approach to heart disease. He related his personal crisis to the interconnectedness of stress, depression, self-esteem, and heart disease.

THE FALLEN HERO

Ornish's transformation, not unlike that of one of our heroes—Achilles—represents a personal attempt to become a different kind of man. You will recall that in shared mourning with King Priam—the king grieving for his son, the warrior grieving for his dearest friend—Achilles was able to relinquish his rage and wounded pride. He could then accept his own vulnerability and feel a full range of emotions. He no longer had to stand alone. Though the *Iliad* closes on this note of personal rebirth, Homer leaves no doubt that Achilles would not evade his destiny to die in battle at Troy. Like Oedipus, Achilles is transformed, his arrogant pride burned away, but acquiring self-knowledge does not save either of them from destruction. In the *Odyssey*, Homer carries the transformation of Achilles a step further when Odysseus encounters him in the land of the dead. Achilles tells him:

> *O shining Odysseus, never try to console me for dying.*
> *I would rather follow the plow as thrall to another man,*
> *one with no land allotted him and not much to live on,*
> *than be a king over all the perished dead . . .*
>
> [LATTIMORE, TRANS., BOOK 11, LL. 488–91]

Achilles no longer embraces the warrior value of glory being preferable to long-lived obscurity. To be a fallen hero is a hollow and lonely achievement. He is only concerned with news of his father and his son, and after Odysseus tells him of his son's heroism in battle, Achilles finds solace:

> *So I spoke, and the soul of the swift-footed scion of Aiakos*
> *stalked away in long strides across the meadow of asphodel,*
> *happy for what I had said of his son, and how he was famous.*
>
> [LATTIMORE, TRANS., BOOK 11, LL. 538–40]

Like Hector, Achilles does not have to compete with his son, although his visiting upon him the same warrior values that he has rejected for himself suggests how difficult it is for men to break the transgenerational pattern by which the tradition of masculinity repeats itself.

Just as women need not take on all the worst aggressions and ambitions of men in order to succeed, men need not fear that in order to be both "good" and acceptable to the opposite gender they must become women. Rather, it may be possible to re-create masculinity by building on men's inner callings for self-respect, responsibility, and legitimate authority. Such a re-created masculinity would include reliability, the power to get things done rather than the power over women or other men, and caring for others by doing as well as being able to feel for them. This model of masculinity is logical and instrumental, while remaining open to feelings of all sorts, not anger alone. The re-created man can do; he can actively protect. But he can also recognize that he needs to be part of an intimate circle, in which at times he can be passive, dependent, and needful. For this is a man whose ideals of strength and self-sufficiency are tempered by the awareness of his vulnerability. In the best tradition of sportsmanship, he is a true team player.

Before we are able to re-create masculinity we must better understand how men have fallen from their idealized perch of self-sufficiency. As we have argued throughout the book, we feel that men are forced into an overzealous form of Hemingway-like toughness due to the culture's gender role expectation and out of a need to defend against earlier memories of traumatic hurt, abandonment, and shame. We found that little boys were often prematurely separated from their nurturant maternal figures in a way that little girls were not. In addition, while little girls could continue to identify with their mothers or with other women, little boys were left to seek their fathers, who were usually emotionally unavailable as models. When girls grew into women they were at home with other people while grown-up little boys continued to fend off the need for lost connection and tried ruggedly to do their best on their own. Men's awareness of being a "we" lost out to the priority of feeling like a big "I." Our experience as therapists is that to unlock these men's buried emotions, to help them be more empathic to themselves, and ultimately to the Special Men and Special Women in their lives, requires that we be empathic to them. We must not shame them by implying that they should be different. The approach must begin with "Of course, you have had to act in these ways," recognizing how they have been shaped by their early development as well as society's expectations for them.

Heinz Kohut, the psychoanalyst whose work we described in depth earlier, pointed out how little children need to feel close to a reliable and soothing adult whom they can idealize. But Kohut went on to say that becoming an adult requires that one slowly disillusion oneself of such ideal qualities in the heroes whom we worship. We must face the less-than-perfect turns of fate and human shortcomings. He called this process "optimal disillusionment," which when interrupted or rushed could lead to tragic consequences—Oedipus, for example, is literally blinded by having suddenly to see that he is not the paragon of virtue he had thought himself to be.

If our idealized view of men as superheroes is abruptly tossed into the dustbin of unfortunate societal errors, what are the men already indoctrinated with that perspective of manhood to do? We are not taking issue with women's rightful concerns about the necessity for change. But we must be realistic about how men's personal transformation can be achieved. The cultural anthropologist David Gilmore has found that the need to live up to a test of manhood at pain of a man losing his identity is so common that it appears to be a "deep psychological structure" analogous to Carl Jung's archetypes.

Some would argue that men need to follow women's lead—since women are relational experts, presumably men can learn how to be less competitive and more empathic from them. But the notion that either gender can be a model for the other is part of the problem, not the solution. Men would always be "second-class" women. This approach also denies the healthy aspects of being a man that should be integrated into the "new man." As we have noted, the other most popular solution urges men to search for the wild and primitive roots of masculinity—a kind of psychological homeopathy. We believe that, as in the fairy tale "Rumpelstiltskin," this is a vain attempt to weave straw into gold. Our perspective as therapists who have seen hundreds of men and women struggling with gender issues makes us feel that basic changes in masculine identity cannot be obtained with one weekend workshop or one foray into the wilderness, however seductive this remedy may appear.

Both men and women have been suffering from what Joseph Pleck first called "gender role strain"—the gap between men's ideal self and the real masculine self. Self-esteem will vary in relation to how close our self-image can come to our ideal view of ourself. If Pleck is correct that stereotyped gender expectations for men can never really be met, and that the urge to meet them and the incapacity to do so intensify in a context of historical change, as we have seen between men and women during the last two decades, we can expect that men who continue to strive to meet such gender expectations will be demoralized, depleted, and sad. They will also become easily enraged when frustrated or criticized. Only when, like the fallen heroes of ancient Greece, men can question the societal expectations for them that have contributed to so much of their stress and pain and realize that an inward journey of self-discovery is worth making can there be a re-creation of masculinity.

WHAT HEROES REALLY WANT

While it is not our intention to resurrect the heroes of the past such that masculinity can strengthen its sovereignty, women may fear that the invocation of "heroes" is a narcissistic yearning for patriarchy. At best, men's admiration of the heroic—a model so imbued with competitive striving and self-reliance—may feel foreign to women's experience. The ancient Greek poet, Sappho, may provide a helpful bridge between male and female perspectives.

John Winkler, in *The Constraints of Desire*, points out that Sappho at times uses Homeric passages as a contrast to highlight women's consciousness. For example, in one poem she evokes a scene from the *Iliad* in which a wounded warrior pleads for a goddess's aid and Sappho uses it as a metaphor for wounded *love*. Sappho makes an even more explicit commentary on the connections between men's and women's worlds in another poem:

> *Some an army of horsemen, some an army on foot*
> *and some say a fleet of ships is the loveliest sight*

> *on this dark earth; but I say it is what-*
> *ever you desire . . .*

> [BALMER, TRANS., P. 21]

In this poem Sappho goes on to use Helen of Troy as a bridge to link men's love for the military to her own erotic yearnings for a specific woman. As John Winkler points out:

> Sappho speaks as a woman opponent entering the lists with men, but her proposition is not that men value military forces whereas she values desire, but rather that *all valuation is an act of desire.* Men are perhaps unwilling to see their values as erotic in nature, their ambitions for victory and strength as a kind of choice. But it is clear enough to Sappho that *men are in love with masculinity and that epic poets are in love with military prowess.*

> [WINKLER, P. 177, ITALICS OURS]

We are back to the question raised in the beginning of this book of what men want or need, and also *how,* in contrast to women, men deceive themselves about the depth of their longings. Sappho, in her dual consciousness of men's and women's experience, reveals their differences while at the same time showing how, at their essence, they are joined. Such a respectful appreciation for gender differences is what we need to cultivate in our own time.

THE VIRTUES OF MASCULINITY

In our new understanding of men, we need to appreciate the faults of their virtues, and, likewise, the virtues of their faults. Although David Gilmore believes that the "deep structure" of masculinity is a barrier that societies must erect against chaos, human enemies, and any human weakness that endangers group life, he also found that men can be far more nurturing and generous than this dark destiny would portend. As we have pointed out, "male mothering" may be less direct than female-style nurturing, more instrumental than emotional, but still a vital form of caretaking that sustains human life.

Robert Weiss, in his book *Staying the Course*, studied a representative sample of male professionals from the ages of thirty-five to fifty-five during the years of 1983 to 1987, utilizing an in depth, semi-structured interview process. He was impressed by these men's capacity to "stay the course": to engage in a responsible form of protectionism for their wives and children while attempting to be respected with reasonable authority in their work lives. These are men who are struggling to "pass the test" of reliable manhood over and over again. They had idealized the personality characteristic of "resilience, determination, competence, and self-sufficiency as the basis of manhood." [Weiss, p. 255] They were struggling to be *good men*:

> The men of this study want not only to have a good life, but to be good men, men they themselves respect. . . . Being a good man means being able to maintain a respected place among men, being able to serve as head to a family and as a model for one's children, and being able to raise one's children properly and help them make a life for themselves. Being a good man is not consistent with behavior that men cannot respect: at work, falling down on the job, or making things harder for others or stealing credit that belongs to someone else; at home, letting down your wife when she's been doing her part or letting down your children. It is inconsistent also with being disloyal to a friend who has a right to expect better.
>
> [WEISS, PP. 253–54]

Indeed, then, the nature of male assertiveness, the need to succeed, compete, the need to be respected at work, and the need to, at times, even aggressively challenge others in order to be a responsible provider and protector may have their roots in a reasonable and caring masculine form of nurturing and societal support. Like Hector and Odysseus, men continue to struggle to fulfill their modern-day *aidos*—their call to duty to family and community. That men's sense of duty can be distorted into workaholism such that human values become subservient to perverse forms of achievement should not cause us to mistrust the fundamental masculine sense of duty.

In this time when men's self-sufficiency is in disrepute, when men's autonomy is construed as a Narcissus-like self-absorption that takes men away from close relationships he is presumably ill-equipped to have, we should remember that there are two developmental pathways to aloneness. True, one of them is a defense against failed relationships and, at worst, leads to isolation. But the other begins under the close but not too close watchfulness of a loving parent who is then felt as a presence throughout a man's life even when the Special Man or Special Woman is no longer there. *Such a man is able to be alone, but he does not have to be.* Such a man has much to teach us about the value of boundaries—the kind that "make good neighbors" and that are set with an awareness of what is being walled out and walled in. Such a man who is able to but does not have to be alone can teach us about the difference between healthy self-respect and making a cult out of the self. He can be self-motivated though he does not ignore the needs of others. In adversity and even in the absence of a father, he is able, like Telemachus, to take charge of his life, or in the modern-day advertising exhortation, to "Just do it."

One man in his forties told us that he recently had to move to another city and he decided to rent a twenty-foot truck for the four-hundred-mile trip. Though he had never driven a truck, he just assumed he would be able to do it. He said that when he first climbed into the truck cab to adjust the mirrors, he felt queasy and wondered, "What the hell am I doing?" But he just told himself he had to do it and that he could. He made the trip without incident, and while he felt relieved when he dropped off the truck, he felt good that he had made the journey instead of hiring someone.

The neophyte truck driver suggests something about men's capacity to surmount their fears. Rites of passage evidently do not end with adolescence. Throughout their lives, men must, figuratively or literally, rise to the occasion. We can admire Achilles' bravery even while we can see how his ardor in battle was fueled also by emotional weakness. The warrior spirit does not require that one go to war. The best of warriors can act not only in spite of their fears, but know when it is sensible to withdraw from the field—in the words of the country-western song, to "know when to hold 'em, know when to fold 'em."

We have pointed out how men's attempt to wield power is often due to a failure to define a role of legitimate authority. In challenging men's exercise of power over them, women have helped to raise the standard of leadership, for unquestioned power is power without social value, without fairness, without legitimacy, and often without reason. In the necessary effort to redefine equity between men and women, we should not lose an appreciation for the value of authority. Men's capacity to assert themselves, to set an agenda, to lead is an admirable trait when tempered by the responsibility of leaders to be governed not by their appetites but by the social welfare.

We have highlighted before men's need to live out their Dream. At its best, we would liken this urge to the Greek ideal of *arete*—the pursuit of virtue and excellence. This desire is linked to a sense of specialness but the endpoint is not the immortality of the self, but the transcendence of the self's limits. The mature articulation of a Dream, the courage to stand by one's convictions, and, most difficult, to strive to bring one's life and one's world into some accord with one's vision is, like the other virtues of masculinity, not the sole province of the male gender, but is a quality that has, in our culture, been most often carried by men.

In the re-creation of masculinity, men do not have to model themselves after women. They should not be Eve's Rib. They also do not have to start fashioning themselves out of unformed clay. They can be proud of their own version of caretaking and duty, their firm appreciation for the sanctity of the self, and their many forms of courage. There is also much to be valued about their knowledge of legitimate authority and their dedication to a Dream.

NECESSARY TRANSFORMATIONS

We believe that men do not have to throw away parts of themselves as much as they need to transform them. The qualities that are often associated with traditional definitions of masculinity, such as autonomy and aggressiveness, are not in themselves bad except as they become exaggerated, reducing men's complex humanity into a caricature. Throughout his life, a man has opportunities to grow beyond earlier solutions. He is shaped by his early development but he need not be enslaved by it. To become as free as possible of the limiting influences of old pain and the overly rigid cultural prescriptions about what it means to be a man requires certain transformations. Since we consider these changes a natural part of men's normal development and essential to their well-being, we call them *necessary* transformations.

Men's autonomy, although valuable, needs to be tempered by the acknowledgment of the importance of connection. Many of the men we see in our practices conduct their lives as if intimate relationships were not all that important. When asked, they often say that family is central, but, sadly, their wives and children mostly feel their absence. They appear in our consulting rooms after an affair, or when their wives are threatening them with divorce, or when their marriages have deteriorated to the point that they don't know what to do. Only when they are faced with the real possibility of the loss of the Special Woman in their life or of their children are they able to ask for help and to consider how they have not tended well enough to those they really love. In many of the couples we see the men complain how hurt they are by their partners, not appreciating the extent to which their own difficulty in communicating about their needs has led to their disappointment. As one wife put it, "I never realized that he cared enough about me that it would matter if I left him."

Jim was a successful lawyer in his forties who had first come for therapeutic help several years before because of struggles with colleagues at work and an inability to maintain an emotional commitment with a woman. Over the course of therapy it had become clear that Jim's parents, although well-intentioned, had substituted "rules for living" for an empathic understanding of their children's needs. Jim's father would often pull away when his son was upset and his mother would preach to him about what he *should* be doing.

One day, in talking about his worry that his deepest fears would never be resolved, his therapist took up in a careful manner the possibility that some questions of trust were still unresolved in the treatment. Jim responded feelingly and directly: "It's not really that I don't trust you, I've known you for quite a while now and you've really helped me. It's that I feel too vulnerable to have needs, to really show my needs and maybe it's to show that I need you. It makes me feel weak and very scared." Therapist: "Yes it's frightening, but it's part of the human condition to depend on each other, isn't it?" Jim: "*Is it?* You know, when they talk about those homeless people sleeping alone out in the cold and how can they do it . . . I sort of know how they can do it. It's their way of keeping themselves private, of not having to let anyone in. You know it's not just letting someone in once, it's needing them and then feeling they won't be there, or they are expecting that they can come in again, it leaves you with no private sense, no private sense of yourself . . ."

Jim's dilemma, although personally tied to his own early experience, is a paradigm for the pain that many men feel in relationships. Men are constantly seeking and yearning to be connected, often with women, but also with fellow men. However, they are terribly frightened of the shameful vulnerability that such connection will bring. Too often the psychology of men has been a means to suppress the anxiety and fear that such connections elicit and to replace them with a withdrawal or angry frustration that tends to cloud the real issues. Men are not self-sufficient loners, who care for no one else. They are frightened searchers, looking to connect, but very unsure of what "insurance" they need should the connection go awry.

Our thesis is that due to the early, abrupt loss of a man's first love and the shame attending the yearnings to recapture it, a man feels that he must keep a safe distance and deny that he has needs. The adult relationships men and women have with each other become much like Narcissus and Echo's—connection and autonomy are the special province of one gender alone. Only when he can come to terms with the wounds caused by these early separations and with the ways he has developed a protective armor can a man be open again to love and to be loved. He must rediscover the submerged peninsulas that once linked him to the mainland. Like Odysseus, he must find a way back home from the corporate battlefields, from his forgetfulness, from his fears about a return. Deep inside every man is a buried longing to return home, to recapture what in Spanish is referred to as *querencia:* "*Querencia* means affection for the place one calls home and the sense of well-being that that place gives one. . . . It means the sense of being nourished by a place in which you belong. It means needing that place and having it. . . . Immediacy is the essence of *querencia.*" [*New Yorker*, September 26, 1977, pp. 27–28]

To re-create himself, a man must be able to make journeys toward and not just away from relationships, seeking help from a variety of Special Women and Special Men. Only then can he interrupt the recurring pattern by which sons forever yearn for fathers, deny their need for mothers, and absent themselves from yearning partners, daughters, and sons.

Men's aggressiveness must also be transformed. The need to prove one's manhood, when it becomes a compulsive urge, results, like Evel Knievel, in a sad and even dangerous caricature of courage. The urge to be manly is severed from a meaningful social context, and, like pumping iron, no matter how strong one becomes, something false adheres to it. Courage has a dark side in that the suppression of fear and empathy, unchecked, can lead to great destruction. We have described how both Achilles and Hector tempered the warrior spirit to be able to have more tender connections. Hector must remove his armor so as not to frighten his young son; Achilles transforms his rage through mourning a beloved friend. We believe that men's aggressiveness is, in part, biologically driven, but that cultural prescriptions that restrict men's expression of emotion to anger make them far more aggressive than nature destines them to be. Achilles' shame was transformed into rage; so at first was his grief at losing Briseus and then Patroclus; so too was his fear of having to endure an early death. The task for men today is to transform their anger back into the various emotions whose nature has been disguised. We have suggested that sports and sex are two of the primary activities in which men struggle, albeit not always successfully, to transmute their anger into love. We believe that playfulness, whether in the bedroom or on the playing field, is a model for transformation. In the safety of the pretend, with the focus solely on the present moment and not some future goal or consequence, risk-taking becomes possible.

One of us has found that couples can modulate aggression through play. This is not a matter of laughing off serious problems. It is also not the same as Albee's George and Martha in *Who's Afraid of Virginia Woolf?*, who have a sadistic appreciation of the ridiculous but no sense of humor. Rather, it includes playful teasing and exaggerating, which enables couples to vent hostility in safe and mutually enjoyable ways against each other and ghosts of the past. For example, Jean dubbed her husband, John, "the invulnerable hero" to refer to his need to be self-sufficient. When at times he was able to show his vulnerability and to share his fears she would joke, "But of course we know you're really an invulnerable hero and that you're not really feeling afraid." This repeated acknowledgment in an accepting way helped them to come to terms with a central problem between them. As Jean put it:

> Things that are revealed as sensitive, vulnerable points in the other person during a fight, which are difficult to talk about, can later be played with from different directions, such as teasing or exaggerating. It is the recurring play around that issue which makes it easier to receive. We never joke about a problem while one of us is really angry, but play is a probing to see if it still hurts and brings it back

slowly without its being a crisis issue. It helps us to integrate a solution in our relationship.

[BETCHER (1981), P. 25]

The example of Jean and John suggests a playful model for women and men to try to address men's "heroic" stance, to gradually moderate their being cut off from their feelings and from intimacy. It cannot be a substitute for serious discussion, even confrontation, but as couples struggle toward a new model of gender relations, they need to have ways of keeping the issues alive between them without constantly beating each other over the head. Play is a way of touching the truth lightly.

A man's sense of duty must be transformed from a Sisyphean sentence to a set of personal obligations. He must be motivated by moral conviction, not guilt. Neither lost in a role, nor remaining a wanderer who is neither a "who" nor a "what," like Odysseus, his task is to refind his rightful place in the social order. Only when a man can restore a proper balance among his duties to country, community, work, and family can he be content. We believe that to find this integration, most men will need to rediscover the roots of their involvement with work and their specific career choice. In particular, they will need to reexamine their relation to their fathers, so many of whom labored as "organization men," like Sisyphus, too long and with too little joy, leaving their sons wondering who their fathers really were.

A man's Dream must also be transformed. Too often the Dream has been an illusory goal, split off from the job descriptions and domestic urgencies of daily life. Such Dreams become harsh indictments of what has never been or fragile glass menageries whose tenuous relation to the present can be sustained only by escapist fantasies. A man must keep alive a Dream that guides him along the twists and turns of his growing up, providing continuity, yet flexible enough to change. The Dream must be reconciled with loss and limitations such that a man can feel without resignation that he is a "good-enough" father and partner, a good-enough man.

RITES AND WRONGS OF PASSAGE

Jewish tradition, like all the cultures and subcultures that David Gilmore studied, has a clear boyhood-to-manhood transition in the ritual right of the Bar Mitzvah. Here the thirteen-year-old child is inculcated into the religious world of his elders. But the distinction between becoming a man on the day of the boy's Bar Mitzvah and being a real man—a *mensch*—is clear. Freely translated, this word means "man." But to the initiated it means so much more. For being a *mensch* is more than moving from boyhood to manhood: it is a sense of being a more *full* person. In fact, as the term has been adopted into English usage, it has also come to mean "a decent and responsible person."

Men are struggling to be decent and responsible. Men are struggling to exist in connection with women without fear. A new psychology of men, a re-creation of masculinity would recognize the heroic effort inherent in such a struggle. It would replace the fanciful and grandiose notions of heroes from afar, with the painful realities and sweet successes of everyday life.

Barbara Ehrenreich, in writing a critique of the so-called new man, states:

> So it is not enough anymore to ask that men become more like women; we should ask instead that they become more like what both men and women *might* be. My new man, if I could design one, would be capable of appreciation, sensitivity, intimacy—values that have been for too long, feminine. But he would also be capable of commitment, to use that much-abused word, and I mean by that commitment not only to friends and family, but to a broad and generous vision of how we might all live together.
>
> [EHRENREICH (1990), P. 137]

How can men be transformed in our society, or, better, how can men *transform themselves*? We are not nostalgic for the drumbeat of primitive masculinity. Further, in a true rite of passage, something important must be at stake. Telemachus went on a hazardous voyage to seek news of his absent father, not because he was a member of Outward Bound. A weekend workshop or wilderness "experience" has value only when it goes beyond play-acting and becomes integrated into the meaningful activities and relationships of a man's daily life. Psychotherapy shares with such rites elements of play. As in a sporting contest or sexual encounter, in psychotherapy intense feelings are expressed in a safe, bounded place. It is set off from the rest of life, but to have value must somehow be integrated with it. We are not suggesting that all men need psychotherapy or that therapy is the only legitimate path of transformation. But its modes of change may be useful benchmarks for men who wish to transform themselves and for their loved ones who seek to support them.

In psychotherapy we see many men who are frightened about some aspect of their work or love life that they cannot master. These men are most afraid of the very fact that they are afraid. They have been brought up to believe that a man must not seek help at a time when he needs it most. So they deny their dependence upon the therapy or the therapist, and if pushed prematurely to face the truth will resort to more drastic protection of their independence—they will run from treatment or devalue the therapy or the therapist. If the therapist remains calm and does not criticize in return, if he or she recognizes and supports men's need to save face when receiving help, then internal changes of great consequence may occur. We must be sensitive to men's shame and not further shame them.

D. W. Winnicott wrote that one should never ask a child the question, "Did you conceive of this or was it presented to you from without?" He meant that it would be premature to ask a child, or an adult patient, whether he is finding answers himself or whether it is the therapist who is giving him support. If we can sustain the process of change without putting demands upon men before they can accept them, transformation can occur. This is not very different from the theory of how to get a "good idea" accepted by an organization. Consultants know that the best way to help others is to enable them to feel they have come to the "good idea" themselves. They can then "own" it and empower its implementation. The case of Burt, a successful businessman in his mid-thirties who was helped by a such a treatment approach, may be instructive.

BURT HAD SOUGHT a consultation with the therapist because he was concerned about the ethics of his work in a highly sophisticated legal firm. In addition, he had vague but deeply painful feelings that "something is terribly wrong in my life." He had observed the therapist during a seminar on business leadership and felt comfortable with him.

The "consultation" developed into a weekly psychotherapy, now continuing into its third year. During the first few sessions, which consisted of Burt responding to the therapist's questions about his history, several traumas during his early life emerged that he had not known about until becoming a young adult. However, Burt saw no connection at the time between these painful events and his present-day anxieties. When the therapist tried to make such connections, Burt looked frightened and launched into discussion of his work, his leadership capacities, and his guilt.

Rather than arguing with Burt or trying to confront his apparent "denial," the therapist felt strongly that Burt was doing his best to maintain his sense of dignity while developing a new form of dependent relationship with him. He continued to listen to Burt's work concerns and helped him to cope with a number of competitive struggles with senior partners. The patient appeared to become more comfortable and was complimentary of the help he received. But he was often careful to say that this was a "consultation" in which he was putting his own "spin" on what the therapist offered. He also managed to be away often from the therapy due to "important business matters."

In the second phase of the treatment, Burt began to describe difficulties in his marriage and in parenting. The therapist helped Burt to realize that although he appeared angry at times he was also very sad. As Burt began to feel that "it's okay to have needs," he also seemed to have a more complex understanding of his wife's concerns and had greater empathy for her. He stopped blocking her effort to find a couples therapist and started to feel that "maybe this marriage can work out."

As a result of what Burt was learning about his marriage, he realized that some of the issues he was struggling with as an adult were frighteningly similar to those from his early life. Even some of his work conflicts began to remind him of situations in his family growing up. He asked somewhat sheepishly, "Isn't this what some people do in psychotherapy?" and whether they could explore these connections in their sessions. The therapist concurred and reminded him that in the very first sessions he had talked about his premature separation from his family due to a hospitalization as a child for a life-threatening illness. Burt began to cry and by the end of the session was discussing the effects of this trauma on his development, a linkage that the therapist had alluded to two years earlier but had been held in abeyance until the time was right.

THE BURDENS OF masculinity cannot be lifted by insisting that men give up their stoic stance of autonomy, for it is this very underpinning that men need to maintain at all costs. They feel they must be true to themselves. If men have fallen from their heroic pedestals, we must offer to help them off the ground without asking for an immediate thanks. We must allow them to talk about their fall while saving face so that eventually they may reach the sadness they have so long avoided in the effort to appear so independent.

We recognize that the Special Women in men's lives cannot be expected to act like "consultants." For too long, women have had to put their own needs on hold to serve the needs of men. But men's sensitivity to criticism must be reckoned with. Both men and women need to "stay the course" if our tired models of gender are to change.

LIKEMINDEDNESS

In Chapter 6 we mentioned that Odysseus, just before reaching home, is tempted one last time to forsake his wife for another woman—Nausicaa "of the white arms." In Odysseus's speech to Nausicaa, we have a glimpse of his (and, presumably, Homer's) ideal marriage:

> *And may the gods grant you what your heart wants most,*
> *a husband and a home, and may there be*
> *accord between you both: there is no gift*
> *more solid and more precious than such trust:*
> *a man and woman who conduct their house*
> *with minds in deep accord . . .*
>
> [MANDELBAUM, TRANS., P. 121]

The Greek word "homo-phrosunê" has been translated by Allen Mandelbaum as "accord," by W. H. D. Rouse as "one heart between two," and by Robert Fitzgerald as "sweet agreement in all things," but perhaps John Winkler's term "like-mindedness" is most succinct.

Recall that Odysseus is a master of deceit. His wife, Penelope, is no less cunning. Her most famous ruse is putting off the suitors for three years by saying she had to weave a shroud for her father-in-law before remarriage, unweaving each night what she had woven during the day. In their essential nature, Penelope and Odysseus are truly "likeminded." Winkler points out that in the couple's reunion, after each has tricked the other into proving their faithfulness, Homer suggests the merger of their two selves through a simile that begins with an image of Odysseus's feelings and ends with a picture of Penelope's:

> *She spoke, and still more roused in him the passion for weeping.*
> *He wept as he held his lovely wife, whose thoughts were virtuous.*
> *And as when the land appears welcome to men who are swimming,*
> *after Poseidon has smashed their strong-built ship on the open*
> *water, pounding it with the weight of wind and the heavy*
> *seas, and only a few escape the gray water landward*
> *by swimming, with a thick scurf of salt coated upon them,*
> *and gladly they set foot on the shore, escaping the evil;*
> *so welcome was her husband to her as she looked upon him,*
> *and she could not let him go from the embrace of her white arms.*
>
> [LATTIMORE, TRANS., BOOK 23, LL. 231–40]

Despite the formalized social roles within which men and women of Homer's time were constrained to live, Penelope and Odysseus manage a partnership based on some sense of equality. Are we so different today, men and women still bound by our upbringing and by social conventions about masculinity and femininity, struggling to respect each gender's different consciousness and yet to find "likemindedness?"

THE "BETTER HALF"

As Virginia Woolf observed in 1928:

There is a spot the size of a shilling at the back of the head which one can never see for oneself. It is one of the good offices that sex can discharge for sex—to describe that spot the size of a shilling at the back of the head.

[A ROOM OF ONE'S OWN, P. 90]

Woolf suggests that although a woman is limited in her knowledge of men, just as a man is limited in his knowledge of women, each needs to learn to laugh at the other sex's peculiarities, and in so doing has something to offer.

We believe that Aristophanes was essentially correct in seeing men as painfully split, endlessly searching for meaning and wholeness in their "other half." So we do not wish to celebrate men but manhood in its best sense, or rather, *manhoods*, since we believe that becoming men should be understood as many, not a single pathway. We are also suggesting that *both* men and women become trapped when the personality characteristics necessary for mature involvement in our complex industrialized world become bifurcated along gender lines. It is no more useful for a man to be a protector and provider, without the capacity for deep empathic feeling or the sharing of sadness with his mate, than it is for a woman to be the nurturant caregiver to her child but be denied the capacity for competitive achievement at work. The time has come to recognize that what men do well and what women do well are *both* good. Both feminine and masculine are "the better half."

Indeed, Pruett has shown that fathers can be excellent primary nurturing caregivers. When researchers watched male and female subjects care for a child, women appeared to be more involved. However, when biological measures of heart rate and blood pressure were taken on males and females responding to the urgent cries of a young infant, there were no gender differences. In other words, it appears that men and women have a full range of biologically based empathic capacities for responsiveness, which later become skillfully shaped in adult women caretakers, and socially suppressed in adult males. As one research group concluded: "These findings lend some support to the contention that females are socialized to be more expressive while males are encouraged to deny their feelings and emotions . . . and further emphasize that physiological measures may be a truer index of male response to infant signals than behavioral observation or attitudinal measure" (Jones and Thomas; see also Frodi and Lamb).

Men are not only able to experience a full range of feelings including love, sadness, and empathic responsiveness; they have the inborn biogenetic equipment to do so. Just as women can compete, men can feel. They are not so much "wounded" as they have been hurt and have lost something. They have lost the inborn capacity for empathic relatedness that they share with all members of their species—male and female. As men come to see that we are still yearning to make what is now only half whole again, our anger will be turned into a sense of grief, which is the harbinger of transformation.

From early childhood boys are told to "Be a *man*" without much direction in how to do it. Once achieved, they feel that their manhood is like a shiny sports car—to be shown off and coveted by others, but easily damaged or stolen. This book describes multiple pathways toward becoming men and a variety of ways of defining male adequacy. It is more accurate to describe it as a process in which men are always becoming men rather than manhood as a static achievement. Men and women need to see manhood more realistically as a balance of strength and vulnerability. Inevitably, men will sometimes fall short of this ideal, and both sexes need to acknowledge these failures without seeing them as catastrophic or traumatic.

Having left (or been expelled) from the Garden of Eden— the paradise of unambivalent connection—the progeny of Adam and Eve are struggling to resolve their conflicting views of "heaven" on earth. This is an era of great strain between men and women as both sexes reassess old roles and men try to come to terms with changes demanded by women. It is also a time of opportunity for men to redefine themselves in accord with their own values and needs. Men need to look within as well as look toward women in order to find out who they are and who they may wish to become. If they can discover the true nature of this new male and explain themselves better to women, both men and women will gain.

The message of this book is that it is men's turn to define themselves, and in so doing to "make their half better." Above all, this means that they must understand how boys become men and what they need from women and from other men. When we are clearer about who men are and women are, each sex can acknowledge their feminine and masculine parts. Then a man could be tender and a woman firm, and sex would be an act of sharing rather than domination. *Men need not love in the same ways that women do, but they need to love.*

The re-created man will be able to be soft and be less prone to destructive bursts of rage. He will have legitimate authority and respect. Such a man's power will flow from his inner balance between a sense of independence and intimate connection. Of him we may truly say, as Mark Antony said in Shakespeare's *Julius Caesar*:

"His life was gentle, and the elements so mixed in him that Nature might stand up and say to all the world, '*This* was a man!' "

BIBLIOGRAPHY

Aries, Elizabeth. "Interaction Patterns and Themes of Male, Female, and Mixed-Sex Groups," *Small Group Behavior*, Vol. 7, 1976, pp. 7–18.

Balint, Michael. *Primary Love and Psychoanalytic Technique*. London: Liveright, 1965.

Bank, Stephen, and Kahn, Michael D. "Sisterhood-Brotherhood Is Powerful: Sibling Sub-systems and Family Therapy," *Annual Progress in Child Psychiatry and Child Development*, 1976, pp. 493–519.

———*The Sibling Bond*. New York: Basic Books, 1982.

Barnett, Rosalind C., and Marshall, Nancy L. *Men, Family-Role Quality, Job-Role Quality, and Physical Health*. Manuscript submitted for publication, 1991.

Barnett, Rosalind C., Marshall, Nancy L., and Pleck, Joseph H. "Men's Multiple Roles and Their Relationship to Men's Psychological Distress," *Journal of Marriage and the Family*, Vol. 54, May 1992, pp. 358–67.

Benedek, Therese. "Parenthood as a Developmental Phase: A Contribution to the Libido Theory," *Journal of the American Psychoanalytic Association*, Vol. 7, 1959, pp. 389–417.

———. "Discussion of Parenthood as a Developmental Phase," *Journal of the American Psychoanalytic Association*, Vol. 23, 1975, pp. 154–65.

Betcher, William. *Intimate Play: Creating Romance in Everyday Life*. New York: Viking Penguin, 1987.

———. "Intimate Play and Marital Adaptation," *Psychiatry*, Vol. 44, 1981. pp. 13–33.

———, and Macauley, Robie. *The Seven Basic Quarrels of Marriage.* New York: Villard, 1990.

Bissinger, H. G. *Friday Night Lights.* New York: Addison-Wesley, 1990.

Block, J. "Psychological Development of Female Children and Adolescents," in *Women: A Developmental Perspective*, ed. P. W. Berman and E. R. Ramey. Bethesda, Md.: National Institutes of Health, 1982.

Blumstein, Philip, and Schwartz, Pepper. *American Couples.* New York: William Morrow, 1983.

Bly, Robert. *Iron John.* New York: Addison-Wesley, 1990.

———. *Selected Poems.* New York: Harper & Row, 1986.

Brentlinger, John, ed., and Groden, Suzy Q., trans. *The Symposium of Plato.* The University of Massachusetts Press, 1970.

Boszormenyi-Nagy, Ivan, and Spark, Geraldine M. *Invisible Loyalties.* New York: Harper & Row, 1973.

Bremmer, Jan, ed. *From Sappho to De Sade, Moments in the History of Sexuality.* London: Routledge, 1989.

Brod, Harry, ed. *The Making of Masculinities.* Boston: Unwin Hyman, 1987.

Brody, Leslie R. "Gender Differences in Emotional Development: A Review of Theories and Research," *Journal of Personality*, Vol. 53, 1985, pp. 102–49.

Broverman, Inge K., et al. "Sex-Role Stereotypes and Clinical Judgments of Mental Health," *Journal of Consulting and Clinical Psychology*, Vol. 34, 1970, pp. 1–7.

Buber, Martin. *I and Thou.* Trans. by Walter Kaufmann. New York: Charles Scribner's Sons, 1970.

Budgen, Frank. *James Joyce and the Making of Ulysses.* Bloomington: Indiana University Press, 1960.

Bulfinch, Thomas. *Bulfinch's Mythology.* New York: Gramercy Books, 1979.

Burstein, Alvin G., and Berthenthal, Michael. "A Note on Everyday Psychopathology and Narcissism," *Psychoanalytic Psychology*, Vol. 3, 1986, pp. 269–76.

Campbell, Joseph. *The Hero with a Thousand Faces.* Princeton, N.J.: Princeton University Press, 1949.

Camus, Albert. *The Myth of Sisyphus and Other Essays.* New York: Alfred Knopf, 1955.

Cavafy, C. P. "Ithaka," in *Six Poets of Modern Greece.* Trans. by

Edmund Keeley and Philip Sherrard. New York: Alfred Knopf, 1960.

Chaucer, Geoffrey. *Canterbury Tales*. Trans. by Theodore Morrison. New York: Penguin, 1949.

Chodorow, Nancy. *The Reproduction of Mothering*. Berkeley: University of California Press, 1978.

———. *Feminism and Psychoanalytic Therory*. New Haven: Yale University Press, 1989.

Chorbajian, Leon. "The Social Psychology of American Males and Spectator Sports," *International Journal of Sport Psychology*, Vol. 9, 1978, pp. 165–75.

Coen, Stanley J. "Sexual Interviewing, Evaluation, and Therapy: Psychoanalytic Emphasis on the Use of Sexual Fantasy," *Archives of Sexual Behavior*, Vol. 7, 1978, pp. 229–41.

Coffin, Tristam P. *The Old Ball Game*. New York: Herder and Herder, 1971.

Cohen, Marcia. *The Sisterhood*. New York: Fawcett Columbine, 1988,

Coover, Robert. *The Universal Baseball Association*. New York: Random House, 1968.

David, D., and Brannon, R., eds. *The Forty-nine Percent Majority: The Male Sex Role*. Reading, Mass.: Addison-Wesley, 1976.

Demos, John. "The Changing Faces of Fatherhood: A New Exploration in American Family History," in *Father and Child*, Stanley H. Cath, Alan R. Gurwitt, and John Munder Ross, eds. Boston: Little, Brown & Co., 1982.

Dervin, Daniel. "A Psychoanalysis of Sports," *Psychoanalytic Review*, Vol. 72, 1985, pp. 277–99.

Diamond, M. J. "Becoming a Father: A Psychoanalytic Perspective on the Forgotten Parent," *Psychoanalytic Review*, Vol. 73, 1986, pp. 445–60.

———. "Fathers and Sons: A Psychoanalytic Perspective on Good Enough Fathering Throughout the Life Cycle." Unpublished paper.

Douthitt, R. A. "The Division of Labor Within Homes: Have Gender Roles Changed?" *Sex Roles*, Vol. 20, 1989, pp. 693–704.

Dover, K. J. *Greek Homosexuality*. Cambridge: Harvard University Press, 1989.

Durrell, Lawrence. *Justine*. New York: Pocket Books, 1961.

Ehrenreich, Barbara. *The Hearts of Men*. New York: Doubleday Anchor, 1983.

———. *The Worst Years of Our Lives*. New York: Harper Perennial, 1990.

Eisler, Riane. *The Chalice and the Blade.* New York: Harper, 1987.

———, and Skidmore, J. R. "Masculine Gender Role Stress," *Behavior Modification*, Vol. 2, 1987, pp. 123–36.

———, and Blalock, Janice. "Masculine Gender Role Stress: Implications for the Assessment of Men," *Clinical Psychology Review*, Vol. 11, 1991, pp. 45–60.

Emerson, Ralph Waldo. *Self-Reliance, The Wisdom of Ralph Waldo Emerson as Inspiration for Daily Living.* Ed. by Richard Weldon. New York: Bell Tower, 1991.

Erikson, Erik. "Identity and the Life Cycle," in *Psychological Issues*, Vol. 1. New York: International Universities Press, 1959.

———. *Childhood and Society.* New York: W. W. Norton, 1963.

Euripides. *The Medea.* Trans. by Rex Warner, ed. by David Grene and Richmond Lattimore. Chicago: University of Chicago Press, 1944.

Fairbairn, W. Ronald D. *Psychoanalytic Studies of the Personality.* London: Routledge & Kegan Paul, 1952.

Farrell, Michael P. "Friendship Between Men," *Marriage and Family Review*, Vol. 9, 1985, pp. 163–97.

———, and Rosenberg, S. D. "Friendship Groups and Male Development," in *Men at Midlife.* Boston: Auburn House Publishing Company, 1981.

Finley, M. I. *The World of Odysseus.* New York: Viking Press, 1954.

Firestone, Shulamith. *The Dialectic of Sex: The Call for Feminist Revolution.* New York: Bantam, 1981.

Friedan, Betty. *The Feminine Mystique.* New York: Norton, 1963.

Frodi, A. M., and Lamb, M. E. "Fathers' and Mothers' Response to the Faces and Cries of Normal and Premature Infants," *Developmental Psychology*, Vol. 14, 1978, pp. 490–98.

———, "Sex Differences in Responsiveness to Infants: A Developmental Study of Psychophysiological and Behavioral Responses," *Child Development*, Vol. 49. 1978, pp. 1182–88,

Freud, Sigmund. *The Collected Papers of Sigmund Freud*, Vols. 1–5. Ed. by James Strachey. London: Hogarth Press, 1950.

———. *The Interpretation of Dreams.* Trans. by James Strachey. New York: Avon, 1965.

———. *Introductory Lectures on Psychoanalysis.* Trans. by James Strachey. New York: W.W. Norton, 1966.

Gearing, Frederick O. *The Face of the Fox.* Chicago: Aldine, 1970.

Giamatti, A. Bartlett. *Take Time for Paradise.* New York: Summit, 1989.

Gilligan, Carol. *In a Different Voice*. Cambridge: Harvard University Press, 1982.

Gilmore, David D. *Manhood in the Making*. New Haven: Yale University Press, 1990.

Glass, Leonard L. "Man's Man/Ladies' Man: Motifs of Hypermasculinity," *Psychiatry*, Vol. 47, 1984, pp. 260–78.

Goethals, George W. "The Evolution of Sexual and Genital Intimacy: A Comparison of the Views of Erik H. Erikson and Harry Stack Sullivan," *Journal of the American Academy of Psychoanalysis*, Vol. 4, 1976, pp. 529–44.

Googins, Bradley. *Work-Family Stress—Private Lives, Public Responses*. Westport, Ct.: Greenwood Press, 1991.

Graves, Robert, trans. *The Golden Ass*. New York: Farrar, Straus, and Young, 1951.

———. *The Greek Myths,* Vols. I and II. New York: Penguin, 1960.

Greer, Germaine. *The Female Eunuch*. New York: Bantam, 1972.

Grene, David, and Lattimore, Richmond. *The Complete Greek Tragedies*, 4 vols. Chicago: University of Chicago Press, 1959–60.

Grossman, Frances K., Eichler, Lois, and Winnickoff, Susan. *Pregnancy, Birth, and Parenthood*. San Francisco: Jossey-Bass, 1980.

Grossman, Frances K., Pollack, William S., and Golding, Ellen. "Fathers and Children: Predicting the Quality and Quantity of Fathering," *Developmental Psychology*, Vol. 24, 1988, pp. 82–91.

Grossman, F. K., Pollack, W. S., Golding, E. R., and Fedele, N. M. "Autonomy and Affiliation in the Transition to Parenthood," *Family Relations*, Vol. 36, 1987, pp. 263–69.

Guttman, Allen. *From Ritual to Record*. New York: Columbia University Press, 1978.

———. *Sports Spectators*. New York: Columbia University Press, 1986.

———. *A Whole New Ball Game*. Chapel Hill: University of North Carolina Press, 1988.

Hall, Donald. *Fathers Playing Catch with Sons*. New York: Dell, 1985.

Hamilton, Edith. *Mythology*. New York: New American Library, 1953.

Harris, Mark. *Bang the Drum Slowly*. Lincoln: University of Nebraska Press, 1956.

Harrison, J. "Warning: The Male Sex Role May Be Dangerous to Yourself." *Journal of Social Issues*, Vol. 34, 1978, pp. 65–86.

Hempel, Amy. *Reasons to Live*. New York: Penguin, 1985.

Herdt, Gilbert H. *Guardians of the Flutes: Idioms of Masculinity*. New York: Columbia University Press, 1987.

———, and Stoller, Robert J. *Intimate Communications*. New York: Columbia University Press, 1991.

Herzfeld, Michael. *The Poetics of Masculinity*. Princeton: Princeton University Press, 1985.

Herzog, James M. "On Father Hunger: The Father's Role in the Modulation of Aggressive Drive and Fantasy," in *Father and Child*, Stanley H. Cath, Alan R. Gurwitt, and John Munder Ross, eds. Boston: Little, Brown & Co., 1982.

Hesse, Hermann. *Demian*. Trans. by Michael Roloff and Michael Lebeck. New York: Bantam, 1968.

Hiller, Dana V., and Philliber, William W. "The Division of Labor in Contemporary Marriage: Expectations, Perceptions, and Performance," *Social Problems*, Vol. 33, 1986, pp. 191–201.

———. "Predicting Marital and Career Success Among Dual-Worker Couples," *Journal of Marriage and the Family*, Vol. 44, 1982, pp. 53–62.

Hite, Shere. *The Hite Report on Male Sexuality*. New York: Ballantine Books, 1981.

Hochschild, Arlie, and Machung, Anne. *The Second Shift*. New York: Penguin, 1989.

Homer. *The Iliad*. Trans. by Robert Fagles. New York: Viking, 1990.

———. *The Iliad*. Trans. by Robert Fitzgerald. New York: Anchor, 1975.

———. *The Iliad of Homer*. Trans. by Richmond Lattimore. Chicago: University of Chicago Press, 1951.

———. *The Odyssey*. Trans. by Robert Fitzgerald. New York: Anchor Books, 1963.

———. *The Odyssey*. Trans. by Richmond Lattimore. New York: Harper, 1975.

———. *The Odyssey*. Trans. by Allen Mandelbaum. New York: Bantam, 1990.

———. *The Odyssey*. Trans. by W. H. D. Rouse. New York: Mentor, 1937.

Horney, Karen. "On the Genesis of the Castration Complex in Women," *International Journal of Psychoanalysis*, Vol. 5, 1924, pp. 50–65.

Isenberg, Phillip. "An Essay," *Harvard Magazine*, November–December, 1980, pp. 6–10.

Jacklin, Carol Nagy. "Female and Male: Issues of Gender," *American Psychologist*, Vol. 44, 1989, pp. 127–33.

Jacques, Eliot. "Death and the Midlife Crisis," *International Journal of Psychiatry*, Vol. 46, 1965, pp. 502–14.

Jones, L. Colette, and Thomas, Sue Ann. "New Father's Blood Pressure and Heart Rate: Relationships to Interaction with Their Newborn Infants," *Nursing Research*, Vol. 38, 1989, pp. 237–41.

Jordan, Judith. "Clarity in Connection: Empathic Knowing, Desire and Sexuality." Paper presented at Stone Center Colloquium, May 1987.

———. "Relational Development: Implications for Psychotherapy." Paper presented at Stone Center Colloquium, April, 1989.

Jordan, Judith V., Kaplan, Alexandra G., Miller, Jean Baker, Stiver, Irene P., and Surrey, Janet L. *Women's Growth In Connection*. New York: The Guilford Press, 1991.

Jung, Carl G. "The Structure and Dynamics of the Psyche." Vol. 8, Trans. R. F. Hall. *Collected Works*. Princeton: Princeton University Press, 1969.

———. *Memories, Dreams, Reflections*. New York: Vintage, 1961.

Juster, F. T., and Stafford, F. P. *Time, Goods, and Well-Being*. Ann Arbor, Mich.: Institute for Social Research, 1985.

Kaplan, Helen Singer. *Disorders of Sexual Desire and Other New Concepts and Techniques in Sex Therapy*. New York: Brunner-Mazel, 1979.

———. *The New Sex Therapy*. New York: Brunner-Mazel, 1974.

Keegan, John. *The Face of Battle*. London: Penguin, 1978.

Keen, Sam. *Fire in the Belly*. New York: Bantam, 1991.

Kernberg, Otto. "Boundaries and Structure in Love Relations," *Journal of the American Psychoanalytic Association*, Vol. 25, 1977, pp. 81–114.

———. "Mature Love: Prerequisites and Characteristics," *Journal of the American Psychoanalytic Association*, Vol. 22, 1974, pp. 743–68.

———. "Barriers to Falling and Remaining in Love," *Journal of the American Psychoanalytic Association*, Vol. 22, 1974, pp. 486–511.

Kimura, Doreen. "Sex Differences in the Brain," *Scientific American*, September 1992, pp. 119–25.

Kitto, H. D. F. *The Greeks*. London: Penguin, 1957.

Klein, George S. *Psychoanalytic Theory: An Exploration of Essentials*, New York: International Universities Press, 1976.

Knox, Bernard M. W. *The Heroic Temper: Studies in Sophoclean Tragedy*. Berkeley: University of California Press, 1964.

Kohlberg, Lawrence. *The Psychology of Moral Development: The Nature and Validity of Moral Stages.* San Francisco: Harper and Row, 1984.

Kohut, Heinz. *The Analysis of the Self.* New York: International Universities Press, 1971.

———. *The Restoration of the Self.* New York: International Universities Press, 1977.

Kraines, Gerald A. "Stress in the Workplace," *Directions in Psychiatry,* Vol. 11, Lesson 7, pp. 1–7, 1991.

Krugman, S. "Male Vulnerability and the Transformation of Shame," in *On Men: Redefining Roles.* The Cambridge Series, Cambridge Hospital, Harvard Medical School, Cambridge, Mass., October 1991.

———, and Osherson, Sam. "Shame and Its Role in Male Development." Unpublished paper.

Kuhn, Thomas S. *The Structure of Scientific Revolutions.* Chicago: University of Chicago Press, 1970.

Lamb, Michael E. "Fathers: Forgotten Contributors to Child Development," *Human Development,* Vol. 18, 1975, pp. 245–66.

———, ed. *The Role of the Father in Child Development.* New York: Wiley, 1981.

Laqueur, Thomas. *Making Sex: Body and Gender From the Greeks to Freud.* Cambridge: Harvard University Press, 1990.

Laumann, E. D. *Bonds of Pluralism.* New York: John Wiley & Sons, 1973.

Lawrence, D. H. *Women in Love.* New York: Bantam, 1969.

Levant, Ronald F. "Psychological Services Designed for Men: A Psychoeducational Approach," *Psychotherapy,* Vol. 27, Fall 1990, pp. 309–15.

———. "Toward the Reconstruction of Masculinity," *Journal of Family Psychology,* Vol. 5, 1992, pp. 379–402.

Lever, J. H. "Sex Differences in the Games Children Play," *Social Problems,* Vol. 23, 1976.

———. "Sex Differences in the Complexity of Children's Play and Games," *American Sociological Review,* Vol. 43, 1978, pp. 237–50.

Levinson, Daniel. *The Seasons of a Man's Life.* New York: Knopf, 1978.

Levinson, Harry. *Executive.* Cambridge: Harvard University Press, 1968.

———. *Psychological Man.* Cambridge, Mass.: Levinson Institute, 1976.

Lidz, Theodore. "The Riddle of the Riddle of the Sphinx," *Psychoanalytic Review*, Vol. 75, 1988, pp. 35–49.

Low, Natalie S. "Projective Identification and Gender." Paper presented at annual meeting of Division 39, American Psychological Association, 1989.

Maccoby, Eleanor E. "Gender and Relationships: A Developmental Account," *American Psychologist*, Vol. 45, 1990, pp. 513–20.

——, and Jacklin, Carol. *The Psychology of Sex Differences*. Stanford: Stanford University Press, 1974.

Malcolm, Janet. *Psychoanalysis: The Impossible Profession*. New York: Alfred A. Knopf, 1981.

Marshall, S. L. A. *Men Against Fire*. New York: Morrow, 1947.

McHale, Susan, and Crouter, Ann. "You Can't Always Get What You Want: Incongruence Between Sex-Role Attitudes and Family Work Roles and its Implications for Marriage." *Journal of Marriage and the Family*, Vol. 54, 1992, pp. 537–547.

Michael, Richard. "Hope: Curative Factor or Resistance?" Workshop presented at annual meeting of the American Group Psychotherapy Association, Boston, 1990.

Michalopoulos, Andre. *Homer*. New York: Wayne Publishers, 1966.

Michels, Robert. "Oedipus and Insight," *Psychoanalytic Quarterly*, Vol. 55, 1986, pp. 599–617.

Miller, Arthur. *Death of a Salesman*. New York: Penguin, 1976.

Miller, Frank Justus, trans. *Ovid III, Metamorphoses I*, 3rd ed. Revised by G. P. Goold. Cambridge: Harvard University Press, 1977.

Miller, Jean Baker. *Toward a New Psychology of Women*. Boston: Beacon Press, 1976.

Miller, Stuart. *Men and Friendship*. Boston: Houghton Mifflin, 1983.

Millett, Kate. *Sexual Politics*. Garden City, N. Y.: Doubleday, 1970.

Mitscherlich, Alexander. *Society Without the Father*. New York: Harcourt, Brace, and World, 1963.

Modell, Arnold H. *Psychoanalysis in a New Context*. New York: International Universities Press, 1984.

Morrison, Andrew. *Shame: The Underside of Narcissism*. Hillsdale, N.J.: The Analytic Press, 1989.

Morrow, Lance. *The Chief: A Memoir of Fathers and Sons*. New York: Random House, 1984.

Neruda, Pablo. *Twenty Love Poems and a Song of Despair*. Trans by W. S. Merwin. New York: Penguin, 1976.

Novak, Michael. *The Joy of Sports*. Lanham: Hamilton Press, 1988.

Osherson, Samuel. *Finding Our Fathers*. New York: Fawcett Columbine, 1986.

———, and Krugman, Steven. "Men, Shame, and Psychotherapy," *Psychotherapy*, Vol. 27, pp. 327–39, 1990.

Paglia, Camille. *Sexual Personae: Art and Decadence From Nefertiti to Emily Dickinson*. New York: Vintage, 1991.

Pasick, R. S., "Raised to Work," in R. L. Meth and R. S. Pasick, eds., *Men in Therapy: The Challenge of Change*. New York: Guilford, 1990.

Pedersen, Loren E. *Dark Hearts*. Boston: Shambhala, 1991.

Person, Ethel S. "The Influence of Values in Psychoanalysis: The Case of Female Psychology," *Psychoanalytic Inquiry*, Vol. 3, 1983, pp. 623–46.

———. "Male Sexuality and Power," *Psychoanalytic Inquiry*, Vol. 3, 1986, pp. 3–25.

———, and Ovesey, Lionel. "Psychoanalytic Theories of Gender Identity," *Journal of the American Academy of Psychoanalysis*, Vol. 11, 1983, pp. 203–226.

Philostratus. *Imagines*. Trans. by Arthur Fairbanks. London: William Heinemann, 1931.

Pindar. *Pindar's Odes*. Trans. by Roy Arthur Swanson. New York: Bobbs-Merrill Co., 1974.

Pittman, Frank. "The Secret Passions of Men," *Journal of Marital and Family Therapy*, Vol. 17, 1991, pp. 17–23.

———. "Beyond the Drumbeating. Staggering Through Life as a Man." *Psychology Today*, Jan/Feb. 1992.

Plato. *The Symposium*. ed. B. Jowett. New York: Tuder Publishing, 1956.

Plato. *The Works of Plato*. Irwin Edman, ed., Benjamin Jowett, trans. New York: McGraw-Hill, 1956.

Pleck, Joseph. *The Myth of Masculinity*. Cambridge, Mass.: The MIT Press, 1983.

———, and Sawyer, J., eds. *Men and Masculinity*. Englewood Cliffs, N.J.: Prentice-Hall, 1974.

Pollack, W. S. *"I"ness and "We"ness: Parallel Lines of Development*. Unpublished doctoral dissertation, Boston University, 1982.

———. "Object-Relations and Self Psychology: Researching Children and Their Family Systems," *The Psychologist-Psychoanalyst*, Vol. 4, 1983, p. 14.

———. "Boys and Men: Developmental Ramifications of Autonomy and Affiliation." Paper presented at the midwinter meetings of the

Division of Psychotherapy, American Psychological Association, Orlando, Florida, February 1989.

―――. "Men's Development and Psychotherapy: A Psychoanalytic Perspective," *Psychotherapy*, Vol. 27, 1990, pp. 316–21.

―――. "Can Men Love? Psychoanalytic and Developmental Perspectives on Men and Intimacy." Paper presented at the Symposium on Men and Intimacy at the 99th Annual Meeting of the American Psychological Association, San Francisco, August 1991.

―――. "No Man Is an Island: Reframing the Psychology of Men." Invited address to the Division of General Psychology (Division 1) of the American Psychological Association. Presented at the Centennial Meeting of the American Psychological Association, Washington, D.C., August 1992.

―――. "Boys Will Be Boys: Developmental Traumas of Masculinity—Psychoanalytic Perspectives." Paper presented as part of a symposium, "Toward a New Psychology of Men," at the Centennial Meeting of the American Psychological Association, Washington, D.C., August 1992.

―――. "Should Men Trust Women? Dilemmas for the Male Psychotherapist: Psychoanalytic and Developmental Perspectives." *Ethics and Behavior*, Vol 2, 1992 pp. 39–49.

―――. "Managers as Fathers," *Levinson Letter*, 1991.

―――, and Grossman, Frances. "Parent-Child Interaction," in L. L'Labate, ed., *The Handbook of Family Psychology and Therapy*. Homewood, Ill.: Dorsey, 1985, pp. 586–622.

Pollak, Susan, and Gilligan, Carol. "Images of Violence in Thematic Apperception Test Stories," *Journal of Personality and Social Psychology*, Vol. 42, 1982, pp. 159–67.

Pollock, George H., and Ross, John Munder, eds. *The Oedipus Papers*. Madison: International Universities Press, 1988.

Pruett, Kyle D. *The Nurturing Father*. New York: Warner Books, 1987.

―――. "The Nurturing Male: A Longitudinal Study of Primary Nurturing Fathers," in *Fathers and Their Families*, Stanley H. Cath, Alan Gurwitt, and Linda Gunsberg, eds. Hillsdale, N.J.: The Analytic Press, 1989.

Rank, Otto. *The Myth of the Birth of the Hero and Other Writings*. New York: Vintage Books, 1964.

Rapoport, Rhona. "The Transition from Engagement to Marriage," *Acta Sociologic*, Vol. 8, 1964, pp. 36–55.

―――, Rapoport, Robert N., and Strelitz, Ziona. *Fathers, Mothers and Others*. London: Routledge & Kegan Paul, 1977.

Redfield, James M. "The Wrath of Achilles as Tragic Error," in *Essays on the Iliad*, John Wright, ed. Bloomington: Indiana University Press, 1978.

Redican, William K. "Adult Male-Infant Interactions in Nonhuman Primates," in *The Role of the Father in Child Development*, M. E. Lamb, ed. New York: Wiley, 1976.

Rexroat, Cynthia, and Shehan, Constance. "The Family Life Cycle and Spouses' Time in Housework," *Journal of Marriage and the Family*, Vol. 49, 1987, pp. 737–50.

Rose, H. J. *A Handbook of Greek Mythology*. New York: E. P. Dutton, 1959.

Rossi, Alice. "Gender and Parenthood," *American Sociological Review*, Vol. 49, 1984, pp. 1–19.

Rubin, Lillian B. *Just Friends*. New York: Harper & Row, 1985.

Russo, Joseph, and Simon, Bennett. "Homeric Psychology and the Oral Epic Tradition," in *Essays on the Iliad, Selected Modern Criticism*, John Wright, ed. Bloomington: Indiana University Press, 1978.

Sappho. *Poems and Fragments*. Trans. by Josephine Balmer. Secaucus N.J: Meadowland, 1988.

Satinover, Jeffrey. "The Myth of the Death of the Hero: A Jungian View of Masculine Psychology," *Psychoanalytic Review*, Vol. 73, 1986, pp. 149–61.

Scharff, David E. *The Sexual Relationship*. Boston: Routledge & Kegan Paul, 1982.

Schein, Seth L. *The Mortal Hero*. Berkeley: University of California Press, 1984.

Schwartz, Richard S.; Olds, Jacqueline; Eisen, Susan; Betcher, William; and Van Neil, Anthony. "A Study of the Effects of Differing Parental Work and Child Care Responsibilities on Marital Satisfaction and Stability." Paper presented at annual meeting of the American Psychiatric Association, 1987.

Seif, Nancy Gordon. "Otto Rank: On the Nature of the Hero," *American Imago*, Vol. 41, 1984, pp. 373–84.

Shane, Morton, and Shane, Estelle. "The Struggle for Otherhood: Implications for Development in Adulthood of the Capacity to be a Good-Enough Object for Another," in *New Dimensions in Adult Development*, Robert A. Nemiroff and Calvin A. Colarusso, eds. New York: Basic Books, 1990.

Shapiro, David. *Neurotic Styles*. New York: Basic Books, 1965.

Shapiro, Edward R., and Carr, A. Wesley. "Disguised Countertransference in Institutions," *Psychiatry*, Vol. 50, February 1987, pp. 72–82.

———. *Lost in Familiar Places.* New Haven: Yale University Press, 1991.

Sherrod, Drury. "The Bonds of Men: Problems and Possibilities in Close Male Relationships," in *The Making of Masculinities*, Harry Brod, ed. Boston: Unwin Hyman, 1987.

Silverman, Doris K. "What Are Little Girls Made Of?" *Psychoanalytic Psychology*, Vol. 4, 1987, pp. 315–34.

Simon, Bennett. "The Hero as an Only Child: An Unconscious Fantasy Structuring Homer's *Odyssey*," *International Journal of Psychoanalysis*, Vol. 55, 1974, pp. 555–65.

———. *Mind and Madness in Ancient Greece.* Ithaca: Cornell University Press, 1978.

———. *Tragic Drama and the Family: Psychoanalytic Studies From Aeschylus to Beckett.* New Haven, Ct.: Yale University Press, 1988.

Sophocles. *The Oedipus Plays of Sophocles.* Trans. by Paul Roche. New York: Mentor, 1986.

Stechler, Gerald. "Gender and the Self: Developmental Aspects," *Annual of Psychoanalysis*, Vol. 14, 1987 pp. 345–55.

———, and Kaplan, Samuel. "The Development of the Self: A Psychoanalytic Perspective." *Psychoanalytic Study of the Child*, Vol. 35, 1980, pp. 85–105.

Steiner, George, and Fagles, Robert, eds. *Homer: A Collection of Critical Essays.* Englewood Cliffs, N.J.: Prentice-Hall, 1962.

Stiver, Irene. "The Meanings of 'Dependency' in Female-Male Relationships." Works in Progress, Stone Center, 1984.

Stockham, Alice B. *Karezza.* Chicago: Leonidas Publishing Company, 1986.

Stoller, Robert J. "Sexual Excitement," *Archives of General Psychiatry*, Vol. 33, 1976, pp. 899–909.

———. "Symbiosis Anxiety and the Development of Masculinity," *Archives of General Psychiatry*, Vol. 30, 1974, pp. 164–72.

Stone, Michael H. "Traditional Psychoanalytic Characterology Reexamined in the Light of Constitutional and Cognitive Differences Between the Sexes," *Journal of the American Academy of Psychoanalysis*, Vol. 8, 1980, pp. 381–401.

Sullivan, Harry Stack. *Conceptions of Modern Psychiatry.* New York: W. W. Norton, 1953.

———. *The Interpersonal Theory of Psychiatry.* New York: W. W. Norton, 1953.

Toulmin, Stephen. "Divided Loyalties and Ambiguous Relationships," *Social Science and Medicine*, Vol. 23, 1986, pp. 783–87.

Vaillant, George E. *Adaptation to Life*. Boston: Little, Brown, 1977.

Waelder, Robert. "The Psychoanalytic Theory of Play," *Psychoanalytic Quarterly*, Vol. 2, 1933, pp. 208–224.

Weiss, Robert S. *Staying the Course: The Emotional and Social Lives of Men Who Do Well at Work*. New York: Fawcett Columbine, 1990.

Winkler, John J. *The Constraints of Desire, The Anthropology of Sex and Gender in Ancient Greece*. New York: Routledge, 1990.

Winnicott, D. W. "The Capacity To Be Alone" (1958) in *The Maturational Processes and the Facilitating Environment*. London: Karnac Books, 1990, pp. 29–36.

———. *Collected Papers*. London: Tavistock, 1958.

———. *The Maturational Processes and the Facilitating Environment*. New York: International Universities Press, 1974.

———. *Playing and Reality*. New York: Basic Books, 1971.

Woolf, Virginia. *A Room of One's Own*. New York: Harcourt Brace Jovanovich, 1989.

Wright, John, ed. *Essays on the Iliad*. Bloomington: Indiana University Press, 1978.

Yogev, Sara, and Brett, Jeanne. "Patterns of Work and Family Involvement Among Single- and Dual-Earner Couples," *Journal of Applied Psychology*, Vol. 70, 1985, pp. 754–68.

INDEX